ENDOGENOUS GROWTH

INTERNATIONAL SYMPOSIA IN ECONOMIC THEORY AND ECONOMETRICS

Series Editor: William A. Barnett and Bruno S. Sergi

Recent Volumes:

Volume 17:	Topics in Analytical Political Economy. Edited by Melvin Hinich and William A. Barnett
Volume 18:	Functional Structure Inference. Edited by William A. Barnett and Apostolos Serletis
Volume 19:	Challenges of the Muslim World: Present, Future and Past. Edited by William W. Cooper and Piyu Yue
Volume 20:	Nonlinear Modeling of Economic and Financial Time-Series. Edited by Fredj Jawadi and William A. Barnett
Volume 21:	The Collected Scientific Works of David Cass – Parts A–C. Edited by Stephen Spear
Volume 22:	Recent Developments in Alternative Finance: Empirical Assessments and Economic Implications. Edited by William A. Barnett and Fredj Jawadi
Volume 23:	Macroeconomic Analysis and International Finance. Edited by Georgios P. Kouretas and Athanasios P. Papadopoulos
Volume 24:	Monetary Policy in the Context of the Financial Crisis: New Challenges and Lessons. Edited by William A. Barnett and Fredj Jawadi
Volume 25:	Banking and Finance Issues in Emerging Markets. Edited by William A. Barnett and Bruno S. Sergi
Volume 26:	Asia-Pacific Contemporary Finance and Development. Edited by William A. Barnett and Bruno S. Sergi
Volume 27:	Advanced Issues in the Economics of Emerging Markets. Edited by William A. Barnett and Bruno S. Sergi
Volume 28:	Recent Developments in Asian Economics. Edited by William A. Barnett and Bruno S. Sergi
Volume 29A:	Environmental, Social, and Governance Perspectives on Economic Development in Asia. Edited by William A. Barnett and Bruno S. Sergi
Volume 29B:	Environmental, Social, and Governance Perspectives on Economic Development in Asia. Edited by William A. Barnett and Bruno S. Sergi
Volume 30:	Quantitative Analysis of Social and Financial Market Development. Edited by William A. Barnett and Bruno S. Sergi
Volume 31:	Comparative Analysis of Trade and Finance in Emerging Economies. Edited by William A. Barnett and Bruno S. Sergi
Volume 32:	Overlapping Generations: Methods, Models and Morphology. Authored by Stephen E. Spear and Warren Young
Volume 33A:	Macroeconomic Risk and Growth in the Southeast Asian Countries: Insight from Indonesia. Edited by William A. Barnett and Bruno S. Sergi
Volume 33B:	Macroeconomic Risk and Growth in the Southeast Asian Countries: Insight from SEA. Edited by William A. Barnett and Bruno S. Sergi
Volume 34:	The Finance-Innovation Nexus: Implications for Socio-economic Development. Edited by William A. Barnett and Bruno S. Sergi

INTERNATIONAL SYMPOSIA IN ECONOMIC THEORY AND ECONOMETRICS VOLUME 35

ENDOGENOUS GROWTH: THEORY, METHODS AND MORPHOLOGY

BY

PETER GALBÁCS

Budapest University of Economics and Business, Hungary

STEPHEN E. SPEAR

Carnegie Mellon University, USA

AND

WARREN YOUNG

Bar-Ilan University, Israel

emerald PUBLISHING

United Kingdom – North America – Japan
India – Malaysia – China

Emerald Publishing Limited
Emerald Publishing, Floor 5, Northspring, 21-23 Wellington Street, Leeds LS1 4DL.

First edition 2026

British Library Cataloguing in Publication Data
A catalog record for this book is available from the British Library

ISBN: 978-1-83662-197-3 (Print)
ISBN: 978-1-83662-196-6 (Online)
ISBN: 978-1-83662-198-0 (Epub)

ISSN: 1571-0386 (Series)

Printed and bound by CPI Group (UK) Ltd, Croydon, CR0 4YY

CONTENTS

LIST OF FIGURES AND TABLES

Figures

Tables

ABOUT THE AUTHORS

Peter Galbács is a Fulbright- and Bolyai-awarded Economist and Visiting Researcher of the Kenneth C. Griffin Department of Economics, the University of Chicago. His research area covers the mathematics of microfounded macroeconomics with a special interest in the role dynamic optimization techniques play in the formation of recursive competitive equilibria and the applications of these techniques to the problems of human capital formation and endogenous growth. His previous works were mainly related to various methodological questions raised by Robert E. Lucas' economics.

Stephen E. Spear is a Professor of Economics at Carnegie Mellon University's Tepper School of Business. His research and teaching include both economic theory applications to general equilibrium and macroeconomic analysis, and industrial organization issues that have come to the fore in the past decade on the economic impact of the internet and digital information technologies. He holds an AB from Beloit College (1974) and a Ph.D. from the University of Pennsylvania (1982). He has spent his whole career at Carnegie Mellon.

Warren Young is Professor Emeritus, Economics, Bar Ilan University. He holds a Ph.D. and D.Litt. from the University of Cambridge. He has published extensively on the history of modern economics.

INTRODUCTION: ENDOGENOUS GROWTH IN PERSPECTIVE

Much has been written on *modern* growth theory, the various forms it has taken since its inception in the first half of the 20th century, and the various phases regarding its impact on economic inquiry. Let us briefly outline how thinking on growth evolved in the 20th century. The precursor nodes are Frisch (1933) – because of his recognition that economic processes would transform the stochastic nature of random shocks – Ramsey (1928) and von Neumann (1937, 1945). This led to Harrod (1939, 1948) and Domar (1946) and the follow-on improvements by Swan (1956) and Solow (1956, 1957). This in turn led to the Cass–Koopmans–Malinvaud characterizations of optimal growth and a full endogenization of the *general equilibrium* effects in the growth model (Spear & Young, 2015).

However, one of the originators of the neoclassical growth model, Robert Solow, when asked about developments *after* his own seminal contributions to growth theory, replied that the period 1970–1986 reflected "intellectual diminishing returns" (Solow in Snowden & Vane, 1999, p. 276). Regarding subsequent developments in growth theory, a number of prominent observers, such as Fischer (1988a, 1988b), Stern (1991a, 1991b), and McCallum (1996), maintained that after significant progress in the 1950s and 1960s, economic growth theory "received relatively little attention for almost two decades" (Fischer, 1988a, 1988b, p. 329) and that "by the late 1960s early 1970s, research on the theory of growth more or less stopped" (Stern, 1991a, 1991b, p. 259). Stern (1991a, 1991b) went on to say however, that "the latter half of the 1980s saw a rekindling of growth theory, particularly in the work of Romer ... and Lucas" (p. 259) in the form of "endogenous growth" models. McCallum (1996), for his part, wrote, "After a long period of quiescence, growth economics has in the last decade (1986–1995) become an extremely active area of research" (p. 41).

In 1985, Lucas (1988) gave his Marshall lectures on growth and a year later, in 1986, Romer published his first paper relating to increasing returns and growth, based upon his 1983 thesis, and *the intellectual tide then turned.* Putting it somewhat more sharply, Hahn (1995, p. 85) wrote:

Endogenous Growth: Theory, Methods and Morphology
International Symposia in Economic Theory and Econometrics, Volume 35, 1–9

ISSN: 1571-0386/doi:10.1108/S1571-038620260000035002

> *Growth theory flourished in the 1950s and 1960s,* **died**, *and has now been resurrected.* Romer (1986b) led the way, but it needed Lucas; (1988 [1985]) uncanny knack of creating followers to beget the now large and growing literature. The aim of the ***new growth theories*** is to have an account of an economy's growth rate which is not exogenous to the theory [our emphases].

What, then, characterizes and constitutes the *new* endogenous growth theories Hahn mentioned? First, let us distinguish between the *notion* of endogenous growth and its use as a *description* of growth; the former recently developed, the latter dating back to classical political economy. Endogenous growth can be defined alternatively as (i) when the growth rate is the equilibrium outcome of a model *per-se*, or (ii) when there is *explicit* modeling of technical progress, or (iii) some combination of (i) and (ii) above. This enables us to distinguish various models ranging from "Neoclassical endogenous" and "R&D-based (semi) endogenous," to "Schumpeterian endogenous" and even "Keynesian-type endogenous" growth models, as seen in this volume.

Indeed, the *growth* in the endogenous growth literature was the subject of a critique by one of its originators, Paul Krugman (as will be seen in this volume), who in a *New York Times* column from August 18, 2013, asked the question: "Whatever happened to endogenous growth?" He started the column by stating that from the late 1980s through the 1990s, endogenous growth was touted as "The Next Big Thing" in economics. But he went on: "And here we are, a couple of decades on, and the whole thing seems to have fizzled out…"

As Fig. 1 shows, however, even a casual examination of a Google Scholar search for the phrase "endogenous growth" should convince the reader that the subject has hardly "fizzled out" as a subject of inquiry among scholars of growth. Indeed, over the period 1985–2005 – what Solow (2000) presciently called the "second wave" of studies on endogenous growth (p. 153) – the number of ECONLIT citations rose from 153 (1985–1990) to 843 (1991–1995) to 2,402 (1996–2005).

Even if we interpret Krugman's assertion that the new growth theories have fizzled as meaning they have not had much impact in economists' understanding of macroeconomics, this interpretation is contradicted by the large body of research on endogenous growth and business cycles. Where Krugman's assertion does seem to have weight, though, is in the lack of impact that the new growth theories have had on macroeconomic policy. Indeed, a Google Scholar search for "endogenous growth" and "policy impact" returns two pages of general work on the subject, and none of the articles returned generates more than a few dozen citations.

We believe this lack of policy impact can be traced ultimately to the new theory's failure to embrace realistic models of imperfect competition in general equilibrium. While models of monopolistic competition achieve the needed positive profit accumulation for on-going R&D, they can't capture the degree of oligopolistic concentration we see in modern developed economies. Nor can they capture the effects of such concentration on income and wealth distribution, and the feedback effects this generates in the market.

Following on from Spear and Young's volume in the ISETE series entitled *Overlapping Generations* (Spear & Young, 2023), we present this volume on *Endogenous Growth*. As Spear and Young did for the OLG model, we will pursue the question of how the historical development of endogenous growth theory

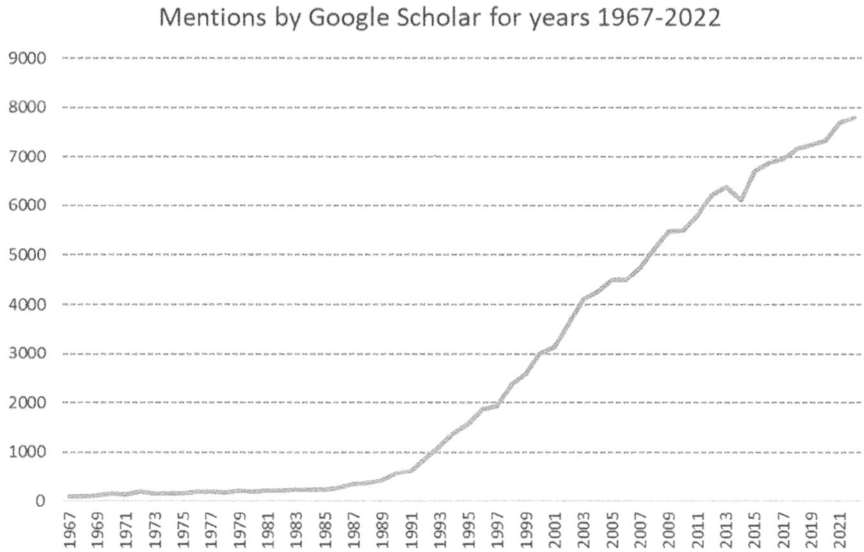

Fig. 1. Records for the Search Term "endogenous growth" 1967–2022 in Google Scholar. *Source*: Compiled from Google Scholar.

led to the neglect of more ***realistic*** models of imperfect competition, and their effect on endogenous growth by focusing on the origins, evolution, development, and dissemination of endogenous growth with emphasis on: (i) the mathematical methods underlying the approach, such as how the application of Hamiltonians and dynamic programming enabled the approaches to develop; (ii) the application of models of returns-to-scale, such as decreasing, constant, and increasing types; (iii) models of competition applied by those who developed the models; (iv) approaches to equilibrium advocated and used by the model-makers; (v) changes in the nature and use of capital in the models, and the implications of these approaches for the success or failure of the models as developed.

The story of endogenous growth begins, for our purposes, with the story of how modern economists sought to explain the remarkable expansion of standards of living that started in the late 1800s with the onset of the industrial revolution and continued full tile into the 20th century. As many previous authors have noted, interest in growth among economists goes back at least as far as Adam Smith. Barro and Sala-i-Martin (1992, p. 9) state that Smith (1776), Ricardo (1895), and Malthus (1926), and, much later, Ramsey (1928), Young (1998), Knight (1944), and Schumpeter (1996) provide many of the basic elements that appear in modern endogenous theories of economic growth. These include forms of competition and equilibrium; externalities, returns to scale and accumulation of physical and human capital; income, education, and population growth; technological progress and specialization of labor; discoveries of new goods and modes of production; monopoly power and the role of government.

Moreover, as Kenneth Arrow (1998, p. 403) noted, "there has been a long tradition, going back to Adam Smith (1776), that technological progress is somehow intrinsically associated with increasing returns." Arrow continued to say that this link was later recognized by Young (1998) and Kaldor (1957), and "more recently, by Arrow (1962), Shell (1966), and Romer (1990a, 1990b)."

The first formal attempts to construct models of economics growth, which would delineate the various drivers of growth, go back to Roy Harrod and Evsey Domar and their development of what we now call the Harrod–Domar model. The Harrod–Domar (HD) model grew out of an attempt to put the recently defined aggregates of national income developed in the early 1930s by Simon Kuznets in some semblance of economic order that would explain economic growth. The basis for the model was a set of what Nicholas Kaldor would later characterize as the "stylized facts of economic growth." Foremost among these was the relative constancy of aggregate the savings rate and the relative constancy of the capital-output ratio in production. Based on this, the HD model specifies the following behavioral relationships:

$$\dot{K} = v\dot{Y}I = \dot{K} + \delta K = v\dot{Y} + \delta v Y = sY,$$

where K is the aggregate stock of capital, Y is the aggregate output (and income), v is the capital–output ratio, s is the savings rate, and δ is the rate of depreciation. As is standard, dots over variables are time derivatives. If we divide the second equation by Y, this yields

$$\dot{y} = \frac{\dot{Y}}{Y} = \frac{s}{v} - \delta.$$

For reasonable values of the parameters s, v, and δ, this equation yields plausible growth rates. Thus, for example, with $s = 0.2$, $v = 3$, $\delta = 0.04$, this implies a growth rate of 3%.

The only problem with this model lies in the fact that the parameters were taken as behavioral specifications. As such, the steady-state equilibrium of the model, where $\dot{y} = 0$, exhibits knife-edge stability: a slight increase in the savings rates (other parameters constant) implies the economy grows explosively, while a slight decrease implies that it implodes. This implied instability led Solow (1956), after his seminal paper "A contribution to the theory of economic growth", to introduce the possibility of capital–labor substitution in production in Solow (1957). This introduction effectively endogenized the capital–labor and capital–output ratios in the HD model, leading to a very different characterization of the growth properties of the economy. The famous Solow differential equation states that

$$\dot{k} = sy - (\delta + n)k$$

where all of the variables and parameters are as in the HD model, with the addition of n which is the rate of population growth. If we work with a simple Cobb–Douglas production function, we can write this equation as

$$\dot{k} = sAk^{\alpha} - (\delta + n)k,$$

where α is the share of output going to capital. From this, one can easily determine that the steady-state equilibrium, where $\dot{k} = 0$, is stable under perturbations of k.

Solow's advancement dispelled the instability problem with the HD model and showed that it was possible for the economy to keep pace with the growing population in a way that kept *per capita* output constant along a balanced growth path, which dispelled the dismal predictions about economic growth going back to Thomas Malthus. But Solow took the analysis a step further in Solow (1957), where he did a careful analysis of how well the new neoclassical growth model explained actual growth data. Solow's procedure here was to posit that the aggregate production function exhibited long-run constant returns to scale in capital and labor, combined with some other exogenous driving factor. By then working in *per capita* terms and taking account of Euler's theorem on homogeneous functions, he reduced the implications of the model to a differential equation relating the growth of output to that of the *per capita* capital stock and the exogenous factor:

$$\frac{\dot{y}}{y} = \frac{\dot{A}}{A} + w_k \frac{\dot{k}}{k},$$

where y and k are as above, w_k is the share of income going to capital (with $1 - w_k$ going to labor), and $A(t)$ is the exogenous forcing factor. Solow then carefully filtered the available data on GNP, labor employment, and expenditures on capital to get the measured quantities to line up with the inputs in the model. This was not a straightforward undertaking, since, for example, measured capital expenditures capture the full capital stock, while the model calls for capital in use to be counted.

What Solow found is the now famous "residual." *Per capita* growth in output for the United States between 1909 and 1949 averaged 1.5% more per year than could be explained purely in terms of increased population and growth in the capital stock. The measured residual, of course, accounts for the persistent increases in standard of living that have occurred since the industrial revolution. As to the question of where this residual comes from, Solow answered this question in the title of his paper: technical change was making workers and their tools more productive over time. Implicit in this characterization of the growth driver was the idea that scientific knowledge and applications of this knowledge to economic processes created the tools and conditions needed for the economy to grow at rates faster than population increase. Solow did not pursue the implications of his discovery further, seemingly content to assert that science happens, so it fell to the next generation of growth theorists to begin a fuller exploration of Solow's discovery, founding the area of study we know call endogenous growth theory, also known as the "new theory of growth."

After Solow's early work, increasing returns to capital began to be linked to innovation. What Solow called "second wave" endogenous growth theorists extended the argument that capital investment, if correctly modelled, could also exhibit IRS, if it was used for innovative purposes, such as investment in R&D,

and human capital: knowledge and skills. Indeed, as Solow (1994) noted in the *Journal of Economic Perspectives* (p. 45, 51):

> The current wildfire revival of interest in growth theory was touched off by articles by Romer (1986a, 1986b from his 1983 thesis) and Lucas (1988 from his 1985 Marshall lectures) ...I think that the real value of endogenous growth theory will emerge from its attempt to model the endogenous component of technological progress as an integral part of the theory of economic growth. Here too the pioneer was Romer (1990a, 1990b). Many others have followed his lead: my short list includes Grossman and Helpman (1991), Aghion and Howitt (1992), Stokey (1992) and Young (1991, 1993) ...

Other "second wave" models included factors such as real interest rates (Gelb, 1989); convexity (Jones & Manuelli, 1990; Rebelo, 1991); fiscal policy (Barro, 1990; Barro & Sala-i-Martin, 1992); inflation (Bruno & Easterly, 1998); real exchange rates (Rodrik, 2008); and international productivity differences (Klenow & Rodriguez-Clare, 1997). A year after Solow's *JEP* article, Charles Jones dealt with "R&D-based models of economic growth," in which he developed the notion of "semi-endogenous growth" (SEG) (Jones, 1994), later stating that "essentially any model that possesses IRS is likely a SEG model" (Jones, 2022b, p. 135). The SEG approach will also be dealt with in this volume.

Our object is this book is not to provide a history of endogenous growth per se, as several conventional narratives have already appeared in the literature since 1990, including by those involved – indirectly or directly – in its evolution. These range from accounts presented in working and published papers, to survey articles, Festschrift chapters and textbooks (Aghion & Durlauf, 2005; Aghion & Howitt, 1998, 2006; Dixit, 1990; Jones, 2022a; Romer, 1984, 2014; Stiglitz, 1990, among others).

Rather, the approach we take here focuses on individual, institutional, and thematic research programs related to the development of endogenous growth. Individual programs were those where one or more researchers were involved and based upon dissertations or collaborative efforts, such as between graduate students and their supervisors, or colleagues. Institutional programs originated in specific settings – seminars, workshops, research centers and sponsored projects, and intra- or inter-university collaboration. Thematic programs reflected focus on specific theoretical elements or their combination such as technology and innovation, learning processes, externalities and returns, the nature of competition, and human capital. We deal here with the evolution and dissemination of watershed published papers, and the institutional settings in which they developed by referring to their *unpublished, working*, and *conference* versions accordingly.

Moreover, as we have shown in previous work, elements of the *evolution* of economic ideas may be described via analysis of their respective *morphologies* (Spear & Young, 2023). And, as will be seen regarding endogenous growth theory and models, *morphologies* can reflect several economic premises and predictions. These include, for example, assumptions regarding:

(i) behavior of economic agents,
(ii) externalities related to human capital,
(iii) learning-by-doing on the economy-wide level,

(iv) innovation spin-offs,
(v) "Creative destruction."

The book chapters are organized as follows:

CHAPTER 1: ENDOGENOUS GROWTH THEORY AND MODELS: THE "FIRST WAVE"[1]

This chapter deals with the development of what can be called "endogenous growth models" over the period 1952–1973. It surveys the works of early endogenous growth theorists and goes on to deal with the Stanford–Chicago–MIT–Yale nexus of growth theorists, graduate students, and seminars. The impact and output of conference sessions at AEA and Econometric Society Meetings on growth, technical progress, and innovations over the period 1964–1968 are discussed, and the important volume edited by Karl Shell (1966) is dealt with. Contributions over the period 1961–1973, including dissertations, working papers, technical reports, conference presentations, book chapters, and papers, are surveyed, including the Shell (1966)'s *watershed* realization of *the incompatibility of competitive equilibrium with increasing returns* (p. 73). Moreover, the prescient, albeit *unrecognized* contributions of Phelps in papers as early as 1961–1962 that anticipated *stochastic* versions of the AK model, will be discussed.

CHAPTER 2: THE INTERREGNUM: EXTENSIONS OF THE CANONICAL GROWTH MODEL[2]

In the immediate aftermath of Solow's discovery that the canonical growth model couldn't explain the growth in *per capita* output and income observed since the Industrial Revolution, the logical research program was that undertaken by Frankel (1962) and Shell (1966, 1973) where they incorporated what Shell called "inventive activity" into the growth model. But this research program never took off and this early work is often overlooked. The result was an interregnum in the development of growth theory which saw the development by Cass and Shell of the so-called Hamiltonian approach to analyzing the growth model, its replacement in most applications by dynamic programming techniques, the development of first two-sector growth models in the work of Uzawa (followed by general multi-sector models), and the development of stochastics extensions of the growth model by Brock and Mirman that became the workhorse for real business cycle models. This chapter surveys the key developments during this period.

Uzawa's work on two-sector dynamics also influenced Lucas; early work on human capital via the obvious inclusion of an education sector in addition to the usual production sector (something which Uzawa himself anticipated). Finally, many current models of endogenous growth have factored in the effects of risk and uncertainty on growth and the investment in new knowledge, so the early work on modeling equilibrium stochastic processes has been important.

CHAPTER 3: LUCAS AND GROWTH: ORIGINS, METHODS, AND MODELS

The thesis of the chapter is that *Lucas' early papers in the microeconomics of the firm form a family of models with which Lucas gave an effective answer to the challenges growth theory faced after Solow's early contribution*, referred to as an exogenous theory of growth. It is argued that the literature of the 1950–1960s expressed a need for a micro-founded growth theory to treat technological investment as the result of optimal resource allocation. In answer to this suggestion, Lucas, in his oft-neglected papers of the mid-1960s, described technological change as a variant of investment in physical capital. His famous 1988 endogenous growth theory paper is analyzed in comparison to this set of his *early* models to highlight their similarities and differences. The connection between Uzawa (1965) and the development of Lucas (1988) is also assessed here, mainly in the context of Lucas; participation in Uzawa's University of Chicago growth theory seminar, based on archival research and interviews with attendees.

CHAPTER 4: ROMER AND THE "NEW GROWTH THEORY"

This chapter deals with Romer's contributions to endogenous growth, starting with his job market paper and 1983 dissertation, in which he applied Hamiltonians, and *demarcated his approach from that of Cass-Koopmans*. His Rochester Center for Economic Research (*RCER*) *Working Papers* over the period 1983–1986 on *increasing returns and growth* are analyzed, and a comparison is made between his 1983 and 1986 models and presentation. We then survey the evolution in Romer's approach from his December 1986 *RCER* WP (in which he recognized the Euler theorem problem earlier mentioned by Shell (1966) [the incompatibility of competitive equilibrium with increasing returns] and instead applied the Dixit-Stiglitz imperfect competition approach), and deal with variorum drafts of what became his 1990 JPE paper, such as his 1988 little-known Buffalo Conference presentation and the reaction to it, are presented here for the first time. His retrospective 1994 *JEP* and other post 1990 papers are discussed and put in the perspective of Romer's growth research program.

CHAPTER 5: AUGMENTED AK, POST-LUCAS AND POST-ROMER MODELS, AND RESEARCH PROGRAMS

This chapter deals with the Jones *critique* (1995) regarding scale effects in the "first generation" of endogenous growth (EG) models, of Romer, Grossman and Helpman, and Aghion and Howitt vintage, as the data showed a "Red Queen effect," that is to say, keeping the growth rate of the economy constant at a positive level requires devoting every increasing amounts of resources to research and development. The *modification* Jones proposed in the form of the semi-endogenous growth (SEG) approach is discussed. We go on to describe Jones; *conundrum* (1999) regarding SEG and *population growth*, and the subsequent models which deal with it (Deonpoulous and Thompson; Peretto; Young; Peretto and Smulders; Howitt; Li). Cozzi (2017)'s *hybrid* approach and the earlier work of Weitzman (1998) regarding recombinant growth of ideas are also dealt with.

CHAPTER 6: UNDERSTANDING RESEARCH

While all endogenous growth models are based on the notion that new ideas lead to new technologies which are operated by economic agents who embody these new ideas as human capital, the way in which economies organize and incentivize the creation of new knowledge has focused predominantly on the process of applied R&D, and the associated intellectual property protections applicable to the outcomes of these processes. This contrasts with clear empirical evidence that it is basic research that generates the most important new ideas, so in this chapter, we examine recent research into the economic organization of basic research and the ways in which it is incentivized. This will include new work on modeling the fact that university faculty simultaneously engage in both basic research and teaching activities that embed the new knowledge generated by research in human capital.

CHAPTER 7: UNIFYING THE APPROACHES? TOWARD A MORPHOLOGY OF ENDOGENOUS GROWTH

This chapter sets out a comparative morphology to deal with EG and SEG models of 1st to 4th ***generation*** vintage. This is done by highlighting: sectors and returns to scale; areas of focus of "first generation" models; "stylized facts" and "new" stylized facts of growth; "generations" of models and *population decline*; and *generalization* of models. Morphological analysis of the characteristics of 1st to 4th generation models is undertaken via focus on both EG and SEG types in comparative perspective.

NOTES

1. This chapter is a modified version of the paper "Macroeconomic Dynamics Survey: Endogenous Growth Theory and Models: The 'First Wave,' 1952–1973" by Spear and Young (2018) and reprinted here with the Journal's permission.
2. This chapter is a modification of the paper "Two-sector growth, optimal growth, and the turnpike: Amalgamation and metamorphosis" by Spear and Young (2015) and reprinted here with the Journal's permission.

CHAPTER 1

ENDOGENOUS GROWTH THEORY AND MODELS: THE "FIRST WAVE"

INTRODUCTION: SCOPE AND METHOD

In previous papers (Spear & Young, 2014, 2015), we surveyed the origins, evolution and dissemination of optimal growth, two sector and turnpike, and stochastic growth models. In this paper, we focus on *endogenous* growth theory and models. However, in contrast to our previous findings regarding optimal growth theory and its offshoots, which exhibited fairly direct lines of conceptual development, the endogenous growth story, as will be seen, is multifaceted, with a more complex pattern of intellectual evolution.

Our object here is not to provide a history of endogenous growth per se, as a number of conventional narratives have already appeared in the literature since 1990, including by those involved – indirectly or directly – in its evolution. These range from accounts presented in working and published papers, to survey articles, Festschrift chapters, and textbooks (Aghion & Durlauf, 2005; Aghion & Howitt, 1998, 2006; Dixit, 1990; Romer, 1984, 2014; Stiglitz, 1990, among others).

Rather, the approach taken here focuses on individual, institutional, and thematic research programs related to the development of endogenous growth. Individual programs were those where one or more researchers were involved and based upon dissertations or collaborative efforts, such as between graduate students and their supervisors, or colleagues. Institutional programs originated in specific settings – seminars, workshops, research centers and sponsored projects, and intra- or inter-university collaboration. Thematic programs reflected focus on specific theoretical elements or their combination such as technology and innovation, learning processes, externalities and returns, the nature of competition, and human capital. We deal here with the evolution and dissemination of watershed published papers and

Endogenous Growth: Theory, Methods and Morphology
International Symposia in Economic Theory and Econometrics, Volume 35, 11–29

ISSN: 1571-0386/doi:10.1108/S1571-038620260000035005

the institutional settings in which they developed by referring to their *unpublished, working*, and *conference* versions accordingly.

The paper surveys the development of what can be considered endogenous models *from 1952 to 1973*, that is to say, the "first wave" of the endogenous approach,[1] including the works of Abramovitz, Haavelmo, Kaldor, Kaldor and Mirrlees, Arrow, Frankel, Phelps, Phelps and Drandakis, and Uzawa. We then focus on the Stanford–Chicago–MIT–Yale (SCMY) nexus of growth theorists and their contributions. The graduate student summer seminars organized by Uzawa in Chicago over the period 1964–1967 are dealt with, including recollections of participants, who besides SCMY students, also included graduate students from Rochester and other institutions.

In addition, AEA and Econometric Society (ES) sessions on growth and capital theory, technical change, technical progress, and theory of innovations over the period 1964–1968 are discussed. The 1967 volume edited by Shell, which included papers emanating from the Chicago groups and AER and ES meetings, by Sheshiski, Norhaus, Cass and Yaari, and Shell himself, will be discussed. The contributions of Shell, Von-Weizacker, Sheshinski, Inada, Aoki, Nordhaus, Stiglitz, Atkinson and Stiglitz, Sidrauski, Calvo, Razin, and Nelson and Phelps, Uzawa and others, over the period 1965–1973, are also surveyed. These include dissertations, working papers, technical reports, conference presentations, book chapters, and papers published by them.

We then turn to the early development of some of the building blocks of what became the "second wave" of the endogenous approach, that is, endogenous technical progress, human capital, increasing returns to scale (IRTS), and imperfect-competition approaches. Finally, the importance of the realization that a competitive equilibrium was not compatible with increasing returns (Shell, 1966, 1973) is discussed.

MODELS IN THE 1950S AND EARLY 1960S

Central Questions, Inventive Activity, Stylized Facts, Learning, and the "AK" Mark 1 Model

Approaches to economic progress date back to Smith and Ricardo. Capital and population theories, as they affected long run change – combined with theories of decreasing and increasing returns – provided the basis for studies of growth. Abramowitz (1952) set out what he saw as the "central questions in the theory of growth" (pp. 135–144). These were (i) supplies of factors of production; (ii) psychological and qualitative attributes of population; (iii) industrial, commercial, and financial organization; (iv) legal and political framework of economic life;

[1]We do not discuss the origins of the application of the notion of increasing returns here, as the idea goes back to Smith (1776) and Marshall (1890). For one of the earliest *modern* views, see Young (1928). For an assessment of the idea seven decades after Young, see the papers in Arrow et al. (1998).

and (v) discovery and exploitation of knowledge. He then set out what he saw as the parallel between the increase in the stock of knowledge and capital stock. As he put it: "Insofar as new applied knowledge results from the deliberate devotion of resources to its discovery and use, the stock of knowledge is increased by a process identical with that which produces an increase in the stock of material equipment" (Abramowitz, 1952, p. 146).

Despite its importance for the endogenous growth story, his 1952 paper is not widely cited. His 1956 *American Economic Review* paper, on the other hand, is widely cited, from Arrow (1962) to Romer (1990a, 1990b), and by many others. In this paper, Abramowitz sets out, in a prescient manner, what he saw as "the central problem" facing growth theorists and analysis. As he put it:

> To identify the causes which explain not only the rate at which are opportunities to raise efficiency increase but also the pace at which we take advantage of those opportunities will, no doubt, remain the central problem in both of history and theory... of economic growth. (Abramowitz, 1956, pp. 13–14)

But, while in his paper Abramowitz (1956) analyzed the data for historical trends in output and the utilization of resources in the U.S. case, he did *not* provide a formal model or method for modeling them. It was left to Solow and others to fill the gap.

Another early approach to endogenizing technical change and knowledge was presented by Haavelmo (1956) in his book *A Study in the Theory of Economic Evolution*. Arrow (1962) later cited this work in his famous "Learning" paper. According to Arrow (1962), Haavelmo's model was one of those that influenced the "production assumptions" of his own approach (p. 160). Arrow described Haavelmo's model in concise and lucid terms. As he put it, in Haavelmo's approach, output depended on the stocks of capital and knowledge, while investment was dependent on output and both the capital stock and stock of knowledge. The stock of knowledge, in the simplest form of Haavelmo's model, was a "function of time"; while in its "more sophisticated version," it was the outcome of investment, with "the educational effect of each act of investment decreasing exponentially in time" (p. 160).

In a 1962 NBER volume, Arrow and Fellner, among others, dealt with what Nelson (1962), who edited the volume, called "crucial conceptual problems" regarding inventive activity (pp. 3–4). According to Nelson (1962)'s introduction, the papers were originally given at a Spring 1960 University of Minnesota conference jointly sponsored by the NBER and SSRC (p. 3). In the introduction to the conference volume, Nelson noted a number of reasons for renewed "interest in inventive activity": (i) technological change, (ii) impact of research and development, (iii) new views on competition and the competitive process, and (iv) shift in focus from "short term Pareto optimality" to conditions of the "long run." He then made the prescient statement that "in a sense these developments represent a renaissance of Schumpeter" (Nelson, 1962, pp. 3–4); a tendency recalled three decades later by Aghion and Howitt (1992). Fellner (1961) had published an abridged version of his conference volume paper with the title "Two propositions in the theory of induced innovations" in *Economic Journal*. Arrow (1962)'s oft-cited conference volume paper "Economic welfare and the allocation of resources for invention" had earlier appeared under the same title as a RAND paper in December 1959 (Arrow, 1959). Interesting enough, in the RAND version, Arrow (1959) had set out one of reasons for the "possible failure of perfect competition to achieve optimality in resource allocation" as "increasing returns" (pp. 1–2). In the conference volume version, he changed this to read "indivisibilities" (Arrow, 1962, p. 609). We will return to this issue later in this paper.

Moving forward, a decade after Abramowitz set down what he saw as the five "central questions," Kaldor set out what he called six "stylized facts of economic growth" which he saw "as a starting point for the construction" of growth models. In his view, "none" of the "facts" could "be plausibly explained by the theoretical constructions of neoclassical theory" then extant (Abramowitz, 1961, pp. 178–179).

Kaldor and Mirrlees (1962) linked "technical progress" and what they called the "technical progress function" to a "purely 'endogenous' growth rate," and "endogenous factors," such as "surplus labor and underemployment" so that "continuous growth" as determined by these factors will "necessarily lead to full employment" (p. 175, p. 190). They continued on to stress the need for more scientific education and expenditure on research, and higher quality business management which would be more alert in searching for technical improvements (p. 190).

In his paper on "learning," Arrow (1962) suggested "an endogenous theory of the changes in knowledge which underlie … shifts in production functions" (p. 155). After presenting the model, he set out a research agenda for its further development. In his words:

> It has been assumed here that learning takes place only as a by-product of ordinary production. In fact, society has created institutions, education and research, whose purpose is to enable learning to take place more rapidly. A fuller model would take account of all these additional variables. (Arrow, 1962, p. 172)

Arrow (1962) is one of the most widely cited papers in economics. In contrast, Frankel published in the *AER*, in the same year, a "rarely cited paper" (Ljungqvist & Sargent, 2018, p. 459) which, according to Aghion and Howitt (1998, p. 27) among others, presented *one* of the *earliest recognizable* versions of what later came to be known as the "AK model" or "AK paradigm" (Aghion & Durlauf, 2005, p. 4), and it is to this curiosum that we now turn.

One of the difficulties in our effort to make sense of Frankel's contribution is that, on the one hand, it was *ostensibly* "a neglected early contribution to the theory of economic growth" with the "only recent reference … in Aghion and Howitt (1998)," according to Cannon (2000, p. 292, p. 294, note 4); while on the other hand, *even prior to 1998*, Frankel's approach was mentioned by Aghion, Banerjee, and Piketty in CEPR symposium papers (1996, 1997), *before* the publication of their well-known paper in *QJE* (1999). Another difficulty is that observers have linked Frankel (1962)'s approach to those of Romer (1986b) and Lucas (1988) and also to that of Rebelo (1991). Romer (1983) outlined his approach in his thesis; Lucas (1985) in his Marshall lectures (published 1988); and Rebelo (1991), as noted. Aghion and Howitt (1998), for their part, maintained that while

Frankel's "basic idea," that is, "his AK model" can be found in Romer and Lucas, they added the caveat that their respective approaches "actually laid out more than an AK model" (p. 27, note 2). An additional problem is that while some observers have talked about a linkage between the approaches of Romer and Lucas, others have linked Lucas (1988) with the earlier work of Uzawa (1965); again, we will deal with this below. Moreover, still others have maintained the AK story to have started with Harrod (1939) and Domar (1946), linking their approaches to that of Frankel (1962) *including Frankel himself, who significantly modified the Harrod-Domar model to essentially develop his own* (p. 1009). *Finally Frankel's approaches to growth and technological change are not limited to his 1962 AER paper* (Frankel, 1955, 1961, 1965).

When queried regarding the development of his approach, Frankel replied that his interest in growth models evolved out of his Ph.D. work. His 1953 Berkeley thesis dealt with Industrial Development Councils in Britain. He wrote "one of the concerns of the Councils, as I recall, was the productivity of British industry" (personal communication, 2013, October 8). In 1955, he published a paper in the *AER* entitled "Obsolescence and Technological Change in a Maturing Economy." In this, he attempted to assess the "degree to which ... innovation is retarded" according to the technological level of industries (Frankel, 1955, pp. 306–309). His paper "Producer goods, consumer goods and acceleration of growth" was published in *EJ* in 1961. In this, he presented "a two-sector growth model..." which integrates and sets forth the relations between the capital stocks and the respective outputs in the investment and consumption sectors (Frankel, 1961, p. 2). His 1962 *AER* Paper and AK model have been extensively dealt with by others and thus will not be discussed here. Albeit limited in its applicability (Aghion et al., 1999), greatly supplemented by Rebelo's work, and ostensibly supplanted by the approaches of Lucas, Romer, and others, suffice it to cite Aghion et al. (2015) who recently wrote that "Frankel is the true father of the AK model the way we teach it" (personal communication, October 22).

In 1965, Frankel published a paper in *Kyklos* entitled "Home vs. Foreign Investment: A Case Against Capital Exports." In this, he applied his AK approach to suggest "a framework in which the relation between investment decisions by enterprises, the returns to factors and the indirect development benefits to the economy can be explicitly shown" (Frankel, 1965, p. 413). As he put it, "the main elements in this approach were presented" in his 1962 *AER* paper (Frankel, 1965, p. 414, note 6).

Over the period 1964–1966, Phelps and Drandakis, individually and jointly, wrote papers focusing on technical progress, induced invention and growth. Phelps (1964, 1966) dealt with the "Golden Rule ... where technical progress is endogenous" in his Cowles Foundation *Discussion Paper* 176 "Models of Technical Progress and the Golden Rule of Research" (p. 4, 11) and in its published version of the same title in *RES* (p. 134, pp. 137–138). Drandakis and Phelps dealt with a model in which the "absolute time rate of change of the (proportionate) growth rate of capital" is "an endogenous variable." They went on to base their "induced invention hypothesis" on this accordingly in their Cowles Foundation *Discussion Paper* 128 entitled "A Model of Induced Invention, Growth and Distribution"

(Drandakis & Phelps, 1965, pp. 9–11, p. 28), which later appeared under the same title in *EJ* (1966, pp. 828–829, p. 838). At the September 1965 World Congress of the ES, Drandakis and Phelps gave an amended version of their Cowles Foundation *Discussion Paper* at the session "Investment and technological change" chaired by Goodwin. Interestingly enough, at the same World Congress, Inada presented a paper entitled "Business Cycles and Endogenous Factors for Economic Growth" at the session "Cycles and growth"; we will return to Inada's contributions below (Program of September 1965 meeting, *Econometrica* 1966, p. 7, p. 10).

In January 1965, Uzawa published a paper in the *IER* entitled "Optimum Technical Change in an Aggregative Model of Economic Growth" which became the basis for what has been called the Uzawa–Lucas model. A number of details regarding this path-breaking paper should be noted here. First, according to the *IER*, the manuscript was "received August 25, 1963, revised April 20, 1964" (Uzawa, 1965, p. 18). Uzawa (1965) was first at Stanford, moving to Chicago in 1964, so he cited both as his institutional affiliation (p. 31). Moreover, Uzawa acknowledged that he was "greatly indebted for valuable comments and suggestions" to Domar (at MIT), which he had briefly visited. In a footnote, Uzawa set out the object of the model he presented in his 1965 paper. As he put it (Uzawa, 1965, p. 19, note 3):

> A number of studies, in particular by ... Shultz [at Chicago] have been made recently on the implications of the improvement in the quality of labor upon the pattern of economic growth. The model presented below has been intended primarily to serve as a basis for discussions on the economic effects of education.

And this, in the context of the notions of "optimum" and "technical change" that reflected Uzawa's interests as manifest in some of his Stanford Technical Reports between 1960 and 1963.

CHICAGO AND MIT SEMINARS, AEA AND ES SESSIONS, PAPERS, AND PH.D. THESES

Uzawa's Chicago Summer Seminars, 1964–1967

In contrast to the intellectual dissonance between "saltwater" and "freshwater" economists starting in the mid-1970s, the period from 1964 until this "great divide" was characterized by cross fertilization and positive interaction between growth theorists and graduate students based at Stanford, Chicago, MIT, and Yale, among other places. This is manifest in the graduate student summer seminars organized by Uzawa at Chicago sponsored by the NSF (1964–1966) and MSSB (1967); in AEA and ES sessions on growth and capital theory, and technical change and innovation over the same period; and in seminars, and publications based upon them, such as the 1967 volume edited by Shell – based on MIT seminars on optimal economic growth, 1965–1966 – and the November 1967 Chicago growth seminar led by Uzawa (later published in *JPE*, 1969). Output of the seminars included University of Chicago Technical Reports, presentations by seminar participants over the period 1965–1968 at AEA and ES sessions, dissertation chapters, published papers, and book chapters.

Now, Uzawa (1965)'s Chicago graduate student summer seminar has been recounted by Stiglitz (1990) in a number of places, asserting "among the topics of discussion was how to incorporate endogenous technological change into growth theoretic models" (p. 63, note 12). It has also been dealt with by Warsh (2006, p. 155). In addition, the 1966 seminar was mentioned by Lucas, who participated (2001). But the 1964 and 1967 Uzawa Chicago graduate student summer seminars, however, *have been overlooked*, despite their importance.

The 1964 Uzawa Chicago summer seminar included Cass, Ryder, Douglas, Oniki, Goldman, Shell, and Teubal. All were Stanford Ph.D. students, with the exception of Teubal, who was at Chicago (communication from Shell, 2013, October 26) (see Appendix 1 for a listing of their dissertations). As Stiglitz (1990, p. 63, note 12) recalled, Uzawa (1965)'s summer Chicago seminar included Stiglitz, Akerlof, Chaudhuri, Sheshinski, Nordhaus, Lamalfa, Levy, and Krishna. In other words, the group consisted of MIT Ph.D. students, with the exception of Lamalfa, an MIT research fellow, Levy, a Yale Ph.D. student, and Krishna, a Ph.D. student at Chicago. Attending the 1966 Summer seminar was, among others, Lucas, then an Assistant Professor at Carnegie Tech. Cass, then an Assistant Professor at Yale, also attended, as did Lav, a student from Johns Hopkins; the recollections of Lucas will he presented below (Lucas, 2001, p. 14).

The 1967 Chicago summer seminar was characterized by the fact that Uzawa did not actively participate at the beginning of the period, as he was obliged to be in Japan that time, and thus the seminar was led, until his return, by his former Chicago Ph.D. student, Sidrauski, who was then an assistant professor at MIT. Graduate students included Calvo, Ethier, Mirman, Narayanan, Nissen, Onitsuka, Razin, and Rhee and comprised the most diverse group of participants in the seminar's brief history. The group included Ph.D. students from Chicago, Yale, Berkeley, Rochester, and even the University of Kansas (Cutler, MSSB Projects Summary Report, July 12, 1973).

AEA AND ES SESSIONS, 1964–1967: PRESENTATIONS, THESIS CHAPTERS, AND PAPERS

As mentioned above, between 1964 and 1967, papers by student members of Uzawa's summer seminars, and others, were presented at ASSA meetings, at sessions on growth and capital theory and technical change, sponsored by the AEA and ES, respectively. For example, at the Chicago December 1964 meetings, in the ES session "Growth models," chaired by Amartya Sen, Douglas, a 1964 Uzawa group participant from Stanford, presented "A two sector growth model with inside money," discussed by Ando, which was based upon his thesis on monetary dynamics (1966). At the December 1964 session "Optimal growth theory," chaired by Phelps, Cass presented a paper entitled "Optimum Economic Growth in an Aggregate Model of Capital Accumulation: The Finite Horizon Case," discussed by Diamond (ASSA 1964 Program, p. 102, p. 169). This was a version of his November 1964 Cowles Foundation *Discussion Paper* 178 (1964, p. 1, note 1), and his thesis chapter III (1965). It was published in *Econometrica* (1966).

At the parallel ES session on "technical change," chaired by Nelson, Shell presented a paper entitled "Invention and Technical Change," discussed by Hurwicz (ASSA 1964 Program, p. 169). According to Shell's recollection, this presentation was partially based on the "endogenous growth" paper he presented at Uzawa (1964)'s August Chicago summer seminar entitled "A Model of Inventive Activity and Capital Formation," circulated as University of Chicago Technical Report 2 (August). This was essentially Chapter III – with the same title – of his Stanford thesis (Uzawa, 1965, April), supervised by Arrow and Uzawa (Shell, 2015); but more about Shell's Ph.D. thesis below.

At the December 1965 New York ASSA meeting, they were a number of AEA and ES sessions relevant to our story. The ES session "Growth theory I" took place on December 28, the AEA session "Capital theory: technical progress and capital structure" on December 29, parallel to the ES session "Growth theory II." The importance of these sessions cannot be overstated: some of the presentations constituted, in our view, fundamental contributions to the ongoing development of the endogenous approach to growth.

The ES session "Growth I" was chaired by Solow. There were three presentations. All of the papers were given by participants in the 1964 and 1965 Uzawa Chicago summer seminars. Cass and Yaari's paper on growth and accumulation was discussed by McManus; the paper by Akerlof and Stiglitz on investment and income by Jorgenson; that by Teubal on monetary policy and growth by Phelps (ASSA 1965 Program, p. 67). An early version of the Cass–Yaari paper had been circulated in November 1965 as Cowles Foundation *Discussion Paper* 198 under the title "Individual Saving, Aggregate Capital Accumulation and Efficient Growth." This later appeared, in revised form, in Shell's 1967 volume. Their paper presented at the ES session dealt with the effects of technical change based on a Modigliani–Brumberg framework that generated aggregate saving which determined capital accumulation (*Econometrica* Report, 1966a, p. 118). The paper by Akerlof and Stiglitz presented a "new model" with "dynamic properties" differing from earlier Harrod–Domar and neoclassical frameworks, based upon endogenous investment (*Econometrica* Report, 1966a, p. 118). Teubal's paper, based upon a chapter from his Chicago Ph.D. thesis "Inflation, Unemployment and Economic growth," was earlier presented at Uzawa's Chicago Summer seminar in August 1964 (communication from Teubal, December 11, 2015).

The second ES session on growth (Growth II), held on December 29, 1965, was chaired by Smyth, and consisted of three presentations. The first was a paper by Uzawa and Sidrauski an entitled "Price Expectations, Inflation and Economic Growth," discussed by Sato. Other papers were given by Mortensen on consumption and growth, discussed by Drandakis, and Britto on "Balanced Growth and Efficiency with Increasing Returns to Scale," discussed by Cass (ASSA 1965 Program, p. 90). We will return to Britto's paper below in the context of a discussion of IRTS; at this point, we focus on that by Uzawa and Sidrauski, which has also not received attention.

With regard to the Uzawa–Sidrauski paper, the following should be noted. First, Sidrauski was Uzawa's Chicago Ph.D. student and later, as a junior faculty member at MIT, led the summer seminar in 1967 when Uzawa was absent from

Chicago. Second, the December 1965 ES presentation was later cited by Sidrauski (1967) with the title "Inflation, optimum consumption and real cash balances" in his May 1967 *AER* Ph.D. thesis summary (p. 544). Third, according to the abstract of the December 1965 paper, as published in the *Econometrica* report of the 1965 ES sessions, their analysis of "the effects of monetary fiscal policies on the pattern of growth, and the structure of the monetary and fiscal policies which result in optimum growth" was conducted "in terms of the techniques of optimum economic growth as recently developed by Koopmans, Cass, von Weiszacker, and others" (*Econometrica* Report, 1966b, p. 128).

However, the December 1965 session that had the most impact on the development of the endogenous approach was the AEA session "Capital theory: technical progress and capital structure" chaired by Solow. It was parallel to the second ES sessions on growth and held on Wednesday, December 29. *In retrospect, presentations at this session comprised two out of the three major papers in the early endogenous growth triad*, that is to say, those by Shell (1965b, 1966) and Nelson–Phelps (1965a, 1965b, 1966) and Uzawa (1965) being the third. Shell's paper, entitled "Inventive Activity and Capital Accumulation" was discussed by Sato; that by Nelson and Phelps, "Investment in Humans, Technological Diffusion, and Economic Growth," was discussed by Hirshleifer (ASSA Program 1965, p. 86).

The Nelson–Phelps paper appeared as a Rand Corporation paper in December 1965, whose abstract read:

> The paper is concerned with the relationship between capital structure and technological progress. The process of education is viewed as an act of investment in people, and educated people are seen as bearers of human capital. According to the models presented, the rate of return to education is greater the more technologically progressive is the economy. This suggests that the progressiveness of the technology has implications for the optimal capital structure in the broad sense. It is concluded that society should build more human capital relative to tangible capital the more dynamic is the technology.

The paper and Hirshleifer's (1966) comments were published in the *AER* (pp. 69–75; pp. 81–82). In his comments, Hirshleifer (1966) focused on the Nelson–Phelps hypothesis "education promotes growth" (p. 81), or as they put it in the paper "education spreads the process of technological diffusion" and thereby economic growth (p. 70).

Shell (1965a, 1965b)'s December paper "Inventive Activity and Capital Accumulation" was based on his August 1964 Uzawa Chicago seminar paper "A model of inventive activity and capital accumulation," which – with the same title – became Chapter III of his thesis. Shell (1965)'s December presentation was discussed by Sato, and the paper and comments by Sato (1966) published in *AER*. According to Shell (2015, communication, December 3), his AEA presentation (1965b) and *AER* (1966) paper "were a specialization of the thesis chapter to the case where the three-sector technology is reduced to one sector, so that research and investment are in the same units as consumption." In his *AER* paper, Shell (1966) put it as follows:

> I treat the one-sector model for ease of exposition. This implies that the production possibility frontier is a hyper-plane in the consumption-investment-invention space (p. 63, note 2).

In his comments on Shell's paper, Sato (1966) wrote:

> Technical progress has been a sort of orphan in capital theory. Even in recent theoretical developments, technical progress has remained largely an exogenous variable. Some have attempted to introduce technical progress functions to rectify this state of affairs. Now Professor Shell attempts to make technical progress an endogenous variable by making the rate of technical progress an increasing function of current expenditure on inventive activity... The close analogy between capital accumulation and augmentation of technological knowledge is the most interesting feature of the model (p. 78).

Regarding the reactions to his AEA presentation, Shell recalled (2015, communication November 28): "Solow served as a neutral chair. Much later (after Romer) he seemed to be very keen on Shell inventive activity...I remember warm vibrations [from] Sid Winter, but not the details. Phelps hired me for Penn after this, so he must have been non-negative on this work." A more detailed look at Shell's early work will be presented below.

At this point, let us turn to the December 1966 ASSA meeting in San Francisco, where others from Uzawa's Chicago summer seminars presented papers. At the ES session on December 27, "Theory of innovations and technical change," chaired by Tang, Nordhaus presented "The theory of invention in the firm," discussed by Cass, and Shell "A Schumpeterian model of induced innovation and capital accumulation," discussed by Phelps. At the 1966 ES session on the theory of economic development, on December 28, chaired by De Vries, Goldman – a member of the 1964 Uzawa Group – presented "Optimal growth and continual planning revision," based on his Stanford Ph.D. thesis. Later that day, the ES session "Growth theory," chaired by Shell, included a paper by Cass and Yaari entitled "Efficient Inter-temporal Allocation of Consumption in the Neoclassical Growth Model," discussed by Hahn (ASSA 1966 Program, p. 80, p. 100, p. 114).

The next year, at the December 1967 ASSA Washington meeting, the ES session "Optimal growth models," chaired by Archibald, included a paper by Goldman "Sequential and continuous planning," discussed by Koopmans (ASSA Report 1967, p. 127). This paper was published in *JPE* (1969). Earlier that year, at the June 1967 ES Tokyo meeting, at the session on "economic growth" chaired by Uzawa, Oniki, another of the members of the 1964 Uzawa group presented a paper entitled "Comparative Dynamics in the Theory of Optimal Growth" (*Econometrica*, Report of Tokyo Meeting, 1968, p. 3).

RECOLLECTIONS OF THE UZAWA GROUPS, 1966–1967: PAPERS, PUBLICATIONS, AND PH.D. THESES

As mentioned above, Lucas attended the 1966 August seminar. In his "Professional Memoir," he recalled (Lucas, 2001, pp. 14–15):

> In 1966 I was invited to a workshop... conducted in Chicago by Hirofumi Uzawa. Uzawa was a charismatic figure, an enormous influence on theoretically minded students, who had moved to Chicago from Stanford just after I had left... Dave Cass spoke about work he and Yaari were doing, trying to understand the logic of a model of an economy with an infinity of overlapping generations that Samuelson had published in 1958. This paper had not been on reading lists of

> mine but I was immediately attracted by its simplicity and the role it had for money. This was the first model I had seen in which paper money had a useful role to perform, and had a command over goods in equilibrium. This was exciting, and the following fall I began to use this setup in my graduate courses in macroeconomics.

The work Cass (1966, September) "spoke about" at the Uzawa seminar was circulated as Cowles Foundation *Discussion Paper* 215 "A note on the role of money in providing sufficient intermediation." This was noted by the authors themselves, who wrote "A preliminary version was presented at the symposium on optimum economic growth held at the University of Chicago during August 1966" (p. 1). Lucas (2001) went on to say "The paper I had written for the Uzawa conference was never finished. I couldn't establish the mathematical result that was to be the paper's centerpiece" (p. 15).

A few months later, Lucas wrote Uzawa (on October 28, 1966) and said:

> I enclose a paper developed from the first two sections of the paper I gave at your symposium in August. As you had suggested, I developed the treatment of the competitive industry in somewhat more detail. In the new version the competitive industry is also analyzed under rational rather than static expectations. (Lucas Papers, Duke, Box 1, File 1966)

And indeed, after the 1966 Uzawa seminar, Lucas started to work with Prescott on the paper he had given there, in order to establish the mathematical result needed via Blackwell's dynamic programming approach. The result was eventually their 1971 joint paper "Investment under Uncertainty" (Lucas, 2001, p. 16).

As noted above, the 1967 Uzawa Chicago summer seminar was composed of a heterogeneous group of a dozen or so graduate students. It was, at first, led by Sidrauski, Uzawa's former graduate student, due to his absence at the beginning of the workshop. Moreover, it was focused, as was the 1965 summer seminar, in the main, on growth. Among the members of the 1967 group who presented papers based upon their Ph.D. work were Calvo and Razin. Ethier and Mirman, attended, and were influenced, to one degree or another by Uzawa. Ethier (2015, communication, November 21) recalled that his "participation was a wonderful experience… that was due to Uzawa himself, who had a great ability to stimulate students." Mirman, for his part (2015, communication, November 20), recalled Uzawa and Cass, who visited the seminar, somewhat discouraging his decision to work on uncertainty. Mirman also specifically recalled Calvo as being "the star of the group." Calvo (2015, communication, November 22) recalled presenting a paper entitled "A Vintage Model of Optimum Economic Growth" at the Chicago seminar. This paper became part of his later 1974 Yale Ph.D. thesis "Efficiency and optimality in a heterogeneous capital model-putty clay," supervised by Koopmans (1976), Chapter IV of which was eventually published in *Econometrica*.

Razin's contributions and recollections are most relevant here. He was a Chicago Ph.D. student of Uzawa's and a member of the 1967 Chicago summer seminar. In a review essay, he recalled (Razin, 2008, p. 132):

> Theories that explain endogenous technological change were known as early as [the] 1960s. Arrow (1962)'s model of learning by doing, Uzawa's (1965) model of human capital driven productivity improvements, and Shell's (1967) model of inventive technological activity. These models are part of the "First Wave" of the literature on [endogenous] economic growth… I contributed to

> developing the theory of the effect of accumulation human capital, in addition to the accumulation of physical capital, on growth, in my doctoral thesis from 1969 [chapters from which were published in *RES* (1972a), and *Metroeconomica* (1972b)].... I noticed that in Uzawa's model private and social returns coincide and applied the Uzawa model to the competitive economy. Years later this theory was extended by Lucas (1988).

Interestingly enough, Razin (1972a)'s *RES* paper "Optimum investment in human capital" was first presented in September 1970 at the Second World ES Congress under the title "The optimum rate of investment in human capital" at the session "Education" chaired by Phelps (Program, *Econometrica* 1971, p. 23). Moreover, as Razin recalled (communication, November 19, 2015) regarding his 1967 paper and 1969 dissertation: "Actually the dissertation was split into a 'normative' version, later published in *RES* (1972a) and the market-based version, later published in *Metroeconomica* (1972b), then a theory journal."

In another recent recollection, Razin (2015) first wrote that:

> Uzawa is well known ... for his seminal contribution to endogenous growth. In his article in the 1965 *IER*, productivity permanently increases as the result of permanent accumulation of human capital. Uzawa was thus a first mover in the new growth theory. (communication, November 20)

He continued: "My Ph.D. dissertation ['Investment in Human Capital and Economic Growth: a theoretical study,' University of Chicago, June 1969] has been an (and the first) application to the market economy of Hiro's [Uzawa's] human capital optimal growth theory." Because of its importance for our narrative, we present Razin's further recollections in detail below (Razzin, 2015, communication, November 20):

> I started to develop the paper at the 1967 summer camp. This summer camp, the 1967 MSSB-NSF sponsored Chicago seminar was led by Uzawa. The student group was: Burton, Calvo, Ethier, Marvy, Mirman, Narayanan, Nissen, Onitsuka, Rhee, Smith, Tsushima and me. Miguel Sidrauski was asked by Uzawa to be in charge. Uzawa was absent most of the time since he began his move from Chicago to Tokyo. There I interacted with several bright young students that were working on cutting edge research projects: Lenny Mirman (Rochester), Bill Ethier (Rochester), Guillermo Calvo (Yale). Hiro got stranded in Japan. He asked Miguel Sidrauski (his former student, and then the young star from MIT, who died from cancer less than two years afterward) to lead the "Summer Camp." We, the students, and Miguel, our leader, were highly interactive. It was an exciting first experience of an interaction within a research group. I started to develop a paper on human capital and economic growth, following an influential paper by Hiro Uzawa, which demonstrates how a centrally planned economy can efficiently affect growth through the allocation of the economy's resources between a sector that produces know how and other productive sectors.
>
> In my paper which turned out to be my Ph.D. Dissertation (1969), I applied these ideas to decentralized, market-based, equilibrium model of an economy which accumulates human capital and physical capital. I noted that "economists have long noticed that people play an important role in the process of production, and in return they are rewarded by an amount which constitutes the largest fraction of income." I guess I heard it from T. W. Schultz. In my model the accumulation of human capital is the driving force behind a permanent rate of increase in income per capita. This feature was dubbed in the 1980s as endogenous growth. I presented an unfinished paper on human capital accumulation and economic growth at a 1967 conference [the November 1967 Uzawa Chicago Conference on Growth, to be discussed below; see *JPE* (1969), 574]. The human capital-physical capital growth paradigm turned out to be important, because one stream of the Endogenous Growth Theory, decade and a half later, in

the mid-1980s, grew out of another Chicago "school" that my endogenous growth model was almost identical to the Lucas' well cited paper on endogenous growth.

Perhaps my contribution which appeared in print (*RES*, 1972), when the profession got a little "tired" of what seems to have been over-occupation in the theory of economic growth after over a decade of significant developments in this area [has been overlooked]. I was extremely successful in terms of visibility and citations with another early endogenous growth paper of mine (in which the endogenous population growth cum education is the driving force for a permanent rise in income per capita because parents trade off "quality for quantity" of their children in the growth model, A*ER* 1975).

MIT SEMINAR ON OPTIMAL GROWTH AND SHELL VOLUME, 1965–1967

Over the period 1965–1966, Shell led a seminar on the theory of optimal economic growth at MIT, papers from which were published in the 1967 volume he edited. The papers were written by members of Uzawa's 1964 and 1965 groups, such as Shell, Cass, and Ryder (1964 group); Sheshinski, Nordhaus, Duta-Chaudhuri, Akerlof (1965 group); and others then at MIT and other institutions, such as Bardhan, Bruno, Chase, and Samuelson (MIT), Marglin (Harvard), and Carter (IBRD).

Some of the papers were based upon chapters from Ph.D. dissertations, such as those of Sheshinski and Ryder; others were based upon working papers, such as that of Cass and Yaari, whose volume paper "Individual saving, aggregate capital accumulation and efficient growth" appeared earlier as Cowles Foundation *Discussion Paper* 198 (November 1965). There were also papers specifically prepared for the Shell seminar, such as that of Bardhan. Finally, Shell contributed two chapters, but more about this below.

Bardhan provided recollections of Shell (2015)'s MIT seminar; again, because of its importance to our narrative, we report his recollections at length here (communications, December 21 and 23). He wrote (Bardhan, 2015a, December 21):

I finished my Ph.D. dissertation in Cambridge University in UK on Economic Growth and International Trade in 1965 under the supervision of James Meade and Frank Hahn. Many of the chapters used optimum growth models, with the use of calculus of variations and Pontryagin's Maximum Principle. A somewhat revised version of my dissertation was published as a book with the title, *Economic Growth, Development, and Foreign Trade: A Study in Pure Theory*, John Wiley Interscience, 1970. I joined MIT in 1966, where I carried out the revisions on the dissertation for publication. Some of the revised chapters were published in *Econometrica, Review of Economic Studies, QJE* and *International Economic Review*.

Karl Shell was then my colleague at MIT. He was running a seminar on optimum growth where he asked me to present a paper, which later became a chapter in his edited book. This paper was written for Karl, it was not a part of my dissertation.

My main inspiration in this period was Robert Solow (whom as well as Ken Arrow I met as a graduate student in Cambridge, UK, when they spent a sabbatical year there). Even before I finished my dissertation, on the basis of reading some of my chapters, Bob invited me to join MIT after the completion of my Ph.D. Bob used to read all my papers and give the most valuable comments. The other person who had helped me throughout in this period was Jim Mirrlees, who was on the faculty in Cambridge, UK (he was also an examiner of my Ph.D. dissertation), and then visited MIT for a semester.

> Optimal Growth and Growth Theory in general was in the air those days in both Cambridge, UK, and Cambridge, Mass. I interacted intensively with the younger growth theory crowd at MIT, particularly Joe Stiglitz, George Akerlof, Eytan Sheshinsky, Miguel Sidrauski, and others. Coming as I did from India, my friends and mentors Amartya Sen, Sukhamay Chakrabarty, and T.N. Srinivasan were also a big influence on my work.

In answer to the question as to whether the recollection by Joe Stiglitz that "endogenous growth" was a subject of discussion at Shell's seminar and at MIT at the time, Bardhan (2015b) wrote (December 23):

> Joe is absolutely right. Endogenous Growth was very much a part of our discussion, particularly with Joe [Stiglitz], George [Akerlof] and Karl [Shell]. Arrow's 1962 Learning by Doing paper was a major inspiration for all of us (I myself published a few papers on that topic), and Learning by Doing is central to endogenous growth. Karl was, however, particularly interested in R&D as a source of endogenous growth, and that was more often discussed in his seminar.
>
> What none of us used much was the link between endogenous growth and imperfect competition, which Paul Romer developed more than two decades later. But American endogenous growth theorists do not remember that the same issue of *Review of Economic Studies* 1962 that carried Arrow's Learning by Doing article also had an article by Kaldor and Mirrlees which developed a theoretical model of endogenous growth with dynamic economies of scale and imperfect competition. (We, graduate students at Cambridge UK, studied that paper intensively.) Many years later when Paul Romer was my colleague at Berkeley, I told him about the 1962 Kaldor-Mirrlees paper, which he had never heard of.

With regard to chapters in Shell (1967)'s volume based on the dissertations of Ryder and Sheshinsky, the following may be said. Ryder (1967a, 1967b)'s paper was based upon work he had presented at the 1964 Uzawa Chicago workshop (Ryder, 1965) and his Stanford thesis "Optimal accumulation and trade in an open economy." Sheshinski's chapter in Shell's volume entitled "Optimal Accumulation with Learning by Doing" is based, in part, on Chapter V of his 1966 MIT thesis "Optimal growth with disembodied learning by doing." His chapter in the Shell volume, however, includes an extension from "closed" and "two sector models" to a two sector "open model" (Sheshinski, 1967, pp. 44–48).

Before proceeding to survey below Shell's contributions over the period 1964–1969 (his work from 1969 to 1973 will be dealt with subsequently), we turn to the November 1967 Chicago Seminar on Growth Theory led by Uzawa, papers from which appeared in *JPE* in 1969. Among these were papers based upon dissertations of two Stanford students, Goldman and Ryder, who attended Uzawa's 1964 Chicago Seminar group, along with Shell. Goldman's November 1967 presentation was titled "Sequential planning and continuous planning revision," discussed by McFadden and Radner. It was then presented at the December 1967 ASSA ES session under the title "Sequential and continuous planning," and discussed by Koopmans, as noted above. Ryder (1967a)'s contribution "Optimal accumulation in a two sector neoclassical economy with non-shiftable capital" was based upon the "second model" presented in his Stanford Ph.D. thesis.

Finally, Teubal, a member of Uzawa's 1964 group, gave a paper to November 1967 Chicago seminar in agricultural and industry development, while Razin, a member of the1967 Chicago group, gave a paper entitled "Investment in Human Capital and Economic Growth," albeit neither paper was included in 1969 *JPE* published version of the November 1967 seminar due to a "editorial considerations," according to Uzawa ("Symposium on theory of economic growth," *JPE* 1969, p. 574). Razin (1972)'s paper was part of his Ph.D. thesis and eventually published in *Metroeconomica* under the same title, also as noted above.

SHELL'S CONTRIBUTIONS AND RECOLLECTIONS, 1964–1969

As recounted above, Shell attended Uzawa (1964)'s Chicago summer seminar for graduate students. The paper he presented there was based upon the first draft of his thesis Chapter III, entitled "A Model of Inventive Activity and Capital Accumulation." This paper was circulated under this title as University of Chicago Technical Report Number 2, dated August 1964. According to Shell (2015)'s recollections, "it was also my job market paper delivered at MIT in Fall 1964" (communication, November 10). We have already discussed Shell's ASSA presentations. What then, is the relationship between his thesis, 1966 *AER* paper, and the two chapters he published in the 1967 volume he edited?

First, his paper that comprises Chapter I of his edited 1967 volume entitled "Optimal Programs of Capital Accumulation for an Economy in Which There Is Exogenous Technical Change" was based on Chapters I and II of his 1965 Stanford Ph.D. thesis, which initially dealt with "the aggregative model" of Solow and Swan (thesis Chapter I) and then with the "two sector model" of growth of Meade and Uzawa (thesis Chapter II). Second, as Shell recalled (communication February 8, 2014) Chapter III of his thesis, entitled "A Model of Inventive Activity and Capital Accumulation":

> is *2-sector* inventive activity and capital accumulation; it is the basis for the 1967 book chapter [volume Chapter IV of the same title]. Chapter III [of the thesis] also has the 1966 [*AER*] *1-sector* phase diagram as a special two sector case. So the *AER* [1966] phase diagram is in Chapter III [of the thesis], but only the *AER* [1966 paper] deals directly and simply with the *1-sector* model. Chapter IV [of the thesis] is some comparative static supporting chapter III.

In May 1967, Shell (1969) attended "The ad hoc meeting of experts on the role of advanced skills and technologies in industrial development," held at the UN in New York, and presented a paper entitled "Technological Knowledge and Economic Growth." He recalled (Shell, 2016, communication, January 16):

> Re-reading the UN conference paper was pleasant for me. It is what I had intended: a provocative think piece with ready references. The main theme is modeling endogenous growth from inventive activity. The sundry theme was "teaching" dynamic optimization in this context. I very much doubt that an untenured 20-something could have published something like this in a major journal. In the conference, Amartya and I formed a coalition of sorts. Amartya was analyzing the development (i.e., poor country) growth model of Arthur Lewis in which the real wage rate is set much higher than market clearing. Profits are saved. Wages are consumed. Then the composition of output (c, z) depends on the technology k. High k means low saving. Low k means low consumption. The "opposition" accused of trying to dump our used cars on poor people. Amartya said that the choice of technique is driven by the social demand price of investment. I showed where that price comes from.

BUILDING BLOCKS: TECHNICAL PROGRESS AND INNOVATION, HUMAN CAPITAL, GROWTH, INCREASING RETURNS, AND IMPERFECT COMPETITION, 1952–1973

A decade after Abramowitz set out the "central questions" in growth theory, as noted above, Kaldor and Mirrlees (1962) describe the relationship between technical progress and endogenous growth, and Arrow (1962) set out his "endogenous theory" of knowledge-based growth. In the years that followed, the focus was, in the main, on the roles of technical progress and innovation in the growth process, as noted above. Some, however, also attempted to bring in other factors, such as the relationship between human capital and growth, and that between increasing returns in a market economy and growth, in *both* static and dynamic frameworks. The human capital approach was ostensibly introduced by Uzawa (1965) and extended by Razin in his Ph.D. – supervised by Uzawa – and published paper, as noted above.

The implications of increasing returns to scale (IRTS) for the market economy are evident in the works of Aoki over the period 1967–1968. Aoki's approach developed out of his 1967 Minnesota Ph.D. thesis, "Increasing returns to scale and the market mechanism" Aoki (1967a) supervised by Chipman . He was then recruited to Stanford by Arrow. At Stanford, he circulated Technical Reports on increasing returns to scale, sponsored by the NSF and Stanford IMSSS, and emanating from Aoki's thesis (1967b, 1968). As he recalled (Aoki, 2013):

> My approach was not explicitly dynamic as in the work of Romer. However it is important to be analytically clear even in [the] static framework about how increasing returns could be consistent with the market economy – either through tax and subsidy schemes (in the case of external economies) or the emergence of the firm (in the case of internal economies) this is what my original contributions did. (communication, October 15)

Interestingly enough, another Ph.D. student *directly introduced* IRTS into a von Neumann type of balanced growth model at about the same time. Britto (1966) "assumed increasing returns to scale" in Chapter IV of his Brown Ph.D. dissertation "Efficient allocation of resources in a growing economy." Moreover, he actually presented his approach of the December 1965 ASSA ES session "Economic Growth II" chaired by Smyth. At that session, as noted above, Uzawa and Sidrauski also gave a paper, as did Mortensen. Britto's paper was entitled "Balanced Growth and Efficiency with Increasing Returns to Scale" and was discussed by Cass.

According to the abstract of his presentation, Britto presented a model "of a two good economy with increasing returns to scale." In the first section, he defined the "the von Neumann path of balanced growth" and demonstrated "its intertemporal efficiency." In the second section, he showed that the von Neumann path "exists…is unique, and…is the only efficient path intertemporally" (Report *Econometrica*, 1966, p. 129).

Returning to the Kaldor-Mirrlees (1962) "new model," *it should be recalled here that their approach "assumed" imperfect competition*. Indeed, as they wrote: "Each entrepreneur, operating in imperfectly competitive markets, aims at the maximum attainable growth of his own business…the share of profits resulting from a model must be higher than a certain minimum (the so-called 'degree of monopoly' or 'degree of imperfect competition')" (Kaldor-Mirrlees, 1962, p. 175, p. 180). We will return to imperfect competition below. At this point, let us survey contributions regarding endogenous growth made by two *additional* important International conferences, the First World Congress of the ES (1965), and the IEA Conference on growth (1970), and also contributions made in the period in between them.

At the First World Congress of the ES held in Rome in 1965, there were a number of sessions dealing with growth, technological change, and technological progress. Of the session on "Cycles and growth," chaired by the Ichimura, a paper entitled "Business Cycles and Endogenous Factors for Economic Growth" was presented by Inada, with Jorgenson and Hansen as discussants (Program First World Congress, Econometica, 1966, p. 7). Inada (1968) continued his interest in the subject as manifest in his subsequent paper "Endogenous technological progress and steady growth" which first appeared as a Stanford Technical Report in 1968 and was subsequently published in the *RES* (1969).

The session "Investment and technological change" chaired by Goodwin included the paper by Drandakis and Phelps "A model of induced invention, growth and distribution," previously circulated in July 1965 as Cowles Foundation *Discussion Paper* 198 and later published in the *EJ*, as noted above (Program First World Congress, Econometrica, 1966, p. 10). The session "Causes and consequences of technical progress," chaired by Mansfield, included Levhari's paper "Extensions of Arrow's learning by doing," and that by von Weizsäcker's "Tentative notes on a two sector model with induced technical progress" (Program First World Congree, Econometrica, 1966, pp. 11–12). Both of these papers later appeared in *RES* (Levhari, 1966a; von Weizsäcker, 1966). Levhari (1966b) also expanded on this in his *RES* paper "Further implications of learning by doing."

In their 1969 *EJ* piece, entitled "A New View of Technological Change," Atkinson and Stiglitz (1969) questioned the approaches of Kennedy (1964) and Samuelson (1965) regarding the impact of "induced invention and innovation on economic growth and distribution" (pp. 577–578). In his paper "An economic theory of technological change," Nordhaus used what he termed a "microtheoretic approach," to provide "a reasonable model of the inventive process." This paper was *originally* presented at the December 1968 Chicago ES session "Theory of innovation," chaired by Phelps, under the title "The sources of productivity change," and was discussed by Domar and Stiglitz. It appeared as Cowles Foundation *Discussion Paper* 265 in February 1969 and was published in AER (Stiglitz, 1969).

The 1970 IEA Conference "Models of economic growth," held in Jerusalem, was attended by leading growth theorists such as Atkinson, Bliss, Bruno, Diamond, Dixit, Hahn, Levhari, Mirrlees, Shell, Sheshinski, Stern, Stiglitz, Teubal, Uzawa, von Weizsäcker, and Yaari, among others. The Conference proceedings were published in 1973. In the introduction to the Conference volume, edited by Mirrlees and Stern, Mirrlees (1973) outlined "some of the uses to which growth models have been put" (pp. xii–xxi). For our purpose here, the most important paper in the volume was by Shell (1973 [1970]), entitled "Inventive Activity, Industrial Organization and Economic Growth." Shell (1973) actually based section II of his paper, which he called "the pure monopoly model," on his paper "The Schumpeterian model of induced innovation and capital accumulation" that he had earlier presented at the ES meeting in December 1965 (p. 80, note 3), as noted above. Moreover, he again stressed what he saw as the limitations of "constant returns to scale" in "contemporary growth theory," which he had been emphasizing from 1965 Ph.D. thesis onward. As he put it (Shell, 1973, p. 80):

> Contemporary growth theory relies heavily on the assumption of constant returns to scale. If technical knowledge is an argument of the production function, then constant returns in *all* factors is not an attractive hypothesis. If the firm doubles its conventional factors, capital and labor, output should be at least doubled since mere replication is always a possibility. Therefore, if the firm doubles its conventional factors and doubles its stock of knowledge (as measured say, in patents held), then the firm's output must be more than doubled. If the firm does indeed face these increasing returns to scale, then it is glaringly obvious that specification of industrial organization will not be straightforward. For example, the competitive model with free entry costs or costless adjustment of inputs will not work. By Euler's theorem, if factors were awarded the marginal products, then payments to conventional factors would exhaust output, leaving no room for inventive activity.

The importance of Shell's assertion here cannot be overstated. In a note to this, Shell (1973) continued (p. 80, note 2):

> This paragraph on increasing returns to scale at the firm level is to be taken as argument by *reductio ad absurdum*. I wish to show the incompatibility of competition and frequently encountered technological assumptions. I do not mean to argue that decreasing returns to scale (especially at the economy level) are impossible.

Shell's underlying message is clear: competitive equilibrium is not viable with increasing returns to scale.

It is somewhat ironic that Shell felt the need to highlight this result. The observation that the price-taking behavior in perfectly competitive markets would generally not be compatible with situations in which there were small numbers of agents goes back to the beginnings of marginalist economic theory and the work of Cournot, Edgeworth, and Walras and is codified in Marshall's *Principles*. The applicability of Euler's theorem on homogeneous functions came along somewhat later but was well-established in Samuelson's *Foundations of Economic Analysis*.

The impetus of Shell's observation and the reason he included explicit taxation in support of research in his own model of external increasing returns to knowledge was the simple fact that if external returns to scale occur without economic costs, models that incorporate these effects are observationally equivalent to the Solow model with exogenous productivity growth.

That Shell's admonition to the profession was necessary is readily apparent in the way that models that build on Marshall's idea of economies of scale external to the actual operation of firms treat the economics of these externalities. Indeed, we can trace a lineage from Allyn Young's 1928 paper through Marvin Frankel's original deployment of the first AK models, to Paul Romer's thesis and Robert Lucas; work on the mechanics of development.[2] It is only with Romer's papers on increasing returns and technological innovation, where he introduces the Dixit–Stiglitz model of monopolistic competition that growth theory finally internalizes Shell's critique.

Once *formalized* by Dixit and Stiglitz (1974, 1977) and Ethier (1982), it is not surprising that "imperfect competition" – *along with IRTS* – became a building block of the *first stage* in the "Second Wave" of the endogenous growth approach, but more about this in the next chapters.

[2]Young (1928)'s treatment of increasing returns is quite nuanced, but he still characterizes the interplay between internal and external returns to scale by noting that returns to specialization lead "the representative firm…to lose its identity…its internal economies dissolve into the internal and external economies of the more highly specialized undertaking which are its success and are supplemented by new economies." (p. 538).

CHAPTER 2

THE INTERREGNUM: EXTENSIONS OF THE CANONICAL GROWTH MODEL

In previous work (Spear & Young, 2014, 2015), we surveyed the origins, evolution and dissemination of optimal growth, two sector and turnpike models up to the early 1970s, and the extension of the canonical growth model to stochastic environments, leading ultimately to the development of real business cycle models and the cementing of the canonical Ramsey–Cass–Koopmans model as the dominant dynamic, stochastic, general equilibrium (DSGE) approach to understanding business cycles.

Most of these developments occurred in the period between the early work of Shell and Frankel on endogenizing growth through the development of new technologies and the ultimate expression of this idea in the work of Lucas and Romer in the late 1980s and early 1990s. We call this period an interregnum because the failure of the economics profession to follow through on the logic of the Solow residual appears to have been driven primarily by unwillingness to confront the issues associated with increasing returns to scale. These issues are threefold. First, increasing returns to scale result in large firms so that the classical assumption of perfect competition does not hold. Second, with imperfect competition, or perfect competition with external increasing returns, the first Welfare Theorem does not hold. As Shell (1966) pointed out, this makes possible the kind of government interventions – in Shell's model, a version of the National Science Foundation – that many mainstream economists of the time were not willing to consider. Third, the mathematical frameworks for analyzing non-convex infinite dimensional optimization problems were essentially non-existent.

On the imperfect competition issue that Shell identified, there were no models available for handling this kind of general equilibrium analysis until the middle of the 1970s, when Dixit and Stiglitz developed their famous model of monopolistic

Endogenous Growth: Theory, Methods and Morphology
International Symposia in Economic Theory and Econometrics, Volume 35, 31–56

Published under exclusive licence by Emerald Publishing Limited
ISSN: 1571-0386/doi:10.1108/S1571-038620260000035008

competition (Dixit & Stiglitz, 1977) and Shapley and Shubik (1977) introduced their extension of the Arrow–Debreu–McKenzie model. Thus, as we've seen, Shell's work relied on assuming that all new knowledge was controlled by a monopolist or was freely available but funded by government taxation.

The problem of being able to show the existence of solutions to infinite dimensional non-convex optimization problems can be simply illustrated by appealing to the well-known log utility/Cobb–Douglas production model of one-sector growth with discounting. In this model, preferences for consumption are given by

$$u(c) = \ln c.$$

And output is given by

$$y = k^{\alpha}.$$

Agents in the economy wish to choose a sequence of savings (which get converted directly into capital) to maximize consumption subject to consumption plus saving being no larger than output. Making the obvious substitution, the problem becomes

$$\max_{\boldsymbol{k}} \sum_{t=0}^{\infty} \beta^{t} \ln\left[k_t^{\alpha} - k_{t+1}\right],$$

where the discount factor $0 \leq \beta < 1$. There is also an assume initial condition $k_0 > 0$.

The solution to this problem is well-known and is given by

$$c_t = (1 - \alpha\beta) k_t^{\alpha}.$$

To see the problem for non-convex optimization, consider the case where $\beta = 1$ and production is constant returns to scale, that is, $\alpha = 1$. In this, we end up with $c_t = 0$ which can't be right because the marginal utility of consumption at $c = 0$ is infinite.

Romer (1983)'s thesis tackled this problem and showed conditions under which certain non-convex optimization problems (including those of most endogenous growth models) could be solved. We state his result from the published version of the thesis (Romer, 1986a),

Theorem: *Assume that* $\delta : [0,\infty) \to \mathbb{R}$ *is nonincreasing, strictly positive, and (Lebesgue) integrable. Assume that* $F : \mathbb{R}^M \times \mathbb{R}^M \times [0,\infty) \to \mathbb{R} \cup \{-\infty\}$ *is [upper semi-continuous] and satisfies the following conditions*:

(i) *For all* $u, v \in \mathbb{R}^M \times \mathbb{R}^M$ *and almost all t,* $F(u,v,\cdot,t) : \mathbb{R}^M \times \mathbb{R} \cup \{-\infty\}$ *is concave.*

(ii) *There exists a constant* $p > 1$ *and a measurable function* $m(t)$*, with* $m(t)\delta(t)$ *integrable, such that for all* $(u,v,z) \in \mathbb{R}^M \times \mathbb{R}^M \times \mathbb{R}^M$ *and almost all t,* $F(u,v,z,t) \leq m(t) - \| z \|^p$.

Then, $W : LI \to \mathbb{R} \cup \{-\infty\}$ *is well defined and there exists an element* $y^* \in LI$ *such that* $\infty > W(y^*) \geq W(y)$ *for all* $y \in LI$.

Here, *W* is the functional being optimized, and *LI* is the space of Lebesgue integrable functions. The proof of this result can be found in Romer (1986a). The import of the result is that it provided conditions on the various functions in the growth model which would ensure the existence of solutions to individual or social optimization problems in situations more general than the canonical convex optimization of Ramsey–Cass–Koopmans models. This included the possibility for increasing returns to scale for some endogenous variables.

In private communication, Romer commented on the role that these mathematical developments played in helping to restart work on endogenous growth:

> Proving these two [existence] results is challenging in an infinite dimensional vector space. Nordhaus says that he gave up. Apparently Mirrlees gave up too. [See Section 1 below.] At that time, there was wide agreement that any analysis that was not supported by the two existence proofs was suspect. After Lucas published his [1988] paper, many people voiced concerns by pointing to the "knife-edge" assumption required by his worked example.
>
> Work almost surely came to a halt because meeting the mathematical prerequisites was so difficult if one was serious about specifying a model that could capture the type of issues raised by Shell, Solow, Nordhaus, Arrow and Young.
>
> The explanation for the restart in this work was that the results from my thesis convinced a few people, including Lucas, that the foundation now existed.
>
> I did it partly by simplifying the problem by ignoring uncertainty and partly by relying on continuous time. Looking back, the critique I would offer is that I did not put enough work into explaining what I had done. (Email of 8/7/2025)

As noted above, this period did see the development of important models and techniques, from Uzawa's introduction of multi-sector models, Cass and Shell's introduction of the Hamiltonian approach, and the stochastic extensions of Brock and Mirman, that played important roles in the work of Lucas and Romer, and modern endogenous growth practitioners. So, in this chapter, we turn to a survey of these developments, starting with the two-sector models of Uzawa and the Cass–Shell work on Hamiltonian functions.

THE EARLY INTERREGNUM

After the early developments in growth theory at the hands of Harrod, Domar, Swan, Solow, Cass, and Koopmans, a number of prominent observers, such as Fischer (1988a, 1988b), Stern (1991), and McCallum (1996), maintained that after significant progress in the 1950s and 1960s, economic growth theory "received relatively little attention for almost two decades" (Fischer, 1988a, 1988b, p. 329), and that "by the late 1960s early 1970s, research on the theory of growth more or less stopped" (Stern, 1991, p. 259). Stern (1991) went on to say "the latter half of the 1980s saw a rekindling of growth theory, particularly in the work of Romer … and Lucas" (p. 259), that is to say, in the form of "endogenous growth" models. McCallum (1996), for his part, wrote "After a long period of quiescence, growth economics has in the last decade (1986–1995) become an extremely active area of research" (p. 41). Moreover, Brock and Mirman's (1972a, 1972b) paper was the sole "extension" of Ramsey–Cass–Koopmans to a "stochastic environment" mentioned by McCallum (1996, p. 49).

This section deals with the evolution of the "classical" growth research program of Ramsey–Cass–Koopmans vintage via its stochastic "variants" and "generalizations" (Samuelson, 1976, note 1). Thus, here, we trace the origins and impact of the stochastic generalization that brought about a paradigm shift in modern economics and still generate significant research in the form of "quantitative macroeconomics," that is to say, "real business cycle theory" (RBC henceforth), and its metamorphosis into the DSGE approaches of both new Classical and new Keynesian vintage.

Our focus, then, is on the origins and development of optimal stochastic growth models in *continuous-time* and *discrete-time* forms. The chapter is divided into three sections. The first section deals with unpublished and published papers by Phelps (1960a, 1960b, 1961, 1962a, 1962b) and Mirrlees (1965a, 1965b). Phelps (1960b, 1961)'s unpublished Cowles Foundation Papers on both continuous-time and discrete-time stochastic optimal growth are also dealt with in this context – the former never published, the latter the basis for his 1962 *Econometrica* Paper.

We then deal with Mirrlees' unpublished papers, dating from 1965, which had *significant* impact on subsequent work in the area of stochastic optimal growth, such as on the contributions of Merton, Mirman, and Brock and Mirman, respectively. Mirrlees' use of the conceptual and mathematical tools provided by Wiener, Doob, and Ito is also dealt with, as they still influence the financial economics developed by Merton, based upon them. Merton (1969, 1975)'s contributions to the continuous-time approach are also dealt with in this section.

The second section deals with the application of the dynamic programming (DP) approach of Bellman and Blackwell over the period 1952–1970, its application to economic planning and growth models, especially by Radner, over the period 1963–1974, and cross-fertilization between Radner, Brock and Mirman, and Radner's Ph.D. student, Jeanjean.

PHELPS, MIRRLEES, AND MERTON: UNPUBLISHED AND PUBLISHED PAPERS, 1960–1975

Phelps: 1960–1962

In his June 1960 RAND paper "Optimal inventory policy for serviceable and reparable stocks," Phelps applied DP to the problem of determining "a unique stockage policy" regarding serviceable and reparable materials that would correspond to specific "decision regions." Phelps (1960a) wrote that "the model developed to treat this sequential decision problem, in being one of the comparatively few two-dimensional dynamic programing models for which the structure of the optimal policy has been ascertained, may be of some methodological interest" (p. 4). He went on to apply Bellman's "principle of optimality" to "current" and "future decisions," such that "all future decisions must be optimal" so as to achieve "overall optimality" (Phelps, 1960a, p. 7). In dealing with "the infinite- stage program," he applied the "fundamental theorems of dynamic programming for decision processes" outlined by Bellman (Phelps, 1960a, p. 11).

In December 1960, Cowles Foundation Discussion Paper (CFDP) 101 entitled "Capital Risk and Household Consumption Path: A Sequential Utility Analysis" by Phelps appeared. The paper presented what Phelps (1960b, 1961) called "a stochastic process of capital growth" (p. 1) in "a continuous time formulation" (p. 1). Phelps' CFDP 101 *was never published.* In our view, the paper is important in three respects. First, it was perhaps the earliest paper to apply an ostensibly continuous time approach to optimal stochastic growth, although Phelps (1960)'s approach will be shown to be problematic, to say the least. Second, it was also one of the earliest papers to apply a DP approach and the Bellman (1957) "principle of optimality" to stochastic optimal growth (Phelps, 1960b, p. 9). Third, Phelps' 1960 CFDP 101 provided the basis for the discrete-time extension of his approach in the form of his subsequent February 1961 CFDP 109, entitled "The Accumulation of Risky Capital: A Discrete-time Sequential Utility Analysis." Now, while CFDP 101 (1960b) *was* cited by Phelps (1961, 1962a) in his 1961 CFDP (pp. 1–3, p. 33), *only* CFDP 109 was mentioned by him in a note in his 1962 *Econometrica* paper, albeit with its title referred to incorrectly as being "identical" to the *Econometrica* paper (p. 733, note 6). This may explain why CDFP 101 has gone uncited and CFDP 109 sparsely-cited accordingly.

But more is involved here than the fact that Phelps' CFDPs have gone virtually unnoticed until now. In correspondence regarding CFDP 101, Phelps (2014, September 23) wrote: "I don't recall any reaction to CF 101 at all… I did not continue with the work that started in CF 101 because it was not clear to me that I had the analytical tools to push it any farther."

With regard to the relationship between CFDP 101, CFDP 109 and his *Econometrica* 1962 paper, he wrote (Phelps, 2014, September 23):

> I did not really "switch" to the discrete-time framework. I had already done all or most of the work for it in my first post-doctoral job at the RAND Corporation.[1] (The great Richard Bellman was there, as you very likely know, so I finally showed it to him. "That's trivial," he exclaimed. "The capital stock goes to infinity!" Of course the whole exercise was aimed at characterizing that path, solving for the consumption function, etc.) When to my surprise I ended right back at Yale in September 1960, I worked on the Golden Rule and what became CF 101.[2] Then, frustrated by how hard CF 101 was, I prepared the discrete-time paper for what became the CF 109.

Turning first to Phelps' 1960 CDFP 101, a number of points stand out. Phelps (1960b, 1961) described what he was analyzing as a "continuous time formulation" of a "stochastic process" (pp. 8–10; p. 1). He then applied DP and the optimality principle (Bellman, 1957) as the analytical basis for his approach (Phelps,

[1]Phelps had utilized Bellman (1960a)'s dynamic programming approach in his RAND papers on "Optimal inventory policy for serviceable and replaceable stocks," as indicated above, and in his paper "Optimal decision rules for procurement, repair or disposable spare parts" (1962b).

[2]There are both priority and multiple discovery issues regarding Bellman's approach. These were raised by colleagues at RAND, in the early 1950s, and recently, by historians of mathematics. On these issues, see Pesch (2012) and Pesch and Plail (2009, 2012).

1960b, pp. 9–17). As Phelps (1960b) put it: "In what follows we take our inspiration from Chapter 9 of Bellman… our continuous-time process can be viewed as the limiting case of a discrete-time process in which the length of each period goes to zero while the number of discrete periods goes to infinity …" (p. 9, pp. 16–17).

A close reading of Phelps' 1960 CFDP 101 reveals the difficulties Phelps faced in attempting to apply and develop his ostensibly "continuous" approach. First of all, he stated that in his model "capital gains and losses occur in unit amounts … fluctuations in the capital stock occur at random times… Thus capital grows according to a **discontinuous** Markov process" (Phelps, 1960b, p. 2) (our emphasis). In other words, this meant that the expected time path of wealth shocks was continuous, even though the underlying random shocks were discontinuous, that is to say, a "mixed model" rather than a pure continuous-time approach.

Second, the result Phelps (1960b) outlined in his 1960 CFDP 101 was that a consumer could end up "ruined" due to "absorbing" states and "cyclic" states, although he noted that there could be both low and high capital persistence states that occur with positive probability, given the finite time horizon he assumed (p. 3, pp. 21–22). If, however, Phelps (1960b) had pushed this through for an infinite horizon setting, he would have ended up with an *ergodic* distribution of the recurrent states, and the high or low capital "traps" would not occur, because there would be no absorbing states (p. 21). Now, while Phelps does in fact consider what happens when the time horizon goes to infinity, and, therefore, the "ruin" probability goes to zero, he does not discuss this in terms of ergodic theory.

We think that the reason for Phelps abandoning the ostensibly continuous-time setting of his 1960 CFDP 101 for the discrete-time framework of his 1961 CFDP 109 may have been to get away from the awkwardness of mixing a discrete stochastic process with a continuous time model. We surmise that he could have chosen to work with a continuous Markov process, as the works of Wiener (1923), Doob (1953), and Ito (1951), respectively – that is, *stochastic* calculus – were available at the time, but the move to a continuous stochastic process would, in turn, *rule out* purely transient and cyclic states, and thereby "trap" behavior, even with finite time horizons, as the continuity of the random shock process would make things look as though there were infinitely many instances of time, so that ergodic behavior would come into play, something Phelps may not have wanted in the context of what he was trying to do in his 1960 CFDP 101.

As noted, Phelps CFDP 109 entitled "The Accumulation of Risky Capital: A Discrete-time Sequential Utility Analysis" appeared in February 1961. In the opening paragraph, Phelps (1961) wrote: "A continuous-time formulation of the same problem was presented in a previous Cowles Foundation Discussion paper" (p. 1). His October 1962 *Econometrica* paper, based on CFDP 109, was entitled "The Accumulation of Risky Capital: A Sequential Utility Analysis." And, although not cited in the references, Phelps did mention CFDP 109 as an "earlier version of this paper" (p. 733, note 8). Indeed, there were many additions, changes and elisions made in the text of CFDP 109 as published in *Econometrica*.

But perhaps the most important addition seen in the 1962 version is the statement made by Phelps, which set out the "vehicle of analysis" for all further work done on discrete optimal stochastic growth models. As he put it in his opening paragraph (Phelps, 1962a, p. 729): "The vehicle of analysis is a stochastic, discrete-time dynamic programming model that postulates an expected lifetime utility function to be maximized."

Mirrlees: 1964–1974

According to Fischer and Merton (1984), "Following the early unpublished work by Mirrlees (1965a, 1965b), Brock and Mirman (1972a, 1972b, 1973), Bourguignon (1974), and Merton (1975) among others, extended the neoclassical growth model to include uncertainty about technological progress and demographics" (p. 58). Over a decade earlier, in their seminal paper, Brock and Mirman (1972a) wrote.

> The only work which is known to the authors which attempts to generalize deterministic optimal growth models to uncertainty... is the work of Mirrlees [1965]. Works by Phelps [1962] and Levhari and Srinivasan [1969] are somewhat related to optimal growth under uncertainty... (p. 481).

They went on to also cite Merton (1969, 1972a) as using "techniques similar to those employed by Mirrlees" (p. 482). We will deal with the Brock-Mirman interpretation of these authors below. At this point, we note that Olson and Roy (2006), in their survey of stochastic optimal growth, wrote (p. 298, note 1): "there is a large literature on stochastic growth in continuous time that built on Merton's ... early work [RES 1975]," and also referred to Brock and Macgill (1979). They did not, however, refer to the seminal, albeit *unpublished* paper by Mirrlees (1965a, 1965b) entitled "Optimum Accumulation Under Uncertainty," which was cited by many who dealt with the stochastic optimal growth model, as will be seen below.

In his contribution to the IEA conference volume entitled *Allocation Under Uncertainty*, edited by Dreze, and published in 1974, Mirrlees (1974) wrote "In the theory of optimum growth it has been found that models with discrete time are easier to treat rigorously than models with continuous time. But continuous-time models often have the advantage of providing simpler results" (p. 36).

Mirrlees worked with both non-stochastic and stochastic models. After his Cambridge Ph.D. dissertation entitled "Optimum Planning for a Dynamic Economy" (Mirrlees, 1964a), he attended a number of Econometric Society and other meetings. At the September Zurich 1964 Econometric Society meeting, he presented a paper entitled "The Structure of Optimum Policies in a Macroeconomic Model with Technical Change" (Mirrlees, 1964c), which later became the core of his 1967 RES paper "Optimum growth when technology is changing" (Mirrlees, 1967, p. 96, p. 124); in essence a continuous non-stochastic extension of Cass; approach, with *exogenous* technical change.

Two months earlier, in July 1964, Mirrlees attended the Rochester conference "Mathematical models of economic growth," sponsored by the SSRC, and led by McKenzie. At this conference, according to McKenzie (1968)'s account, Mirrlees presented two papers; a two-sector extension of Uzawa (1964), and an attempt "to extend the Ramsey model to the case of uncertainty" (p. 5). McKenzie (1968) wrote that in this paper, Mirrlees "apparently met a snag he was unable to overcome" and that while McKenzie later tried to discover "what the difficulty was," Mirrlees "could not recall, and had lost the paper" (p. 5). When asked about his

Rochester presentation, Mirrlees (2014, September 4) replied: "I recollect that at the Rochester Conference I was trying to deal with the discrete-time model, also with the assumption of a random factor multiplying output, not stationary as in the later paper published in the Dreze book. I didn't succeed after the conference any better than I had in Rochester." In a subsequent communication (via email on December 30, 2014), Mirrlees (1964b) also recalled the title of his Rochester paper to be "Optimum Economic Policies Under Uncertainty" and that in "this unfinished paper," he "was trying to work out optimal saving under uncertainty for a discrete-time infinite-horizon model, and finding it remarkably difficult to get any results."

Mirrlees also attended the July 1965 Stanford MSSB Conference on "Optimal Economic Growth" conducted by Arrow and initiated by McKenzie himself "as the economics member of the MSSB." According to McKenzie (1968)'s recollections, Mirrlees presented a paper on "planning in mixed economies with 'surplus labor'" and also led a roundtable discussion "on population and growth" (pp. 6–7).

Mirrlees (1965a, 1965b)'s paper entitled "Optimum Accumulation Under Uncertainty" was presented at the First World Congress of the Econometric Society held in Rome, in September 1965, revised and circulated in December 1965. And, as noted, this paper, *albeit unpublished*, was cited by leading growth theorists, and many of those who developed stochastic optimal growth.

A comparison of the abstract of the September 1965 version of Mirrlees' paper (*Econometrica*, Supplementary Issue, 1966), with parallel text and equations in the December 1965 version shows only very minor differences.

Two interesting points emerge from Mirrlees (1965)'s December paper. The first is its use of Bellman (1957)'s DP in a stochastic setting (p. 27). The second is that it also contains a section entitled "Orders of Magnitude," which comments on the "quantitative implications" of the theory he presents in the paper, linking it to "the interesting values of the parameters and the capital-output ratio" he dealt with in his 1964 Zurich paper (Mirrlees, 1965b, p. 44). Mirrlees' unpublished December 1965 paper was cited by most optimal growth theorists and others (Brock & Mirman, 1972a, 1972b; Dobell, 1970; Fischer & Merton, 1984; Leland, 1974; Levhari & Srinivasan, 1969; McKenzie, 1968; Merton, 1969, 1973, 1975; Samuelson, 1976; Sandmo, 1970; Stiglitz, 1969). What is strange is that two references said that the paper was "forthcoming" in *Econometrica* (Dobell, 1970; Sandmo, 1970).

When asked about this, Mirrlees (2014, June 28) replied:

> *Econometrica* more or less (I don't remember precisely) accepted the paper subject to revision. When I came to revise it, I found an error in the existence proof, and didn't succeed in correcting it. Later I convinced myself that the existence claim was false, and it is old unfinished business for me to sort out the fundamental existence problem with the model used in the paper. The worrying point is that utility discounting seemed to me not enough to deal with it. By the time I realized the problem, my interests had moved well away from optimum accumulation, but I am ashamed of not having sorted the problem out. I have never seen a paper that does.

Mirrlees also attended the July 1971 IEA Bergen conference, where he gave a paper entitled "Optimal Growth with Uncertainty" (Merton, 1975), which he revised and expanded in May 1972, changing the title to "Optimum Growth and Uncertainty" (Mirrlees, 1974, p. 36), and eventually publishing it in the 1974 IEA conference volume edited by Dreze, *Allocation under Uncertainty*, with the title "Optimum Accumulation Under Uncertainty: The Case of Stationary Returns to Investment."

Merton 1969–1975

Merton submitted his MIT Ph.D. thesis, supervised by Samuelson, and entitled "Analytical Optimal Control Theory as Applied to Stochastic and Non-stochastic Economics," in September 1970. The thesis consisted of five chapters, three of which were published in 1969. Chapter II, entitled "Lifetime Portfolio Selection Under Uncertainty: The Continuous-time Case" was published in August 1969 in the *Review of Economics and Statistics*. In the introduction, Merton (1969) wrote

> Phelps (1962) has a model used to determine the optimal consumption rule for a multi-period example where income is partly generated by an asset with an uncertain return. Mirrlees (1965a, 1965b) has developed a continuous time optimal consumption model of the neoclassical type with technical progress a random variable (p. 247).

In the concluding section, Merton (1969) wrote:

> A more general production function of the neoclassical type could be introduced to replace the simple linear one of this model. Mirrlees (1965) has examined this case in the context of the growth model with ... technical progress a random variable. His equations (19) and (20) correspond to my equations (35) and (37) with the obvious proper substitution for variables.
>
> Thus, the technique employed for this model can be extended to a wide class of economic models. However, because the optimality equations involve a partial differential equation, computational solution of even a slightly generalized model may be quite difficult (pp. 256–257).

Two things should be pointed out here. First, Merton was referring to equations in the *unpublished* December 1965 paper by Mirrlees. It would seem, then, that a number of leading economists, and especially growth theorists, were familiar with this paper. Indeed, in the copy of the Mirrlees' paper provided to the authors by Merton, there are marginal notes made by Samuelson, who seems to have given a copy of the paper to Merton. Second, regarding his "equation 19," Mirrlees (1965a, 1965b) wrote:

> It is also interesting to note that (19) generalizes what is often called the Keynes–Ramsey formula for optimum policy... In that case, of course, (19) solves the problem, provided the side conditions are satisfied. Mathematically (19) and (20) are a fairly decent pair of partial differential equations. The trouble is that the side conditions are of such an odd kind, and that creates serious computational difficulties (p. 13).

In the 1971 published version in *Journal of Economic Theory* of Chapter 5 of his thesis – which had earlier been presented at the 2nd World Conference of the Econometric Society – entitled "Optimum Consumption and Portfolio Rules in a Continuous Time Model," Merton (1971) wrote: "By the introduction of Ito's Lemma and the Fundamental Theorem of Stochastic Dynamic Programming ...

we have shown how to construct systematically and analyze optimal continuous-time dynamic models under uncertainty" (p. 412).

Merton's seminal paper on growth "An asymptotic theory of growth under uncertainty" was published in the *Review of Economic Studies* in July 1975. It started as a paper presented "in various forms" at venues such as the December 1971 Yale NBER growth conference, the March 1973 Rochester mathematical economics seminar, and the April 1973 mathematical economics seminar at Columbia (Merton, 1975, p. 375). It was subsequently circulated as MIT Sloan School working paper 673-73 in August 1973 (Merton, 1973). The paper was submitted to the *Review of Economic Studies* a month later and finally accepted in May 1974 (Merton, 1975).

A comparison between the 1973 working paper and 1975 published versions shows a number of significant additions in the published paper in the form of explanatory notes; a result both of editorial suggestion (Merton, 1973, p. 11; Merton, 1975, p. 383, note 1), and Merton's efforts to explain his use of various methods, and issues in the paper. For example, he added notes explaining his use of the Bellman approach and optimality in solving DP problems in continuous time, boundary conditions, and generalizations of maximization to uncertainty (Merton, 1973, p. 14, p. 16; Merton, 1975, p. 384, notes 1 and 2, p. 386, note 1).

In the introduction to his paper, Merton (1973, p. 1; 1975, p. 375) cited works that dealt with "capital accumulation under uncertainty" and "the optimal consumption-savings decision under uncertainty," based upon "a given linear production technology" (Levhari & Srinivasan, 1969; Phelps, 1962a, 1962b, among others). He also cited the unpublished December 1965, and the early version of the 1964 conference volume paper, by Mirrlees, as examples of dealing with "the stochastic Ramsey problem and a continuous time neoclassical one-sector model subject to uncertainty about technical progress." He went on to describe the work of Brock and Mirman (1972a, 1972b), and Mirman (1973) as "important contributions," albeit having "little to say about the specific structure" of "steady state" or "asymptotic distributions" regarding the "capital-labor ratio," when "outcomes are uncertain." And this, as against the model he proposed "where the dynamics of the capital-labor ratio" is "described by a diffusion-type stochastic process."

The Brock–Mirman assessment of Mirrlees–Merton will be dealt with below, in the section on the development of the work of Brock and Mirman from 1970 onward. At this point, suffice it to say that Merton (1969, p. 248; 1971, p. 412; 1973, p. 6; 1975, p. 377), as Mirrlees (1965a, 1965b) before him had utilized an approach based upon "a generalized theory of stochastic differential equations developed by Ito," and extended by Ito and McKean "which is applicable to diffusion processes" (p. 3).

Ito calculus is a variety of stochastic calculus, which extends the normal operations of calculus – differentiation and integration – to stochastic processes. Unlike smooth (i.e., continuous and continuously differentiable) functions, stochastic processes can be discontinuous and non-differentiable, manifesting sudden random jumps in value.

At its core, stochastic calculus operations follow conventional operations, with the difference being the recognition that over even small intervals of time, non-vanishing changes in the value of the stochastic process can occur, and hence need to be included in computations of things like rates of change, in the case of differentiation, or weighted suitably in taking the limits of partitions that define the Riemann integral.

The specific version of the stochastic calculus applied by Mirrlees and Merton, Ito's calculus, was formulated between 1938 and 1945 by the Japanese mathematician Kiyoshi Ito while he was working at the National Statistical Office (Ito, 1942, 1951, 1965; Ito & McKean, 1964).

DP, ECONOMIC PLANNING AND GROWTH: 1948–1973

Bellman, Karlin, and Blackwell

As mentioned above, in their survey on stochastic optimal growth, Olson and Roy (2006) did not cite Mirrlees (1965b)'s seminal, albeit unpublished, paper. They also did not cite Bellman (1957)'s famous book *Dynamic Programming*, although they did cite Blackwell (1965)'s paper "Discounted dynamic programming." *What is important to recall here is that Bellman's 1957 book was based upon his work at RAND and elsewhere, and published and unpublished papers, from 1948 onwards*, and this according to Bellman's own recollections and accounts (Bellman, 1984; Bellman & Lee, 1984, p. 24).

Bellman first visited RAND to attend its 1948 summer program, which was also visited by Morgenstern. Among the other attendees were Dantzig, Karlin, Tukey, Blackwell, Arrow, and Shubick (Assad, 2011, p. 422). Bellman wrote that his introduction to Dantzig's linear programming algorithm while there was his "first exposure to effective numerical solutions," which, as he recalled, "subsequently became a central theme" of his research program (Bellman, 1984, p. 135). He then went to Stanford to take up a position as Associate Professor in its Mathematics Department. In the summer of 1949, Bellman returned to visit RAND again. This time, at the suggestion of a colleague at RAND, he shifted the focus of his research to "multistage decision processes" (Assad, 2011, p. 424; Bellman, 1984, p. 157). During this period, according to his recollections, he had to essentially "find a name for multistage decision processes" (Bellman, 1984, p. 159).

In a July 1951 RAND paper entitled "On a General Class of Problems Involving Sequential Analysis," Bellman (1951)'s set out the basis for what he subsequently called "dynamic programming." As he put it:

> We wish to discuss a general class of multi-stage problems involving a sequence of operations ...This class of problems is characterized by the fact that at each time the problem may be described by a set of parameters which change from operation to operation, which is to say that each operation performs a mapping of the parameter space upon itself, and secondly, that the purpose of the operations is to optimize according to a criterion which has the important property that after any initial number of operations, starting from the state one finds oneself in, one optimizes according to the same criterion. ...this last point ... allows a mathematical formulation by means of recurrence relations which are very useful both theoretically and computationally (p. 1).

Over the period 1952–1957, Bellman produced a significant number of papers on DP and on its applications to many areas, including problems in mathematical economics, as will be seen below. The central message of these papers, as manifest in what he called "the principle of optimality" and the method he developed, as reflected in what became known as the "Bellman equation," eventually appeared in his 1957 monograph. Indeed, as one reviewer said, Bellman's 1957 book brought "under one cover the introduction and development of the theory of dynamic programing, which to a great extent has appeared previously in many papers scattered throughout many journals and pamphlets" (Newhouse, 1958, p. 788).

Now, one of the problems emanating from the fact that Bellman's 1957 book was, in essence, a *compilation* of his previously published papers and RAND reports, is that the focus has been on his 1957 book rather than on his earlier work. This, in turn, has led to some misunderstanding regarding the origin of his central message, that is to say, the principle of optimality. For example, Puterman (1994, p. 155) noted that his book "presented the optimality equations and the principle of optimality together with references to his earlier papers (dating back to 1952) which introduced and illustrated many of the key ideas of dynamic programming."

Acemoglu (2008, p. 222), for his part, wrote "the basic ideas of dynamic programming, including the principle of optimality, were introduced by Richard Bellman in his famous monograph (Bellman, 1957)." And Acemoglu (2008), as Puterman, noted that Karlin (1955) had provided "a formal mathematical structure for the analysis of dynamic programing models" (Puterman, 1994, p. 155) and "a simple formal proof to the principle of optimality" (p. 222).

Both Puterman and Acemoglu, however, overlooked the fact that Bellman's earliest published contribution specifically regarding DP entitled "On the Theory of Dynamic Programming" appeared in the 1952 *Proceedings of the National Academy of Sciences*, "communicated by Von Neumann in June 1952" (Bellman, 1952, p. 716), in which he acknowledges that DP was "intimately related to the theory of sequential analysis due to Wald [1950] (1952, p. 717)."[2] Had they also looked carefully at Karlin (1955, p. 285)'s paper they would have seen that Karlin pointed to the fact that the principle of optimality appeared in Bellman (1954)'s *Econometrica* paper, "Some problems in the theory of dynamic programming," published in January 1954 (p. 47). Moreover, in July 1954, in his RAND paper P-550, entitled "The Theory of Dynamic Programming," Bellman (1954b, 1954c) again presented the principle of optimality, as in the published version of this RAND paper, that appeared in the November 1954 issue of the *Bulletin of the American Mathematical Society* (p. 4, p. 504).

Another interesting aspect of the Bellman–Karlin nexus is that prior to Karlin's paper, published in the December 1955 issue of the *Naval Research Logistics* Quarterly, Bellman (1956a, 1956b) had discussed Karlin's paper "Some aspects of dynamic programming," presented on September 1, 1955, at the Ann Arbor meeting of the Econometric Society, at a session also attended by Koopmans (Report of 1955 meeting, *Econometrica*, p. 208).

What is also important to mention here is that in a number of papers that appeared both before and after his 1957 book, Bellman specifically dealt with the application of DP to mathematical economics. In 1956, his RAND paper "Dynamic programming and its application to variational problems in mathematical economics" appeared (Bellman, 1956a). It was subsequently presented at the Eighth American Mathematical Society's Symposium in Applied Mathematics, held at the University of Chicago in April 1956, and was eventually published in the symposium *Proceedings* in 1958 (Bellman, 1956b, 1958). He wrote (Bellman, 1956b, 1958, p. 115):

> The purpose of this paper is to discuss some variational problems arising from mathematical economics, and some of the methods that can be used to treat these questions both analytically and computationally.
>
> Since the range of mathematical economics is so extensive – and indeed the subject possesses no precise boundaries – and since the array of mathematical techniques which have been borrowed, begged, stolen, or improvised to cope with this field is so imposing, we cannot hope to present any adequate survey in any reasonably sized article. In consequence, we have restricted our attention to two important and interesting classes of processes, allocation and smoothing processes, and to a discussion of the application of the theory of dynamic programming to these processes.

Later, in March 1963, Bellman (1963)'s RAND paper, "Dynamic programming and mathematical economics" (RM-3539-PR) appeared. Here, he toned down his language a bit and wrote (Bellman, 1963, Preface, iii):

> In this memorandum, the author describes the uses and contributions of the mathematical theory known as dynamic programming to certain problems in economics. Examples of these are the optimal allocation of resources, and multistage decision processes that involve planning and learning in the face of uncertainty (i.e., adaptive control processes).

He continued on to say (1963, Introduction, 1)

> The functions of a mathematical theory in the scientific field are to furnish the systematic means of formulation of classes of problems, to indicate various techniques for their analysis, and to provide methods for obtaining numerical answers to numerical questions.
>
> At one point in the nineteenth century, serious doubt was expressed that problems in the field of economics could ever be handled mathematically. The introduction of the digital computer changed the situation drastically. Nevertheless, much remains to be done, and many new approaches must be devised, before we can consider ourselves to have a firm hold in the domain of mathematical economics.
>
> In this memorandum we outline briefly some of the principal contributions of the theory of dynamic programming, the formulation, analysis, and computational treatment of economic processes.

In a series of papers from 1961 onward, Blackwell (1961, 1962, 1964a, 1964b, 1965) also focused on DP. Interestingly enough, as early as 1952, Blackwell had assisted Bellman in obtaining a solution to at least one of the fundamental theorems of Bellman's DP approach (Bellman, 1952, Theorem 7, p. 719). Later, in his 1961 paper "On the functional equation of dynamic programming," Blackwell (1961, p. 274) demarcated stable, optimal, and stable optimal policy and extended Bellman's (1957) treatment to the case of *policy-switching* and its effects on optimal policy and stability. In a subsequent paper entitled "Discrete Dynamic

Programming," Blackwell (1962) turned to simplify the results obtained by Howard (1960) regarding the introduction of discount factors less than and equal to unity into "the general dynamic programming problem" set out in the works, as he put it, of "Dvoretzky, Kiefer and Wolfowitz (1957), Karlin (1955) and Bellman (1957)."

In his 1965 paper "Discounted dynamic programming," Blackwell (1965, 2 to 6) wrote:

> Soon after the appearance of Wald's work on sequential analysis, Richard Bellman recognized the broad applicability of the methods of sequential analysis, named this body of methods dynamic programming, and applied the methods to many problems… The first development of a general theory underlying these methods is due to Karlin (1955), and a rather complete analysis of the finite case was given by Howard (1960)…. Our formulation of the dynamic programming problem is somewhat narrower than Bellman's.

Bellman and Blackwell

We now try to explicate the contributions of Bellman and Blackwell in the context of a discrete time model, but the extensions to continuous time are relatively straight-forward. Let us consider a multi-sector capital model with a single infinite-lived representative agent. The objective function for the planning problem is to maximize an infinite discounted sum of utilities of consumption in each period subject to the constraints that output is produced using labor (fixed) and capital (variable) inputs and that output allocations of consumption goods must be allocated feasibly. Furthermore, assume that the period utility functions are strictly concave, and production functions exhibit constant returns to scale.

Now, look at a sub-problem where we want to do the maximization over some finite number T periods. In this case, since the objective function is a sum of concave functions, and constraint sets are convex, the standard results from concave programming theory will be applicable, once we recognize that we need a terminal condition on what the period T+1 vector of capital stocks should be. One approach, which Lucas and Stokey use to get the standard transversality condition, is to set the terminal stock to zero. If we are interested, however, in looking instead at short-run efficient allocations, we should maximize the sum of utilities up to T plus K(T+1). In between, we can specify whatever terminal condition we like. Once we do this, concave programming theory says that the first-order conditions (more generally, the Kuhn–Tucker conditions) will be necessary and sufficient to characterize the solution.

To get an answer to our original question, we need to let T go to infinity. Doing this formally in a way that answers the original question then requires the techniques of Pontryagin for dealing with the terminal condition and getting the right limiting transversality condition. This is what Cass (1965) did in chapter one of his thesis. What would not be correct, though, would be to claim that in the T = infinity case, we have an infinite discounted sum of concave utilities so that we are in the world of concave programming and the first-order conditions (i.e., the Euler equations) are necessary and sufficient. Indeed, they are not, as Malinvaud's counterexample to Koopmans (1965) showed, even though they are for any finite T. Something is very different in the infinite dimensional case.

To see what is different, one needs to go back to how the concave programming (Kuhn–Tucker theory) result is proven, and what we find when is that it relies, not surprisingly, on applying the Separating Hyperplane Theorem (i.e., Minkowski's theorem). Now, Minkowski's theorem holds in very general spaces, but it does have one stringent requirement: one of the two disjoint, convex sets being separated must have a non-empty interior. One of things that John Tukey (1942) is famous for is having provided a counterexample to the claim that you can dispense with the non-emptiness requirement in Minkowski's theorem. He constructed two disjoint convex sets in l_2 (classic Hilbert space), neither of which had an interior, and showed that there was no linear functional that would separate them.

Since the discounted sum of utilities specification of the capital model necessarily involves looking at something in the positive orthant of an infinite-dimensional space, the interiority criterion becomes relevant, and a direct application of the Minkowski theorem isn't available. So, we are left with the situation in which the Euler equations are necessary, but not sufficient. What Pontryagin et al. demonstrate is how to augment this with the right specification of the terminal conditions to pick out the one correct trajectory satisfying the Euler equations so that the two conditions together are necessary and sufficient.

Now, the forward DP algorithm gets around the problem of terminal conditions by embedding the optimization problem in a recursive time-structure where the future looks like a steady-state extension of the past. Specifically, given a function specifying the continuation value of the DP given the values of the state variables one period hence, we are left with a simple, finite-dimensional programming problem. If all of the functions involved are concave, we have a simple, finite-dimensional concave programming problem, and, of course, the FOCs here are necessary and sufficient.

The genius of Bellman and Blackwell was to recognize that they weren't actually getting rid of the infinities that cause problems in the control theory setting; rather, they were converting the problem of the infinite time-horizon into that of finding one among an infinity of possible continuation functions. In the problems that involve discounting (or other set-ups that satisfy the Blackwell conditions for a contraction), the functional equation that replaces the infinite discounted sum of utilities turns out to be a contraction mapping, and the Banach theorem, therefore, applies, yielding a fixed-point to the Bellman equation, and, via the obvious recursion, a solution to the original optimization problem. Again, because the Bellman equation evaluated at the fixed-point value function is a finite-dimensional concave programming problem, the FOCs are necessary and sufficient.

The solution that comes out of the DP approach can also be used to demonstrate the sufficiency of the transversality condition in the original problem. The ascendance of the DP approach in growth theory is clearly due to the availability of the contraction mapping results and their computational tractability. We think this also explains why the profession brushed aside the whole question of the moral implications of discounting so widely discussed in the Vatican Conference volume (1964), at least until the issue was resurrected in the contemporary discussion of global warming.

THE LATE INTERREGNUM: STOCHASTIC DYNAMICS AND GROWTH

As noted above, Phelps was perhaps the first to introduce Bellman's DP approach in economics in both continuous- and discrete-time settings in his work between 1960 and 1962. Over the period 1963–1974, Roy Radner (1963) also advanced the application of DP in economics. For example, his ONR supported 1963 Technical Report entitled "Notes on the Theory of Planning" utilized DP which, as he wrote "is relatively new to the theory of economic planning" (p. 2). He gave accounts of "the dynamic programming valuation function for various functions and programs" (Radner, 1963, Lecture 4, Sections 2–3). In February 1964, Radner's Berkeley Center for Research in Management Science Technical Report Number 17 (also supported by the ONR) entitled "Dynamic Programming of Economic Growth" appeared. The abstract of the paper read as follows:

> A class of problems of optimal economic growth is formulated in terms of the functional equation approach of dynamic programming (Bellman, 1957). A study is made of the continuity and concavity properties of the state valuation function, i.e., the function indicating a maximum total discounted welfare (utility) that can be achieved starting from a given initial state of the economy. Under suitable conditions this function is characterized by a certain functional equation. Both the cases of a finite and an infinite planning horizon are treated; the latter case being discussed under the assumption of constant technology and tastes. Here iteration of a certain transformation associated with the functional equation is shown to provide convergence to the state valuation function. Exact solutions are given for the case of linear-logarithmic production and welfare functions.

Radner's 1964 Technical Report 17 went virtually unnoticed. It was only cited in his 1966 *International Economic Review* paper "Optimal growth in a linear-logarithmic economy." An abridged version of the report was published in 1967 under the same title, that is, "Dynamic Programming for Economic Growth" (Radner, 1967, pp. 111–141). Now, the introductory paragraph in the 1967 abridged version was identical to the abstract of his 1964 Technical Report. However, in contrast to the "relatively new" description of DP he used in his 1963 Technical Report 9, in his 1967 paper Radner (1967, p. 111) wrote:

> The techniques used are familiar to workers in the field of dynamic programming, although the particular assumptions appropriate to a study of optimal economic growth differ from those commonly encountered in other applications (e.g. inventory and replacement theory) (such as in Phelps, 1960a, 1960b).

Radner continued:

> The interest in such an approach must ultimately derive from its power, if any, in producing new characteristics of optimal growth and/or new and more efficient computational techniques.

Over the period 1971–1973, Radner both presented, at various meetings, and published two important papers relating "optimal steady state" programs and stochastic production. One was presented at the Mathematical Social Science Board (MSSB) workshop at the University of California, Berkeley, July–August 1971, and published in the *Journal of Economic Theory* in February 1973. The other was presented at the symposium on mathematical analysis of economic systems at the Fall 1971 meeting of the Society for Industrial and Applied Mathematics (SIAM), held at the University of Wisconsin-Madison, October 11–13, 1971, and published in *Mathematical Topics in Economic Theory and Computation* (1972). In both his 1972 and 1973 papers, Radner used the *identical* "bibliographic note" in which he cited *two* papers by Brock and Mirman, one a paper they presented at the summer 1971 Berkeley MSSB workshop, the other, their now famous 1972 *Journal of Economic Theory* paper. Radner (1972, p. 89; 1973, pp. 110–111) wrote:

> W.A. Brock and L.J. Mirman (1971), (1972a, 1972b) have studied optimal growth under uncertainty in a model with one commodity and a sequence of independent and identically distributed states of the environment. In particular, in the second paper they considered the problem of optimal stationary programs.

We will return to the MSSB meeting below.

Another work cited by Radner in his *SIAM* (1972) and *JET* (1973) papers, was the unpublished September 1972 Berkeley Ph.D. thesis of Jeanjean, supervised by Radner, entitled *Optimal Growth with Stochastic Technology in a Multi-Sector Economy*. In May, Jeanjean (1971) had circulated his Berkeley Center for Research in Management Science Working Paper 332 entitled "Optimal Growth with Stochastic Technology in a Closed Economy." Interestingly enough, Jeanjean (1974a) published two additional papers, one in French, which was, in effect, the translation of his thesis. The other was a paper published in *JET* entitled "Optimal Development Programs Under Uncertainty: The Undiscounted Case" (Jeanjean, 1974b). In the French translation of his thesis, Jeanjean (1974a, p. 98) cited an unpublished paper by Mirman (1970a, 1970b) entitled "The Steady State Behavior of a Class of One Sector Growth Models with Uncertain Technology." This paper was later published by Mirman in the June 1973 issue of *JET* under the same title. According to Mirman (personal communication to authors, 2014, November 9), he gave the 1970 paper, and other papers, to Radner at the MSSB meeting. This cross-fertilization continued, with Jeanjean's thesis being cited by Brock and Mirman (1972b) in their paper in the volume *Techniques of Optimization*, and in their 1973 *International Economic Review* paper "Optimal economic growth and uncertainty: the no discounting case." They reported that Jeanjean (1972b, 1973) had "extended some" of their "results to multisector models" and that "Recently our results have been generalized to the multisector case by Jeanjean," citing his unpublished thesis accordingly (p. 418, p. 573).

The summer 1971 Berkeley MSSB workshop on "Theory of markets and uncertainty" was conducted by Radner. The participants were William Brock, Leonard Mirman, Peter Diamond, Jerry Green, Theodore Groves, Werner Hildebrand, Michael Rothschild, Jose Scheinkman, Michael Spence, Bernt Stigum, and Shmuel Zamir (Cutler, 1973). Now, according to McKenzie (1999, p. 10), *two* papers by Brock and Mirman on growth with uncertainty, dealing with the undiscounted and discounted cases, were given at Radner's workshop. There are, however, some problems regarding McKenzie's account. First, only *one* Brock–Mirman paper is ever cited as having been presented and discussed at the MSSB meeting, that is, their paper entitled "Optimal Economic Growth and Uncertainty: The Ramsey-Weizacker Case," that is to say, the "undiscounted case." This was later published by Brock and Mirman in the October 1973 issue of *IER* under the title "Optimal Economic Growth and Uncertainty: The No Discounting Case," according to Mirman (personal communication to authors, 2014, November 9). Second, the "discounted" case, that is to say the now classic Brock and Mirman (1972a, 1972b) *JET* paper was "received June 28, 1971" by the journal (p. 479), or in other words, *immediately prior* to the July–August 1971 MSSB conference. Finally, as will be seen below, the Brock–Mirman "discounted" case paper was first circulated as a Rochester/Cornell "mimeo" in 1970, and also presented at an NBER conference at Yale led by Stiglitz, and at the North American Meeting of the Econometric Society in December 1970. And thus, it is to the intriguing story of the evolution and impact of the Brock–Mirman approach that we now.

BROCK AND MIRMAN: FROM THESIS TO *META-SYNTHESIS*, 1970–1973

Brock and Mirman's 1972 *JET* and 1973 *IER* papers are well known, and the former is widely cited. What is less well known is that they also published another joint paper on the stochastic growth model. As Mirman wrote (personal communication, 2014, June 13) "there is a third Brock-Mirman paper, which mirrors the discounted case paper [*JET* 1972]." This paper, albeit not widely cited, was presented at an October 1971 conference on "optimization techniques" and will be discussed below. All *three* Brock and Mirman (1972a, p. 483) papers were the outcome of Mirman's 1970 thesis and their collaboration in developing, as they put it "the unification" of previous approaches to growth or, in other words, their *meta-synthesis*. But before proceeding to a discussion of the evolution of the joint work, we deal with the development of Mirman's approach to uncertainty and growth, his 1970 thesis, and early papers.

MIRMAN, UNCERTAINTY, AND GROWTH: CHICAGO AND ROCHESTER

Mirman's interest in issues surrounding uncertainty and growth started as a graduate student. He recalled (personal communication, June 14, 2015) that his interest in the study of uncertainty in economics "... was a big problem for me early on, so many people – including Hirofumi Uzawa and David Cass – disparaged my interest in uncertainty ...." Mirman recalled that in 1967 he went to the summer workshop on growth at University of Chicago organized by Uzawa, also attended by Ethier, Calvo, and Razin, among others. Mirman also wrote (personal communication, 2014, June 15):

> I was a graduate student, at the end of my second year, just finishing my course work, when I was sent by the department (or by McKenzie) to a summer workshop on growth at the University of Chicago run by Hiro Uzawa. In my early discussions with Hiro about my work he was dead set

> against my working on uncertainty and growth, I had some very preliminary ideas but needed much more thought and work and help before anything could develop from these ideas. I remember he thought that putting uncertainty in a growth model was too hard and not enough was known about certainty and growth to waste time on uncertainty. He didn't let me work on uncertainty all summer, he had me working on a project he found interesting but I had no idea what he was talking about. At the end at the summer I was at wits end because I needed a second year paper for Rochester. Luckily the only thing that made sense to me then was uncertainty and I was able to write a paper on an uncertain Von Neuman growth model. It mimicked the work McKenzie was doing and it began to lay the foundation for my thesis. In any case, I had met Cass at the conferences run by Uzawa and discussed my ideas with him. In my view both Cass (who was a student of Uzawa) and Uzawa were (are) brilliant economists. In fact, Uzawa was a brilliant mentor, too bad he had no use for uncertainty. But lucky for me that was my only idea.

MIRMAN'S THESIS AND EARLY PAPERS

In their *JET* paper, "Optimal Growth and Uncertainty: the Discounted Case," Brock and Mirman (1972a, p. 482) wrote "The basic framework for the paper was developed by Mirman in [9, 10], for discrete time one-sector stochastic growth models." Reference 9 was to Mirman (1970a, 1970b)'s Ph.D. thesis, entitled "Two Essays on Uncertainty and Economics"; reference 10 was to Mirman's as yet "unpublished" 1970 paper, entitled "The Steady State Behavior of a Class of One Sector Growth Models with Uncertain Technology," which emanated from his thesis, and was later published in *JET* in 1973.

With regard to his thesis and influences on it, Mirman recalled (personal communication, 2007, February 9):

> Brock and I overlapped at Rochester, he as an assistant professor and I as a graduate student, for one semester, and he told me he had no idea what I was doing, but we were friends. I turned in my thesis the next spring – I was at Cornell – and he was assigned to read it. My advisor was McKenzie – Brock and Zable were on my committee from economics – but the biggest help I got was from a mathematician named Kemperman, who was also on my committee. A statistician – who taught me stochastic processes – was also on the committee, Keilson. I was really lucky to be surrounded by a group of great scholars.

Another paper Mirman wrote at the time was his 1971 *Econometrica* paper entitled "Uncertainty and Optimal Consumption Decisions," received in March 1969; the final revision dated November 1969. In the first note to the paper, Mirman (1971) acknowledged "the encouragement and advice of Prof. J.H.B. Kemperman" (p. 179).

In January, Mirman (1971) sent his second thesis paper entitled "On the Existence of Steady State Measures for One Sector Growth Models with Uncertain Technology" for publication to *IER*, and after revision in September 1971, it was published in June 1972. Now, in his *IER* paper, Mirman (1972) *cited* his then "unpublished" 1970 thesis paper "The steady state behavior of a class of one-sector growth models with uncertain technology," as having introduced "a stochastic generalization of the concept of a steady state equilibrium for a model of economic growth" (p. 271). However, in his *IER* paper, Mirman (1972) *did not cite his own 1970 thesis* (*as against its citation* in Brock & Mirman, 1972a, 1972b), and in the *IER* paper, Mirman cited his *JET* paper *with Brock* as "forthcoming" (p. 286).

Mirman's *1970 paper*, "The Steady State Behavior of a Class of One Sector Growth Models with Uncertain Technology," finally *appeared* in the June 1973 issue of *JET*. When asked about the differential citations, Mirman replied (personal communication, 2007, February 8):

> This is easy to answer. I think my thesis paper and the ... *IER* paper are almost exactly the same so there was no need to quote the thesis, but then I needed to quote *the not yet forthcoming JET paper* [our emphasis, as Mirman is talking here about the June 1973 *JET* version of his 1970 paper]. But the 1973 *JET* paper and the thesis paper are different – the referee insisted that I change the proof.

And indeed, in the introductory note to the June 1973 *JET* version of his 1970 paper, Mirman wrote: "This paper contains results reported in my Ph.D. thesis... However, the organization of the paper and the proofs of the main theorem have undergone considerable change." In the references to his 1973 *JET* paper, which, as Mirman (1973, p. 219) wrote, was based on his 1970 Ph.D. thesis, both Cass (1965) and Koopmans (1965) are cited, as is Radner (1971). Brock and Mirman (1972a, 1972b), however, only cite Cass and Koopmans, and a paper by Brock entitled "Sensitivity of Optimal Growth Paths with Respect to a Change in Final Stocks" [actually published (Brock, 1971) in the same conference volume as Radner (1971)].

BROCK–MIRMAN: RECOLLECTIONS, PRESENTATIONS, AND META-SYNTHESIS

Over the period 1970–1973, the interaction between Brock and Mirman took place on two levels. The first was the relationship emanating from Brock being Mirman's thesis examiner and intellectual catalyst for extending his approach. The second was as partners in presenting their joint papers at conferences, and publishing them so as to achieve the widest possible audience for what they described as "the unification" of approaches to growth their framework provided.

Above, we discussed the 1973 and 1975 versions of Merton (1973, 1975)'s paper "An asymptotic theory of growth under uncertainty." In *both* versions, he cited a paper by Brock and Mirman entitled "The Stochastic Modified Golden Rule in a One-sector Model of Economic Growth with Uncertain Technology," as being published in the June 1972 issue of *JET* (p. 33, p. 392). Moreover, Samuelson (1976, p. 491) also cited the 1972 *JET* Brock–Mirman paper under the same title used by Merton, that is, "The stochastic modified golden rule in a one-sector model of economic growth with uncertain technology." The title of the oft-cited Brock and Mirman (1972a, 1972b) *JET* paper, however, was "Optimal economic growth and uncertainty: the discounted case."

In their citations, Merton and Samuelson actually referred to the title of the *earlier versions* of Brock and Mirman's watershed paper, which was initially circulated and presented at conferences in 1970. The paper, under its original title, first appeared as a "mimeo" emanating from "Rochester and Cornell," Mirman by then at Cornell, Brock at Rochester.

RECOLLECTIONS

In a series of queries from the authors, and replies from Brock and Mirman, they recounted the evolution of their 1972 *JET* and 1973 *IER* papers, which they identified as "Brock-Mirman I" and "II," respectively (Brock & Mirman, 1973, p. 560, footnote 2). When asked about the origins and dissemination of the 1970 "Cornell/Rochester mimeo" (1970a) and the first version of the 1972 *JET* paper, Mirman recalled (personal communications, 2014, June 12 and August 10): "I do remember that we wrote, what is from hindsight, a preliminary version of the [*1972 JET*] ... The first version of the paper was sent out to a rather wide audience and we did get comments on it" (June 12). He went on to say (August 10).

> I believe that my first communication with Brock ... was in the spring of 1970. I was to defend my thesis in May at Rochester and he was a member of the committee and had just read the thesis. He told me he had an idea for extending my thesis, which was for a positive growth model under uncertainty, to the optimal case. My work used the notion of stochastic technical progress, which was taken from the work of Mirrlees that inspired me ... to study the question of growth under uncertainty ...

Brock, for his part, recalled (personal communication, 2014, June 12):

> Rochester was my first job. I had just arrived there. I was reading Len's thesis and I got very excited about the possibility of generalizing his work on the stochastic Solow type model to the infinite horizon optimization case. I recall not only talking to Len by phone about this problem, but also going to Cornell to visit him, where we worked on this problem and probably the undiscounted one too ... I recall it [the 1970 version of the 1972 *JET* paper] being well known to researchers in growth before it actually was published.

In a subsequent communication (2014, June 13), Mirman expanded his account and recalled:

> I was an assistant professor at Cornell and just finished my defense, when I received a call from Brock who was relatively new in the department at Rochester. He told me that he had been assigned to read my dissertation and was upset because he had just finished reading a dissertation that was very boring and uninteresting. He thought mine would be the same. He told me he was very surprised that my dissertation was very interesting; in fact he was sure that we can generalize it to the optimal case, and he asked McKenzie why he had never told him about my work. My dissertation studied the steady state behavior of a stochastic growth model, similar to what Solow did in his classic paper for the deterministic growth model. So Brock and I did the optimal case, both in the discounted case and in the non-discounted case, the latter never got the audience of the former.

When asked about the citations by Samuelson and Merton and impact of the published paper, Mirman replied (personal communication, 2014, June 14):

> I do remember that Brock got a short note from Samuelson. He praised the work and introduced his student Merton, who was working on similar problem in continuous time. Actually, over time, it turns out that not many people actually read the published version, for several reasons ...

Mirman continued, relating the paper to his later work with Zilcha[3]:

---

[3]The Mirman-Zilcha growth model (1975) is based upon log utility and Cobb-Douglas production with exponential uncertainty. In three seminal papers, Mirman and Zilcha (1975, 1976, 1977) extended and amended the original Brock-Mirman model. Here, we only deal with the origins of Brock-Mirman, and thus we do not discuss the Mirman-Zilcha papers. However, the Mirman-Zilcha papers deserve careful reading by those applying the Brock-Mirman framework.

> There, I think, are two main reasons which are related. The first is that the paper is well known and taught a lot so people think they understand and know very well what's in it. The role of the other is that the books of Sargent cover it in a way that people don't think they need to read it. For example, our paper does not contain any examples. But most people think that a Brock-Mirman model is with log utility and Cobb Douglas production. This is from my paper with Zilcha, and is presented by Sargent as the Brock-Mirman model. So many people I've spoken with have never read the original.

When asked about conference presentations of their 1972 *JET* paper, Mirman recalled (personal communication, 2014, August 10):

> Brock came down to Cornell, where we wrote (what is now) a barebones version of our paper. This is the paper, "The stochastic modified golden rule in a one-sector model of economic growth with uncertain technology." In the fall … we went to a conference on growth theory at Yale at which Brock gave our paper, in a pretty rough form.

Mirman continued:

> In attendance was among others Karl Shell and David Cass. Karl was at MIT the time and I believe that is how the paper got to Samuelson (but I conjecture here) … In the meantime Brock and I corresponded by mail and the paper started to expand with many of the cracks and holes filled in. I would be remiss not to mention that every time he sent me the paper I would send it back with the key inequalities backwards, which drove him crazy … In the meantime Brock and I worked on the paper.

Mirman went on to say:

> My next recollection is a visit by Brock to Cornell, I was writing a proposal for the NSF and he suggested that the introductory material for the grant application be part of the paper. But at the same time Brock had an idea for a second paper, the no discounted case. We realized at this time that the work was more general than just the stochastic technical progress case and that the dynamics played an important part. So we decided that the reference to modified golden rule was too narrow. We then changed the title to take account of the generality of the paper and to link it to the second paper. We continued to fill cracks and holes, as well as added the appropriate diagrams. I think that it was in this form with the name change that we sent it to *JET*.

PRESENTATIONS

Below, we complement the recollections of Brock and Mirman by reference to the published record of conference presentations of the *three* Brock–Mirman papers.

Brock–Mirman I

With regard to their 1972 *JET* paper, they recalled that it was first presented at Yale in the fall of 1970 at a conference on "growth theory." An examination of the record of 1970 conferences shows that the paper was actually presented in November 1970 at the NBER conference on econometrics and mathematical economics funded by the NSF and organized by Joseph Stiglitz (NBER Record, 1970).

The 1970 version of their 1972 *JET* paper was presented to a wider audience at the December 1970 North American regional conference of the Econometric Society held in Detroit (*Econometrica*, July 1971, p. 300) at session 15 "Growth Models," chaired by Stiglitz. The abstract of their paper "The stochastic modified golden rule in a one-sector model of economic growth with uncertain technology" (1970b) read as follows (*Econometrica*, July 1971, pp. 345–346):

> In a discrete time one sector model of economic growth with uncertain technology we show that the distribution functions of optimal consumption and capital stock at time t (which are random variables) converge pointwise to limit distributions. The limit distribution, F, of optimal capital stock is a natural generalization of the modified golden rule. Hence our result is an extension of the Cass, "Optimal Growth in an Aggregative Model of Capital Accumulation," *RES* 1965; Koopmans "On the Concept of Optimal Economic Growth," *Pontficae Academiae Scientiarum Scripta Varia*, 1965, results to the case where technology is uncertain. All of our assumptions are similar to Cass-Koopmans except for the random technology and the planning objective which is assumed to be maximization of the capital value of the discounted sum of utilities. We assume that technology can be represented by $F(K, L, r)$ where F satisfies the usual assumptions for each value of the random variable r, and increases in r for each K, L. We have found an elementary set of techniques to deal with this rather difficult problem. First we follow Levhari and Srinivasan, *RES* 1969, and use dynamic programming to establish the existence of time invariant policy functions, giving optimal consumption and capital stock at time $t+1$ as a function of capital in existence at time t. Hence the evolution of optimal capital stock is given by a stochastic process. This stochastic process is shown to converge in distribution by exploitation of the necessary conditions of optimality.

Brock–Mirman II

In his 1973 *JET* paper "Optimal Stationary Consumption with Stochastic Production and Resources," Radner cited a paper by Brock and Mirman entitled "Optimal Economic Growth and Uncertainty: The Ramsey-Weizacker Case" as Working Paper number 7, emanating from the MSSB Workshop on "The Theory of Markets and Uncertainty," held at the Department of Economics, University of California, Berkeley, in 1971. As noted above, this paper became their October 1973 *IER* Paper "Optimal Economic Growth and Uncertainty: The No Discounting Case" which was received at that journal in January 1972, and revised in November 1972 (Brock & Mirman, 1973, p. 560).

Brock–Mirman III

In October 1971, what Brock and Mirman have called "Brock-Mirman III" was presented by Brock at the 4th International Federation for Information Processing Colloquium on optimization techniques, Los Angeles, October 19–22. This paper was entitled "A One-sector Model of Economic Growth with Uncertain Technology: An Example of Steady State Analysis in a Stochastic Optimal Control Problem." It was published in the 1972 conference volume techniques of optimization edited by Balakrishnan (Brock & Mirman, 1972b, pp. 407–419).

What is interesting about this sparsely cited paper is that it is what could be considered an "executive summary" of their more extensive 1972 *JET* paper. This is evident in the introduction, literature survey, and concluding remarks of the paper. For example, in the introduction to Brock–Mirman III, they pointed to their extension of Cass–Koopmans to the case of stochastic "output or technical progress," while departing from the Cass–Koopmans approach, as Brock and

Mirman deal with "uncertain technology or technological progress," and this "in discrete time"; thereby establishing "a stochastic analog" of steady state convergence, which they termed "the modified golden rule." They then described their approach as "essentially a blend of dynamic programming and discrete-time stochastic optimal control theory" (Brock & Mirman, 1972b, p. 407).

In their literature review, they cited the work of Mirman (1970a, 1970b, Ph.D. thesis) and Mirrlees (1965a, 1965b) as "most relevant." However, they went on to say that "Mirrlees operates in continuous time where the theory of stochastic processes is messy," counterpointing this by then saying "we avoid the messy mathematics by working in discrete time" (Brock & Mirman, 1972b, p. 408).

In their concluding remarks, they cited Mirman's 1971 University of Massachusetts paper "The steady state behavior of a class of one-sector growth models with uncertain technology," which became his 1973 *JET* paper, and their own summer 1971 MSSB Working Paper 7, which became their 1973 *IER* Paper on the "non-discounted case." They also referred to Jeanjeans' 1971 Ph.D. thesis as extending some of "their results to multisector models." Finally, they concluded by saying that in Brock–Mirman III (1972b), "they chose to take the self-contained route in order to delineate the ideas and to reach a wider audience" (p. 418).

METASYNTHESIS

A close reading of Brock and Mirman's seminal 1972 *JET* paper reveals three major issues they dealt with: (i) dynamics of optimal processes and steady states, (ii) the use of DP, and (iii) the synthesis of approaches to optimal growth. The first and second issues set out by Mirman in a communication to the authors (via email on August 12, 2014). He wrote that in the 1972 Brock–Mirman paper, there were:

> Two issues that needed to be dealt with. The first is the dynamics of the optimal process and its corresponding steady state. Mirrlees [1965] dealt with an economy that had a concave technology and thus, although not done, could deal with the stochastic dynamics and corresponding steady state as, say, Cass [1965] does in the deterministic case. The work of Levhari and Srinivasan [1969] and Phelps [1962] deals with a linear technology. Hence, although it might have, the issue of the dynamics and steady state does not arise .... The second issue is the use of dynamic programming. Mirrlees does not use dynamic programming techniques. He takes a deterministic "Euler conditions" and linearizes them .... Both Levhari-Srinivasan and Phelps use dynamic programming techniques, in a very rudimentary form to get at the results, which were done in a linear technology setting. Hence their method at getting at the optimal program is foundationally similar to ours.

The third issue relates to Brock and Mirman's "unification," that is to say, "*metasynthesis*" of previous approaches to optimal growth. This is expressed in what we take to be the *central message* of their 1972 *JET* paper, in a paragraph which, in our view, has been overlooked by most observers up to now, possibly reflecting the situation that they may not have actually read the full text of the paper, as Mirman noted in his recollections cited above. They wrote (Brock & Mirman, 1972a, p. 483):

> The model used in this paper is analogous to the Mirrlees and Mirman model of a one sector economy under uncertainty, which is essentially the generalization of the Cass-Koopmans

> model with a random variable in the production function. *In fact, our methods unify the structure of growth theory*. The dynamic programming formulation makes the Cass-Koopmans results somewhat easier to obtain. It is thus seen that this paper represents a nontrivial extension and unification of the work of Cass, Koopmans, Mirman and Solow. (Our emphasis)

But let us leave the last word regarding the impact of their "unification" to Lucas, who recognized the Brock–Mirman approach as one of the starting points for Kydland and Prescott's own "*metasynthesis*" that led to quantitative or empirical macroeconomics. Indeed, as Lucas (1987) put it, "technically the immediate ancestor of Kydland and Prescott" was the Brock–Mirman 1972 *JET* paper (p. 32, note 1). Just how Brock and Mirman's approach influenced subsequent developments in growth and cycle theory is another story (see Young, 2014, Chapter 1).

With the unification of growth theory around the three elements of optimization, DP, and stochastic control, the modern development of the neoclassical growth model reaches completion in the work of Brock and Mirman. The model that now bears their name has become a workhorse in real business cycle theory and is the basis for models of repeated games and optimal taxation. The basic techniques of stochastic DP have spun off from the Brock–Mirman nexus into areas of applied microeconomics, finance, contract theory, and even in dynamic game theory. But, the underlying theory encapsulated by the model has not changed in the 40 plus years since the Brock–Mirman paper appeared.

It is worth reflecting, then, on what the model and theory deliver, because it is only against the backdrop of these results that we can begin to understand why the neoclassical framework has fallen short as a theory not just of growth but also of micro-founded macroeconomics. The key results we associate with the neoclassical model are

- optimality – the equilibria generated by the model satisfy the first welfare theorem, generating Pareto optimal outcomes;
- determinacy – the application of DP converts the model into one amenable to analysis via concave programming so that optimal trajectories of the model have a saddle-path property that implies the solutions are unique;
- ergodicity – under reasonable specifications of the discount factor, the deterministic steady-state of the model is locally stable; hence, the stochastic extension of the model will exhibit ergodic behavior asymptotically.

While these features seem eminently reasonable (and seem to reflect the fundamental results one obtains from the static Arrow–Debreu model of general equilibrium), when we confront these results with empirical facts, the shortcomings of the model become apparent.

On the question of optimality, particularly in the context of real business cycle theory, the optimality of equilibria means that there can be no such thing as involuntary unemployment of input resources. During the period of the 1980s through the first decade of the 2000s, the so called great moderation in the world macroeconomy relegated this issue to a back burner, since those spells associated with downturns in the business cycle were short, and the world economy, for the most part, spent most of the time near the full-employment threshold. It was also easy to ignore the experience of Japan in the 1990s, blaming their woes on demographic effects or the peculiarities of government regulation. But the financial crisis of 2008 and the subsequent long-lived downturns in the United States and Europe saw the economics profession arguing with itself (as it had in the 1930s) over whether or not there was anything to be done about the slump. Proponents of real business cycle theory stated clearly that the observed unemployment resulting from the crash was entirely due to a marked reduction in productivity that made continuing to work undesirable. This, of course, is part and parcel of the so called freshwater–saltwater divide in macroeconomics, but the distinctly unmoderated effects of the '08 crash and its aftermath have brought the optimality implication of the RBC model and its neoclassical underpinnings to the fore.

A second issue that RBC macro has pushed to center stage is the question of what gives rise to aggregate shocks. While the Brock–Mirman assumption was, as a theoretical construct, entirely acceptable, confronting the mechanism with actual data in the calibrated versions of Brock–Mirmin pioneered by Kydland and Prescott has posed problems. Specifically, actual shocks large enough to impact the economy as whole (particularly large economies such as the United States or European Union) don't occur at anything close to business-cycle frequencies. Sectoral shocks do occur more frequently, but the connectedness of input–output relationships between different sectors leads to the conclusion that the law of large numbers should dampen the overall effect of these shocks on the economy as a whole. So, despite the success of RBC models in explaining many macroeconomic co-movements, the question remains as to what actually drives business cycles.

Finally, as a model of economic growth (independently of any other applications of the model or its methodology), the neoclassical growth model never actually moves beyond Solow's original work and its finding that, except for population growth, nothing in the neoclassical model explains the economic growth experienced since the onset of industrialization on the mid-1700s (i.e., what we now routinely refer to as the Solow residual). This problem is particularly galling, since it means that all of the work that went into the development of optimal growth theory can't actually explain growth, optimal or not. And, in this problem, we find the seeds for the development of a new theory of growth which ultimately leads to the unraveling of the key features of the neoclassical growth model, as optimality gives way to equilibrium in environments in which the perfect competition and complete markets assumptions of the static Arrow–Debreu model, and it's dynamic extension in the neoclassical model must give way to increasing returns and knowledge externalities. So, we turn next to an examination of how the profession finally reoriented toward the logical research program on what has actually driven the remarkable *per capita* increases in production and the concomitant improvements in human lifestyles since the 1770s.

CHAPTER 3

LUCAS AND GROWTH: ORIGINS, METHODS, AND MODELS

The inception of Lucas: 1988 endogenous growth theory paper is abundantly documented in the archives. The notes are contained in five folders. Most of the space is devoted to typed working paper versions to be circulated in Chicago and elsewhere with some basic letters attached in which Lucas asked for comments. The archives also clarify that the paper was solicited: Lucas submitted the final version to Robert G. King and Charles I. Plosser, editors of the *Journal of Monetary Economics*, with a short note but with no submission fee included (Lucas; letter to Robert G. King and Charles I. Plosser. August 27, 1987. Lucas papers. Box 15. Folder 1). We also know from the archives that by circulating the subsequent versions of the model, Lucas effectively called the profession's attention to his work, and the paper "generated widespread interest," intense, and wide-ranging reactions. By the time of publication, the paper had thus been in the limelight, and the one referee report that the archives preserve suggested publication with only minor and technical revisions to keep the paper as close to the circulated version as possible (Anonymous referee report. Undated. Lucas papers. Box 15. Folder 4). In a note written in a personal tone of voice, King and Plosser informed Lucas about acceptance to which they enclosed the report which later Lucas used as a checklist to implement the technical changes the referee suggested. It is obvious from the phrasing of the editorial letter that they invited only one referee (Robert G. King and Charles I. Plosser's letter to Lucas. November 6, 1987. Lucas papers. Box 15. Folder 4). There was a second, formal letter of acceptance by King to inform Lucas of the expected publication date and to reassure fee waiver (Robert G. King's letter to Lucas. March 10, 1988. Lucas papers. Box 15. Folder 1).

More importantly, in the notes Lucas took from 1984 onward when preparing for the presentations of the subsequent versions of the model at various occasions, including his University of Chicago classes, we can track the

Endogenous Growth: Theory, Methods and Morphology
International Symposia in Economic Theory and Econometrics, Volume 35, 57–90

ISSN: 1571-0386/doi:10.1108/S1571-038620260000035011

formations of the underlying ideas. These notes are centered around two core thoughts: focus must be placed on the empirical facts a theory of growth and development should explain, and it is the growth of knowledge that must play the central role in this explanation.

Lucas repeatedly highlighted the empirical facts that drove him to start thinking about growth and development. The archives show that in the years between 1984 and 1988 Lucas used his public appearances to promote the ideas of his endogenous growth theory research. Some of his presentations were rather formal, especially the Marshall Lectures he held at the University of Cambridge in 1984–1985 when he first came out with his models.[1] He thus was ready to keep things short and sweet and omitted the formal parts just to shed light on the nature of the problem. The notes he took in preparation for his lecture at the University of California, Santa Barbara, on May 19, 1986, offer a good example. On this occasion, Lucas avoided all the mathematics to simplify things as much as possible[2] and focused on the distinction between *growth* and *level* effects, the diversity of levels and growth rates across the countries without any notable correlation between the two, the stability of growth rates in the advanced countries, and the possibly sudden changes in the growth rates of middle-income and poor economies (Hand-written notes. 1986. Lucas papers. Box 15. Folder 3). In her summary, Stokey (2025) also highlights that Lucas required his theory to be consistent with specific empirical facts which, of course, is a hallmark of his oeuvre.

In an undated class note (based on the dating of the surrounding materials in the same folder, they might be from 1985), Lucas effectively emphasizes that he believed the central element behind economic development to be the growth in knowledge. This relocates the task of understanding growth to the understanding of how knowledge grows. What Lucas had in mind was a law of motion for the stock of ideas and skills that he sharply distinguished from and did not restrict to academic or scientific ideas. Instead, Lucas emphasized the social nature of knowledge – knowledge about how to do anything, do economies, run a restaurant, or utilize computers in business. Such knowledge is always the property of a group of people or a culture. When people are newly introduced into a culture, as Lucas goes on, they learn the language, start exchanging previously existing ideas, produce new ideas, train new entrants, and so on. Of course, there is also much interaction among cultures, so when it comes to understanding the exchange of ideas, no sharp boundaries among cultures or countries should be assumed.

Knowledge belongs to a culture through the people forming and sharing the culture. Producing knowledge or the accumulation of human capital, as Lucas claims, uses two inputs: time and previously acquired knowledge. Time and knowledge are always personal, so the costs of producing knowledge are private, while benefits, while private, are largely more widespread. By realizing that

[1]In a note, it is Lucas who refers to his Marshall Lectures as rather technical.
[2]In this lecture, Lucas felt it necessary to explain basic concepts like diminishing marginal product with the popular story of shoveling snow – doubling actual workforce while keeping the capital stock, taken as the number of shovels, intact will not double the output. This detail shows that Lucas; public lectures covered a wide spectrum of audience.

the individual cannot exclude others by constraining the positive effects of her knowledge to herself, Lucas identifies an external effect of knowledge. Any individual as a member of society can benefit from the positive external effect of others' human capital, so there is no reason to believe that the individual is driven to have the right amount and mix of human capital. Given this external effect, two problems arise. One is the appropriate way of measuring the extent of the external effects, and the other is the identification of the social institutions that may internalize them. As knowledge generates positive externalities ranging beyond the benefits that an individual agent, be it a firm or individual (at this point, Lucas considers the option that knowledge might be owned by a business unit), can harness, agents might need to be compensated to be interested in producing the right amount and mix of knowledge. In the final version of the paper, Lucas addressed this problem by distinguishing the equilibrium and optimum paths of human capital. With no incentives but with the same initial stocks, the competitive equilibrium path falls short of the optimum path chosen by the social planner.

There is more than one way of understanding human capital accumulation. One is certainly based on the distinction between income-producing and knowledge producing activities. This became the core idea of the Uzawa–Lucas model – the individual shares their available time between work and learning. Here, Lucas confronts two alternative ways of making the choice between today's and tomorrow's consumption. One is through savings – given the choice between work and learning, the individual finds an optimum share between consumption and savings hence investment into physical capital. The other is through human capital accumulation which takes a time input, so this decision directly affects the time the individual devotes to work. Given the time decision, the individual can find an optimum share of output between consumption and investment, but the core problem for Lucas is to find an optimum time investment *and* an optimum investment into physical capital *at the same time*. The individual must make these two decisions simultaneously. Her decision on time investment in human capital affects the productivity of physical capital, while the stock of physical capital constrains the effectiveness of human capital. Too low a level of physical capital does not make it rational to accumulate a high level of human capital – and *vice versa*: too low a level of human capital does not make it rational to accumulate a high level of physical capital. The two decisions are inherently interrelated.

Another facet for understanding human capital accumulation is the idea that knowledge is a by-product of some privately rewarding activity, which Lucas labels as learning by doing. However, as Lucas adds, this way of human capital accumulation might lead to too little or erroneously mixed human capital. This line of thought suggests that of the three models Lucas compared in the 1988 paper, he preferred the model based on the time-sharing problem between two activities to the model of learning by doing (Hand-written notes. Undated. Lucas papers. Box 15. Folder 2).

The archives preserve multiple versions of the learning-by-doing model. In one of them, which is presumably also from 1985, Lucas addresses the problem of human capital accumulation in a learning-by-doing framework formulated in an embryonic discrete-time overlapping generations model. In the title of the notes, Lucas mentions as a source his graduate student Ki Seong Park whose dissertation addressed the problem of on-the-job training (Park, 1987). Besides education with time investment and learning by doing, Park distinguishes on-the-job-training as a third form of human capital accumulation. By so doing, Park subscribed to Lucas; main idea of learning as a social activity distinct from physical capital, while explaining human capital accumulation with interactions between different age groups of workers within a firm. In Park's framework, any firm has junior and senior employees, and when a young worker enters a firm, she as a student learns from her senior fellows regarded as teachers, and the larger the teacher–student ratio, the more human capital she can accumulate relative to young workers in jobs at other firms with lower ratios. As Park assumed, a worker prefers firms which provide better learning opportunities, and hence higher future income signaled by the higher teacher–student ratios, even at the price of lower earnings in the short run. This outlines the familiar trade-off between current earnings and future earnings.

Even though Lucas, notes are incomplete and rudimentary, they are worth attention as the suggested framework falls so far from the final preprint and published versions of the model. Lucas used some elements of Park's idea, though similarities should not be overemphasized. Most importantly, he distinguished two age groups of workers (in contrast with Park's framework with many cohorts) having different levels of human capital, and hence different levels of productivity. He also makes a distinction between individual human capital and the human capital of an industry, which bears close resemblance to Park's distinction between general and firm-specific forms of human capital. In the model, workers are assumed to live for two periods ($t=0,1$). At age 0, a worker has h_0 units of human capital, while at age 1, her stock of capital is $(1+\delta)h_0$, so the growth rate of knowledge is δ. Lucas thus simply treats the rate as a constant, while Park regarded it as a variable to endogenously explain with his framework of on-the-job training. For Lucas' specification of the industry-wide form of knowledge k_t, the dynamics are given by a difference equation:

$$k_{t+1} = k_t + \lambda x_t, \tag{1.1}$$

where x_t is industry output. This shows that in Lucas' framework, a change in human capital at the industry level generated from learning by doing is proxied in the model by the intensity of production. Individuals combine the two forms of knowledge in production, while Lucas assumes away the contribution of physical capital. Hence, the output of the young and old workers is $h_0 k_t$ and $h_0(1+\delta)k_t$, respectively. Total output is then

$$x_t = n_{0;t} h_0 k_t + n_{1;t} h_0 (1+\delta) k_t = h_0 k_t \left[n_{0;t} + (1+\delta) n_{0;t-1} \right], \tag{1.2}$$

where $n_{0;t}$ is the number of young workers at t, $n_{1;t}$ is the number of old workers at t, and of course $n_{1;t} = n_{0;t-1}$. Combining (1.1) and (1.2) yields

$$\frac{k_{t+1}}{k_t} = 1 + \lambda h_0 \left[n_{0;t} + (1+\delta) n_{0;t-1} \right], \tag{1.3}$$

which is the growth rate of industry-wide knowledge stock.

As a next step, Lucas defines the simple inverse demand function for the industry as

$$p_t = Ax_t^{-\eta}, \tag{1.4}$$

with obviously $A > 0$ and $\eta > 0$. To determine the wage rates for the two cohorts of workers, Lucas assumes that the value a worker creates is equal to her wage. On this basis he finds that

$$w_{0;t} = p_t h_0 k_t, \tag{1.5}$$

$$w_{1;t} = p_t (1+\delta) h_0 k_t,$$

where $w_{0;t}$ and $w_{1;t}$ stand for the wage rate of the young and the old at time t, respectively. Hence, the present value of wages for a worker employed in the industry is

$$V = w_{0;t} + Rw_{1;t+1} = p_t h_0 k_t + Rp_{t+1} h_0 (1+\delta) k_{t+1}, \tag{1.6}$$

where R is the discount factor. Lucas assumes a competitive mechanism for entering and leaving the industry that ensures the present value in (1.6) prevails, so he treats V as a constant.

At this point, Lucas introduces a new variable $z_t = p_t k_t$ that appears in (1.6) for both t and $t+1$. As h_0 appears in both parts in the right-hand side of (1.6), with this invention Lucas can express the relative value as

$$\frac{V}{h_0} = z_t + R(1+\delta) z_{t+1}, \tag{1.7}$$

that he rearranges to yield

$$z_{t+1} = \frac{V}{R(1+\delta)h_0} - \frac{1}{R(1+\delta)} z_t, \tag{1.8}$$

which is a first-order difference equation that is supposed to describe the dynamics of $p_t k_t$. If

$$-\frac{1}{R(1+\delta)} > -1,$$

or, simply put, $R(1+\delta) > 1$, then z_t tends toward some $\overline{z}$ with damped oscillations as $t \to \infty$. In the opposite case, when $R(1+\delta) < 1$, the process would show explosive oscillations which Lucas ruled out by explicitly assuming $R(1+\delta) > 1$. Obviously, the case of non-oscillating convergence is not viable as it would require

$$-\frac{1}{R(1+\delta)} > 0,$$

which would be possible only if $R(1+\delta)<0$. Hence, Lucas assumes that $z_t \to \bar{z}$ with damped oscillations. The stationary value $\bar{z}$ is easy to describe based on the parameters in (1.8) as

$$\bar{z} = \frac{V}{\left[1+R(1+\delta)\right]h_0}, \tag{1.9}$$

which is the stable value for $p_t k_t$. Note that even if $p_t k_t$ is constant as $t \to \infty$, it may be consistent with diverse dynamics for p_t and k_t. At this point, Lucas assumes that the industry-wide capital stock grows at a constant rate κ as described by $k_{t+1} = (1+\kappa)k_t$. This is the same assumption he applied in the paper when describing growth patterns along a balanced growth path. Lucas neglects to be clear on the sign of κ, but we can assume that $\kappa > 0$. As in the steady state we have $z_t = z_{t+1} = \bar{z}$, we also have

$$\bar{z} = k_t p_t = k_{t+1} p_{t+1} = (1+\kappa)k_t \frac{p_t}{1+\kappa},$$

in which $k_{t+1} = (1+\kappa)k_t$ implies that

$$p_{t+1} = \frac{p_t}{1+\kappa},$$

in which κ is the rate of price decline. Price change and the rate of change of industry-wide knowledge changes at the same rate κ. Lucas labels this constant as *the rate of external capital accumulation* as it is related to how knowledge grows in the industry without providing a definition or any remarks on this. From the context, we infer that κ is supposed to measure the effect of learning by doing at the industry level. Although Lucas does not use this term, we can say that δ is *the rate of internal capital accumulation* which Lucas planned to describe as dependent upon the ratio of the wages of the old and the young. A higher ratio means that the rise in wages between the two age groups is sharper, which implies higher values for δ. As a final step, Lucas tries to say something intelligent about this rate, but he does not go beyond realizing that from (1.3)

$$1+\kappa = 1+\lambda h_0\left[n_{0;t} + (1+\delta)n_{0;t-1}\right],$$

follows. At this point, the notes discontinue (Hand-written notes. Undated. Lucas papers. Box 15. Folder 2). We all know the end of the story – in the published version of the paper Lucas does not use this model of overlapping generations.

LUCAS; FULL-FLEDGED ENDOGENOUS GROWTH THEORY: ON THE MECHANICS OF ECONOMIC DEVELOPMENT

Lucas (1988)'s endogenous growth theory paper is commonly regarded as the Uzawa–Lucas model and most celebrated for Uzawa's two-sector framework that Lucas implemented to distinguish human capital accumulation and production, some of which is saved and invested as physical capital. In the introduction, Lucas indicates a number of studies he treats as predecessors that address the problem of human capital accumulation and how human capital affects production. By this time, human capital accumulation had received ample attention, and a wide range of approaches were available – suffice it to mention the seminal contribution of Becker (1964) and Schultz (1963). Ben-Porath (1967) examined life-cycle time investment into human capital in a framework where the individual is supposed to find the optimum share of available time she devotes to learning. This time investment inevitably constrains the time she uses in income-related activities, so the trade-off between current and future earnings emerges. Arrow (1962), instead of the time investment of the worker, describes the accumulation of knowledge as a by-product of production. In a version of his two-sector growth model, Uzawa (1965) describes human capital accumulation and technological change as the product of a distinct productive sector exclusively responsible for knowledge creation. As we saw above, in the mid-1960s, Lucas also attempted to interpret technological change as an investment activity of the representative firm. It was easy to reinterpret investment activity of the firm as investment in technology, but this way of thinking does not endow knowledge with any kind of special character – it remains as an immaterial form of capital, as Lucas; referees also highlighted. Most importantly, in Lucas' previous framework, knowledge has no social character, and if knowledge is really of a social nature as Lucas underlined in the 1980s, then his previous attempts missed the point. A related problem is how to fit increasing returns in a model. There are options here, and Lucas, like Romer (1986a), assumed a perfect competition framework in which the effect of knowledge responsible for increasing returns must be external. In this case, however, internalization is an issue; hence, equilibrium and optimum human capital cannot coincide. To reach the optimum, knowledge must be funded by the government.

UZAWA'S CHARACTERIZATION OF TECHNOLOGICAL CHANGE IN A TWO-SECTOR MODEL

Given that Lucas adopted Uzawa's two-sector framework for his analysis of human capital investment, it is worth spending a bit of time elaborating of what Uzawa (1961a) did. His paper postulated a two-sector and two-commodity economy in which each commodity is produced with a production function of two factors of production, physical capital (K), and labor (L). Sector 1 is responsible for the production of investment-goods through the production function $Y_1 = F_1(K_1; L_1)$, while sector 2 produces the consumption-goods by $Y_2 = F_2(K_2; L_2)$. Most importantly, sector 1 creates the capital stock of the whole economy (K), and as production of capital also requires some capital input, Uzawa established a competitive mechanism that forces households to find the optimal allocation of capital between the sectors (i.e., how K is divided between K_1 and K_2, so by assumption $K = K_1 + K_2$). A part of the problem is to optimally allocate the labor force between the sectors on the basis of optimal capital allocation. Both decisions are made by the social planner – with no taxes or other market distortions, the optimal decision of any agent to take a job in one of the sectors exactly coincides with the optimal decision of the benevolent social planner. The technology is described by two standard neoclassical productions functions which are assumed to be twice continuously differentiable, strictly increasing, and concave (with constant returns to scale). By using the constant-returns-to-scale assumption, Uzawa specified technologies in terms of the output–capital ratio as

$$y_i = f_i(k_i), \tag{3.1.1}$$

$$f_i(k_i) > 0;\ f_i'(k_i) > 0;\ f_i''(k_i) < 0 \text{ for all } k_i > 0, \tag{3.1.2}$$

where $y_i = Y_i / L_i$, $k_i = K_i / L_i$, $f_i(k_i) = F_i(k_i;1)$, and $i = 1,2$. Monotonicity properties in (3.1.2) can be restated as compatibility with the familiar Inada conditions. The transition to per-capita terms preserves the differentiability features of the production functions.[3] Two further assumptions are

$$\frac{\partial F_i}{\partial K_i} = \frac{r}{P_i} \text{and} \frac{\partial F_i}{\partial L_i} = \frac{w}{P_i}, \tag{3.1.3}$$

$$P_1 Y_1 = rK \text{and} P_2 Y_2 = wL, \tag{3.1.4}$$

where P_i is the price of the investment-goods and consumption-goods and r and w are the returns to capital and labor, respectively. Assumption (3.1.3) is the usual equilibrium condition according to which the real rate of interest and the real wage are equal to the marginal product of capital and labor, respectively, in both sectors to ensure optimal allocation of factors of production. Condition (3.1.4) ensures that labor spends all its income on consumption with no savings, while capital does not consume. Note that conditions (3.1.3) and (3.1.4) together form a six-equation system in six unknowns (K_1 and L_1, r and w, P_1 and P_2) with given K and L, yielding the optimal allocation for each factor. The system in (3.1.3) is the first-order condition for *static* profit-maximization. The problem in the model is inherently dynamic as today's consumption can be increased only by a reduction in tomorrow's consumption – more consumption today requires more capital and labor input today that, in turn, reduces the inputs devoted to capital accumulation necessary for the production of consumption goods tomorrow. Uzawa, however, used a framework in which he could approach this dynamic problem as an infinite series of momentary static problems – agents, given $K(t)$ and $L(t)$, need to find optimal allocations at every moment of time t. Every such decision implies some dynamics, though, depending on the allocation of factors to capital formation. It may happen that

[3]In this series of papers, Uzawa did not specify the technologies as first-order homogenous Cobb-Douglas production functions, although such functions perfectly fit his assumptions. Lucas (1988) explicitly used a Cobb-Douglas function, and Ljungqvist and Sargent (2018, p. 641) also describe Uzawa's contribution with a Cobb-Douglas technology.

the optimal allocation of factors leads the economy to change its size, resulting in increasing or reducing K. In this approach, the steady state is a specific pair of $K(t)$ and $L(t)$ where optimal allocation results in a change of capital in line with the rise of the population.

If, to keep things simple, in addition to the previous assumptions, we set $\rho_i = L_i / L$, and $\omega = w / r$, we have three further equations:

$$\omega = \frac{f_i(k_i)}{f_i'(k_i)} - k_i, \tag{3.1.5}$$

$$\rho_1 k_1 + \rho_2 k_2 = k, \text{where } \rho_1 + \rho_2 = 1, \tag{3.1.6}$$

$$\rho_1 f_1(k_1) = f_1'(k_1) k, \tag{3.1.7}$$

where $k = K / L$, and ρ_i describes the allocation of labor force in each sector. Equation (3.1.5) is easy to turn into a form that yields a unique k_i for any ω, determining optimal ratios $k_i(\omega)$ as allocations. Note that equation (3.1.5) establishes a monotone increasing function between ω and k_i (the differential of ω with respect to k_i is positive, so $d\omega / dk_i > 0$ implying $dk_i / d\omega > 0$). The introduction of ω helps us to dismiss prices P_i, while it must remain valid that for any k, we have optimal ratios k_i, ρ_i, and ω. Accordingly, now that for any ω, we have the unique optimal ratios $k_i(\omega)$; from (3.1.5) and (3.1.7), it follows that

$$\rho_1 = \frac{k}{\omega + k_1(\omega)}, \tag{3.1.8}$$

so the optimal labor force allocation is also determined within the system. At this point, Uzawa introduces the additional assumption $k_1(\omega) < k_2(\omega)$ according to which sector 2 is more capital intensive than sector 1, which might seem too restrictive an assumption to underpin the model's key results (Solow, 1961). Uzawa defended the assumption as a generalization of experience (Gordon, 1961, p. 948). As a final step, Uzawa shows that, based on (3.1.6) and (3.1.8), we have

$$k = \frac{\omega + k_1(\omega)}{\omega + k_2(\omega)} k_2(\omega), \tag{3.1.9}$$

which yields a unique k to any given ω, denoted as $k(\omega)$. Taking the logarithm of each side, we have

$$\ln[k(\omega)] = \ln[\omega + k_1(\omega)] + \ln[k_2(\omega)] - \ln[\omega + k_2(\omega)],$$

which we differentiate with respect to ω to have

$$\frac{1}{k(\omega)} \frac{dk}{d\omega} = \left[\frac{1}{\omega + k_1(\omega)} - \frac{1}{\omega + k_2(\omega)}\right] + \frac{\frac{dk_1}{d\omega}}{\omega + k_1(\omega)} + \frac{dk_2}{d\omega}\left[\frac{1}{k_2(\omega)} - \frac{1}{\omega + k_2(\omega)}\right].$$

The second bracketed term on the right is obviously positive. Furthermore, $dk_i / d\omega > 0$, as we have seen above. Given that $k(\omega) > 0$, the sign of $dk / d\omega$ clearly depends on the sign of the first bracketed term on the right – which is positive if our assumption regarding the capital-intensity of the sectors holds. This latter result is of crucial importance in terms of the uniqueness of k^* for given this strict monotonicity, $d\omega / dk > 0$ also holds. This is the very condition that ensures the uniqueness of k^* as in the case of $d\omega / d\dot{k} \geq 0$ some ω^* would be compatible with more than one k^*.

Now, the system is closed: to any k, we have a unique ω that in turns determines the optimal allocation for each factor of production. This result is easy to translate into a solution of the original system in terms of K_i and L_i, given any pair K and L. At this stage, the system at any k implies some dynamics through ω and $k_i(\omega)$. On this basis, finding the steady state amounts to finding a unique k^*, where $\dot{k} = 0$.

The solution to this part of the problem directly follows from the way we have ensured that the system can be solved for any k. In this first paper of the sequence, Uzawa only wanted to prove the existence and the uniqueness of a steady-state capital stock k^*, and left the attributes of the convergence process to the subsequent studies. The dynamics of the system is described by two equations. Assuming a constant growth rate of labor, λ, labor force dynamics is easy to describe as

$$\dot{L}(t) = \lambda L(t). \tag{3.1.10}$$

A similar differential equation for the capital stock is also available. Given (3.1.4), the output of the capital-manufacturing sector is

$$Y_1(t) = \frac{r}{P_1} K(t),$$

which is gross investment which, by definition, describes the dynamic implications of optimal factor allocation. Correcting it with depreciation $\mu K(t)$, we have net investment, which is the actual change in the stock of capital. Formally put, it is

$$\dot{K}(t) = \left(\frac{r}{P_1} - \mu \right) K(t), \tag{3.1.11}$$

which is, just like (3.1.10), a homogenous first-order linear differential equation. Equations (3.1.10) and (3.1.11) lead to

$$\frac{\dot{k}(t)}{k(t)} = f_1'\left[k_1(\omega)\right] - \mu - \lambda, \tag{3.1.12}$$

where any capital stock k determines some wage rate ω through (3.1.9), which in turn determines k_1 as $k_1(\omega)$ through (3.1.5), so eventually, it is k that is supposed to determine its own dynamics through (11) based on (3.1.5) and (3.1.9). The steady state is where $f_1'\left(k_1^*\right) = \mu + \lambda$, which leads to a unique pair of ω^* and k^*.

We know that (3.1.5) defines ω as a strictly increasing function of k_1, so through (3.1.5), we have a unique ω^* corresponding to k_1^*, and finally, (3.1.9) gives the unique $k^* \equiv k(\omega^*)$. The steady state exists, and it is unique.

In the next paper of the sequence, Uzawa (1963) replaced the assumption of the pervious paper according to which there is no savings from labor income while there is no consumption from capital gains. Instead, Uzawa assumed a propensity to save parameter $s \in (0,1)$. Uzawa's strategy closely followed the main thread of the previous paper, so his main concern was to show the existence and the uniqueness of a balanced capital-labor ratio k^*, and to describe as closely as possible the convergence properties of the new system. He still conceives the dynamic problem as a chain of momentary static problems, the solution of which always implies some dynamics regarding the system as a whole. So, again, the steady state is a particular state where the solution to the static problem implies some dynamics that leaves the system at rest. It is only in his 1964 paper that he brings genuine dynamic analysis into his work, first via the conventional approach of the Euler equations, followed by the 1965 paper with its Hamiltonian.

In the 1963 study, the economy still consists of the same sectors with the same production functions $Y_1 = F_1(K_1;L_1)$ and $Y_2 = F_2(K_2;L_2)$. Both factors are fully employed all the time, and their allocation between sectors is competitive. The decision problems remain the same: capital is to be allocated between the sectors optimally, and households also allocate their labor optimally. In the absence of market distortions, both decisions are made by the social planner. Output of the capital-goods sector, $Y_1(t)$, is gross investment, so dynamics of the labor force and capital stock are described by a pair of differential equations

$$\dot{L}(t) = \lambda L(t), \tag{3.1.13}$$

$$\dot{K}(t) = Y_1(t) - \mu K(t). \tag{3.1.14}$$

Gross national product is

$$Y(t) = Y_2(t) + p(t)Y_1(t), \tag{3.1.15}$$

where $p(t)$ is the price of investment goods expressed in terms of consumption goods. In addition to (3.1.15), we also assume

$$sY(t) = p(t)Y_1(t), \tag{3.1.16}$$

which equates the portion of income devoted to investment goods with the expenditures on investment to determine the quantity of new capital goods. Instead of (3.1.3), we now have

$$w(t) = \frac{\partial F_2}{\partial L_2}\left[K_2(t);L_2(t)\right] = p(t)\frac{\partial F_1}{\partial L_1}\left[K_1(t);L_1(t)\right], \tag{3.1.17}$$

$$r(t) = \frac{\partial F_2}{\partial K_2}\left[K_2(t);L_2(t)\right] = p(t)\frac{\partial F_1}{\partial K_1}\left[K_1(t);L_1(t)\right]. \tag{3.1.18}$$

As in the previous paper, for simplicity, Uzawa switches to per-capita terms by assuming that $k = K / L$, $y = Y / L$, $k_i = K_i / L_i$, $y_i = Y_i / L$, $\omega = w / r$, and $\rho_i = L_i / L$. Note that assuming $y_i = Y_i / L$ (replacing $y_i = Y_i / L_i$ of the 1961 paper), we have $y_i = f_i(k_i) l_i$. As a result, we have the following system of equations (everything is specified at its time t value):

$$\omega = \frac{f_i(k_i)}{f_i'(k_i)} - k_i, \tag{3.1.19}$$

$$p = \frac{f_2'(k_2)}{f_1'(k_1)}, \tag{3.1.20}$$

$$y = y_2 + p\,y_1, \tag{3.1.21}$$

$$y_1 = f_1(k_1)\frac{k_2 - k}{k_2 - k_1} \text{ and } y_2 = f_2(k_2)\frac{k - k_1}{k_2 - k_1}, \tag{3.1.22}$$

$$p\,y_1 = s\,y. \tag{3.1.23}$$

Equation (3.1.19) is equivalent to (3.1.5) due to which $dk_i / d\omega > 0$ still holds. Equations (3.1.21) and (3.1.23) trivially come from (3.1.15) and (3.1.16), respectively. Starting from (3.1.18), we can express p as a ratio of the marginal products which are easy to describe in terms of k_1 and k_2, leading to (3.1.20). In (3.1.22), optimal labor force allocations ρ_i are determined as functions of k_i, given k. This is the analog of the competitive mechanism in (3.1.8) to allocate the labor force.

The dynamics of k are then given by the differential equation:

$$\frac{\dot{k}}{k} = s\,f_1'(k_1)\frac{k + \omega}{k} - \lambda - \mu. \tag{3.1.24}$$

Now, it is easy to identify the condition that determines the steady state k^* as

$$s\,f_1'(k_1^*)\frac{k^* + \omega^*}{k^*} = \lambda + \mu, \tag{3.1.25}$$

which is the condition for $\dot{k} = 0$ at any $0 < s < 1$. Uniqueness of the solution is ensured by the strict monotonicity of the left-hand side of (25) with respect to ω, to which, again, we need the assumption $k_1(\omega) < k_2(\omega)$. To any $0 < s < 1$, there is thus a unique k^* to which a unique ω^* and k_1^* correspond, and the system starting at this point stays at rest, while starting at any initial k, the system asymptotically converges to k^*.

In the most technical part of the sequence, Uzawa (1964) analyzes the trajectories along which two-sector economies converge to a steady state from initial conditions where the capital stock is too low or two high as compared to the balanced capital stock k*. The economy remains the same as it was in the previous papers, but here, Uzawa assumes that there is a minimum amount of capital that must be devoted to production is sector 2. If population grows at a high rate, he argues, a society with low levels of capital may be trapped in the “vicious circle of poverty," meaning that in order to fulfill society's basic needs there might be no free capacities to be used in capital accumulation. To deal with the problem, Uzawa introduced a new maximand

$$\int_0^\infty \frac{Y_2(t)}{L(t)} e^{-\delta t}\, dt,$$

as the discounted sum of per-capita consumption. Given the initial conditions for $K(t)$ and $L(t)$, of the feasible consumption paths for the economy, the objective of the planner is to maximize the total welfare of the population. Six equations describe the system:

$$\dot{K}(t) = Y_1(t) - \mu K(t), \qquad (3.1.26)$$

$$Y_i(t) = F_i\left[K_i(t); L_i(t)\right], \qquad (3.1.27)$$

$$K_1(t) + K_2(t) = K(t), \qquad (3.1.28)$$

$$L_1(t) + L_2(t) = L(t), \qquad (3.1.29)$$

$$Y_2(t) \geq w_{\min} L(t), \qquad (3.1.30)$$

where (3.1.30) expresses the constraint that consumption (food) is needed at a level where the minimum nutrition requirements of the society are met. Unlike the previous two papers, Uzawa uses a dynamic framework and sets up a Lagrangian with six multipliers belonging to the six constraints above as

$$\int_0^\infty \left\{ \begin{matrix} Y_2(t) - p_1(t)\left[Y_1(t) - F_1\left[K_1(t); L_1(t)\right]\right] - p_2(t)\left[Y_2(t) - F_2\left[K_2(t); L_2(t)\right]\right] - \\ r(t)\left[K_1(t) + K_2(t) - K(t)\right] - w(t)\left[L_1(t) + L_2(t) - L(t)\right] - q(t) \\ \left[\dot{K}(t) - Y_1(t) + \mu K(t)\right] - v(t)\left[w_{\min} L(t) - Y_2(t)\right] \end{matrix} \right\} e^{-(n+\delta)t}\, dt, \qquad (3.1.31)$$

that is to be maximized in terms of $Y_2(t)$ with the constraints given by (3.1.26)–(3.1.30). Here, Uzawa applies the method of the calculus of variations (Gelfand & Fomin, 1963, p. 15) to have the seven Euler equations corresponding to the seven variables $Y_1(t)$, $Y_2(t)$, $K_1(t)$, $K_2(t)$, $L_1(t)$, $L_2(t)$, and $K(t)$ by which the optimal path of variables must abide,[4] and the one necessary condition from the constraint behind $v(t)$ involving a Kuhn–Tucker inequality problem.

Having set up the framework for the analysis, he follows the strategy of the previous papers. First, he transforms the system into per-capita terms and shows that under $k_1(\omega) < k_2(\omega)$ for all $\omega > 0$ there is a steady state k^* and ω^*, where $\dot{k} = 0$

[4]Just as a quick technical reminder, please note that here Uzawa applies the Euler equations to constrain the optimal paths the same way as discrete-time dynamic programming uses Euler equations that optimal paths must satisfy (Stokey & Lucas, 1989, pp. 148–156).

and $\dot{\omega}=0$. Then, he turns to the analysis of optimal trajectories under different assumptions and finds out what dynamics the solutions satisfying the Euler equations imply. First and foremost, he wants to point out the conditions under which an economy converges to the steady state. In this regard, the minimum consumption requirement plays the role of the decisive factor. In the simplest case where $w_{\min}=0$, the economy can proceed with no food production from any low level of capital stock until it reaches a critical level of capital where it can divide its resources between capital accumulation and food production. Specifically, (3.1.5) still applies and combined with the assumption of specialization to capital accumulation, implies the increase in capital stock in sector 1 that in turn implies higher rates ω, so $\omega \to \omega^*$, while $k=k_1 \to k_1\left(\omega^*\right)$. After this point, capacities are allocated to food production. The same is true of the economy where $w_{\min}>0$ with the caveat that the economy can accumulate capital while satisfying the minimum consumption requirement only if its initial capital stock is above a critical level. Starting under that level, the economy cannot devote any resources to capital accumulation, and it converges to the $k=0$ state.

On these foundations, Uzawa (1965) constructs an economy in which physical capital as the product of a specialized industry is replaced by technical progress which he also interprets as the product of an optimal allocation decision. The labor force is allocated between two sectors, the first of which manufactures a commodity to be optimally divided between consumption and investment, and the second of which is responsible for technical progress that, entering the production function as an additional factor, enhances the productivity of labor. Specifically, Uzawa postulated a standard two-variable strictly increasing concave constant-returns-to-scale production function

$$Y(t)=F\left[K(t);A(t)L_P(t)\right], \qquad (3.1.32)$$

where $K(t)$ is the stock of physical capital, and $A(t)$ is the state of technological knowledge interpreted as a factor determining the efficiency of labor force employed in production, $L_P(t)$.[5] The imposition of Inada conditions then guarantees that optimal trajectories will be interior. As in both the 1961 and 1963 papers, when $y(t)=Y(t)/L(t)$ and $k(t)=K(t)/L(t)$, (32) becomes $f(k;uA)=F\left(\frac{K}{L};A\frac{L_P}{L}\right)$, where $u=\frac{L_P}{L}$, and f preserves the monotonicity and concavity of (3.1.32).

[5] An equivalent variant of this production function is $F(K;L;t)=A(t)F(K;L)$, so time affects the production function only through technical change, and the part describing this progress is separable from the part that combines the traditional factors of production. Uzawa (1961b) showed that such a production function is consistent with stable equilibrium in the neoclassical model of economic growth. Some recent contributions pointed out that stability in the sense of dynamic equilibrium with technical progress implies this functional form. This result reverses the line of thought, and it is not the constant rate of technological change that puts the economy into dynamic equilibrium, but with constant returns to change it is the dynamic equilibrium, where $\dot{Y}/Y=\dot{K}/K=g$, that implies a functional form that includes a constant rate of labor-augmenting technological change.

Technological knowledge is affected by a large number of factors ranging from education through health care or other public goods. Uzawa represented this process with a weakly increasing and weakly concave production function ϕ, and labeled it as the educational sector, while assuming that the production of technological knowledge takes labor only. Then, the progress in technological knowledge is determined by the ratio of labor force employed in education through

$$\frac{\dot{A}(t)}{A(t)} = \phi\left[\frac{L_E(t)}{L(t)}\right], \tag{3.1.33}$$

where $L_E(t)$ and $L(t)$ are labor force inputs devoted to the production of technological skills and the total labor force, respectively. It is of course assumed that $L_P(t) + L_E(t) = L(t)$. The dynamics of labor force and physical capital are described by a pair of differential equations:

$$\frac{\dot{L}(t)}{L(t)} = \lambda, \tag{3.1.34}$$

$$\dot{K}(t) = I(t) - \mu K(t), \tag{3.1.35}$$

where, as before, μ is the depreciation rate, and $I(t)$ is aggregate gross investment that together with consumption equals aggregate income. The state variables are $K(t)$, $A(t)$, and $L(t)$, of which the path of $L(t)$ is exogenously determined by (3.1.34), while the dynamics of $K(t)$ and $A(t)$ depend on the allocation of time between production and education, and the allocation of physical output between consumption and investment – they are thus the endogenous states affected by the optimizing decisions of the social planner seeking to maximize total social welfare from consumption. On this foundation, the objective is to maximize

$$\int_0^\infty \left[1 - s(t)\right] y(t) e^{-\delta t}\, dt, \tag{3.1.36}$$

where $s(t) = I(t)/Y(t)$ is the investment ratio, and δ is the rate of interest, so (3.1.35) simply becomes $\dot{K}(t) = s(t)Y(t) - \mu K(t)$. Following the procedures of the previous papers, Uzawa describes the laws of motion as

$$\dot{k}(t) = s(t)y(t) - (\mu + \lambda)k(t), \tag{3.1.37}$$

$$\dot{A}(t) = A(t)\phi\left[1 - u(t)\right], \tag{3.1.38}$$

where $u(t) = L_P(t)/L(t)$ describes the ratio of the labor force allocated to manufacturing. The social planner's control variables are thus $s(t)$ and $u(t)$ so that $0 \le s(t) \le 1$ and $0 \le u(t) \le 1$. Assuming $f(k) = k^\alpha$ with $0 < \alpha < 1$, it is easy to see that $y(t) = A(t)^{1-\alpha} u(t)^{1-\alpha} k(t)^\alpha = A(t)^{1-\alpha} u(t)^{1-\alpha} f\left[k(t)\right]$, which might also be written as

$$y(t) = A(t)u(t)f\left[\frac{k(t)}{A(t)u(t)}\right]. \tag{3.1.39}$$

Note that (3.1.39) can enter (3.1.36), and combined with (3.1.37) and (3.1.38), we can rewrite the optimization problem in terms of a standard Hamiltonian as

$$H(q;v;k;A;u;s;t) = \left\{(1-s)Auf\left(\frac{k}{Au}\right) + q\left[sAuf\left(\frac{k}{Au}\right) - \lambda k\right] + vA\phi(1-u)\right\}e^{-\delta t}, \tag{3.1.40}$$

where q and v are the current-value costates of states k and A, respectively. Deriving the first-order necessary conditions for the Hamiltonian is quite standard, however, Uzawa is very creative in finding some possibilities for simplification. By introducing

$$x(t) = \frac{k(t)}{A(t)} = \frac{K(t)}{A(t)\ L(t)},$$

and recognizing that the fact that in (3.1.40), control s maximizes the expression

$$(1-s)Auf\left(\frac{k}{Au}\right) + qsAuf\left(\frac{k}{Au}\right) = (1-s+qs)\ Auf\left(\frac{k}{Au}\right),$$

the problem boils down to the maximization of $1-s+qs$. The optimal choice for s then depends on what value q takes on. Given that $q \geq 0$ all over the process, we have three distinct cases. When $q=1$, $1-s+qs$ becomes $1-s+s=1$, and s remains indetermined for now. When $q>1$, $s=1$ is optimal, and $1-s+qs$ becomes $1-1+q=q$. Finally, in cases where $q<1$, $s=0$ is optimal, and $1-s+qs$ becomes $1-0+0q=1$. The expression $1-s+qs$ can thus be replaced by a new variable $p(t) = \max\left[1;q(t)\right]$. With these changes in notation, the system of necessary conditions becomes

$$\dot{q} = (\delta+\lambda)q - pf'\left(\frac{x}{u}\right), \tag{3.1.41}$$

$$\dot{v} = \left[\delta - \phi(1-u)\right]v - pu\left[f\left(\frac{x}{u}\right) - f'\left(\frac{x}{u}\right)\frac{x}{u}\right], \tag{3.1.42}$$

$$f\left(\frac{x}{u}\right) - f'\left(\frac{x}{u}\right)\frac{x}{u} \geq \frac{v}{p}\phi'(1-u), \tag{3.1.43}$$

$$\frac{\dot{x}}{x} = s\frac{f\left(\frac{x}{u}\right)}{\frac{x}{u}} - \lambda - \phi(1-u), \tag{3.1.44}$$

where the differential equation (3.1.44) comes from the definition of x and from the laws of motion for $\dot{k}/k$ and $\dot{A}/A$. An initial condition $x(0)=K(0)/A(0)L(0)$ also applies. The solution of the model then means finding the values for the variables where the system is at rest and analyzing the dynamics of the system near the steady state. Uzawa distinguishes three distinct cases on the basis of the distinct values $q \geq 0$ might take and adjusts the system of necessary conditions (3.1.41)–(3.1.44) to the case at hand and solves it for $\dot{x}=\dot{q}=\dot{v}=0$. He then shows that $q=1$ and $x=x^*$ is the state to which the system converges along saddle paths from both the case $x>x^*$ and $q<1$, and the case $x<x^*$ and $q>1$. Of course, the dynamics of x and q, the latter being the shadow price of capital, are closely related. In the steady state, obviously, $x(t)$ and $A(t)$ change at the same rate.

ROMER'S 1986 MODEL OF GROWTH WITH INCREASING RETURNS

Another source Lucas (1988, p. 17) cited as one bearing close technical similarity to his endogenous growth theory paper is Romer's (1986a) model of technical change with increasing returns. As Romer argues, there have been some patterns in economic growth (including the basic fact that the growth in the stocks of physical inputs does not explain the growth in aggregate income, and especially the increasing productivity of the labor force) that need an explanation built on increasing returns in production. To him it means that growth rates are positively related to the level of development. He translates this observation into a requirement that per capita output in a model should grow at a rate monotonically increasing over time because knowledge is constantly accumulated. His key factor in the explanation was thus endogenous technological change or accumulation of knowledge performed by profit-maximizing firms.

Romer describes knowledge accumulation by the firm by assuming it is generated by a concave and first-order homogenous production function

$$\dot{k}=G(I;k)\text{and especially}\frac{\dot{k}}{k}=g\left(\frac{I}{k}\right)=G\left(\frac{I}{k};1\right), \tag{3.2.1}$$

where k is the current level of private (i.e., firm-owned) knowledge, and I is forgone consumption of households offered to firms as inputs in knowledge creation. The dynamic problem thus lies in the circumstance that consumption is satisfied with a production technology that needs knowledge as an input, but tomorrow's knowledge can only be increased at the expense of today's utility of current consumption – or, in other words, today's consumption is dependent upon knowledge previously accumulated. Most importantly, (3.2.1) shows diminishing returns: at any level of k, the doubling of I does not lead to the doubling of the increase in k. To strengthen the diminishing returns feature of technological change, Romer also introduced an upper bound in (3.2.1) so that $\dot{k}/k \leq \alpha$; hence, the level of knowledge can constantly grow, while the growth rate remains finite.

Romer specifies a three-variable production function in k, K, and x as $F(k_i;K;x_i)$ for firm i, where k_i is the firm's knowledge capital, x_i is the set of further factors like physical capital and labor, and $K=\sum_{i=1}^{N}k_i$, where N is the number of firms. The production function exhibits increasing returns to scale as F is increasing in the stock of knowledge K, while it is concave and homogenous of degree one in k_i and x_i at any given K. Function F is thus characterized by

$$\lambda F(k_i;K;x_i)=F(\lambda k_i;K;\lambda x_i)<F(\lambda k_i;\lambda K;\lambda x_i), \tag{3.2.2}$$

which is the same function that Romer (1990a, 1990b) later specified to show how knowledge makes the firm interested in increasing without bound. Of the three variables, it is the role of x that is the easiest to understand as x stands for factors like labor and physical capital available in fixed supply. If the number of firms and the number of households are the same (denoted by S), and all firms are identical, then firm-specific indices can be omitted, and $x_i=\overline{\mathbf{x}}$ in $F(k;K;\overline{\mathbf{x}})$. The external effect K is simply the sum of firm-owned knowledge, so $K=Sk$, and finally, $F(k;K;\overline{\mathbf{x}})=f(k;K)=f(k;Sk)\equiv\mathcal{F}(k)$. As Romer (1986a, p. 1003) argues, assuming positive external effects of knowledge is quite natural as knowledge cannot be made exclusively owned by a patentee. The activity of any firm has a positive spillover effect on the production possibilities of other firms in the industry or in the whole economy (Ljungqvist & Sargent, 2018, p. 637). To strengthen the role that knowledge plays in production, Romer also assumes that k in $f(k;Sk)$ has increasing marginal product; hence, the production function is convex in k. The social planner maximizes social utility given by

$$\int_0^{\infty} e^{-\delta t}\ U\left[c(t)\right]\, dt,$$

with $\delta>0$ and subject to investment into technology given as $I(t)=\mathcal{F}\left[k(t)\right]-c(t)$ going into I/k in $g(I/k)$, where the production function $\mathcal{F}(k)$ is of course globally convex in k. The social planner takes both forms of knowledge as identical, so when deciding on the optimal level of k, she takes its external effect into account. As a typical example, Romer (1986a, p. 1027) assumes $f(k;K)=k^{\upsilon}K^{\gamma}=k^{\upsilon}(Sk)^{\gamma}=S^{\gamma}k^{\upsilon+\gamma}$ with $\upsilon+\gamma>1$, with a given population size S. By solving the social planner's problem summarized in the Hamiltonian,

$$H(k;\lambda)=\max_{c}U(c)+\lambda\left\{kg\left[\frac{\mathcal{F}(k)-c}{k}\right]\right\}. \tag{3.2.3}$$

Romer (1986a, pp. 1022-1023) shows that the social optimum is a trajectory in the $k\lambda$ plane along which k grows with no bound.

Due to the presence of externalities, however, the social optimum does not coincide with a competitive equilibrium. In contrast with the social planner taking the external effect into account, the individual firm regards the external effect as exogenously given, so it optimizes in terms of private knowledge and disregards the social effects of knowledge accumulation. Given $f(k;Sk)$, the social marginal product of knowledge accumulation is $f_1(k;Sk)+Sf_2(k;Sk)$, which can be taken as the competitive equilibrium price of additional intangible capital. If then the firm regards K as exogenously given, its return from technological change appears to be only $f_1(k;Sk)$, while $f_1(k;Sk)+Sf_2(k;Sk)>f_1(k;Sk)$. In other words, the true (i.e., social) price of additional knowledge measured in production units is higher than the direct benefits of investment to the firm, so the firm simply does not undertake the socially optimal investment. If S is high, the firm has an incentive to shirk as its contribution to the external effect is negligible, so even with no private investment, the firm enjoys almost the same positive effect from investment by the rest of the economy. In the second part of the paper, Romer analyzes the suboptimal equilibrium and considers what government policies can equate the private and social marginal products. As he argues, interventions can force a reallocation of goods away from production and towards research; hence, such policies are welfare-improving. Given that the optimizing firm and the social planner taken as the government look at different problems, taxes and subsidies must be chosen so that the after-tax private marginal product is equal to the social marginal product. In this case, the firm does not have an incentive to shirk as the return on its investment is the same as the price of additional knowledge, and the social optimum is thus achieved by the optimizing decisions of the private sector.

In the analysis of the competitive equilibrium, special attention must be paid to the consistency between individual optimization and its economy-wide effects. Any optimizing firm takes the path of $K(t)$ given and solves its own optimization problem. The aggregate level of capital is thus a state variable that affects the production possibilities of the firm, so the firm chooses its private investment with the external effect taken into consideration. However, equilibrium is possible only if $K(t)$ induces private investment decisions the social consequence of which is exactly $K(t)$. So, as also underlined by Lucas (1988, p. 20), in equilibrium $K(t)$ as the social-level outcome of private accumulation and $K(t)$ expected by the firms must be identical. Romer approaches the issue as a fixed-point problem of a function Γ taken as a mapping between K and Sk. A fixed point of this function means that K implies itself as Sk, so private investment in k is such that it generates that very $K(t)$ the expectation of which induces each firm of S to set its capital to k. Romer (1986a, p. 1017) presents a simple two-period model in which the social planner first finds the social optimum for consumption and k as a fixed point of Γ. If then we set K^* as the social level of capital and allow the agents to find their optimum, then they will choose $k^* = K^* / S$. The existence of competitive equilibrium can be demonstrated both in this simple model and its infinite-time version, even if such an equilibrium is not Pareto optimal without the compensating interventions of the government.

After his general analysis of the problem, Romer chooses specific forms for the utility function and the production functions of output and knowledge. These examples are supposed to give clear insights regarding how capital and consumption behave in time in a competitive equilibrium. In the simplest case, which we have already mentioned above, $f(k;K) = k^{\upsilon}K^{\gamma}$, where $0 < \upsilon \leq 1$ (private marginal product of knowledge is non-increasing) and $\upsilon + \gamma > 1$ (social marginal product is increasing). A simple choice for the production function of knowledge is

$$g(I/k) = \frac{\alpha \frac{I}{k}}{\alpha + \frac{I}{k}},$$

with some $\alpha > 0$, which ensures that $g(0) = 0$ (with no investment, there is no growth in knowledge), $g'(0) = 1$ (at a very low level of investment, a small increment creates a unit of capital), and by L'Hôpital's rule, $\lim_{z \to \infty} g(z) = \alpha$; hence, the required upper bound applies. Finally, $U(c) = \ln(c)$. At this point, to learn more about how capital and consumption behave asymptotically, Romer applies the theory of asymptotic exponential introduced by Brock and Gale (1969). In this spirit, he finds functions of which he can show that it is nowhere crossed by the trajectory of the competitive equilibrium in the $k\lambda$ plane (i.e., the plane of the state and costate). The first-order condition regarding c implies that

$$\frac{1}{c} = \lambda g'\left(\frac{f(k;Sk) - c}{k}\right).$$

Note that Romer (1986a, p. 1024 and 1028) here applies the same general procedure as, for instance, Lucas (1988, p. 21) uses when solving for the competitive equilibrium. *After* solving the individual optimization problem with $K(t)$ as an exogenously given state variable, we simple set $K(t) = Sk(t)$. The agents can optimally respond to any $K(t)$, but there is only one path for $K(t)$ that implies itself through individual optimization – finding it means we find the trajectory $K(t)$ that induces agents to choose paths for $k(t)$ that bring about $K(t)$ at the aggregate level. By this procedure, we get a result other than when the social planner *in advance* takes into account the external effect of knowledge as $K(t) \equiv Sk(t)$. By so doing, Romer like Lucas applies the same approach to ensure the consistency between individual optimization and its economy-wide effects.

In addition, in the $\dot{k} = 0$ nullcline $f(k;Sk) = c$, hence $g'(0) = 1$ applies, and $c = f(k;Sk) = \lambda^{-1}$, from which it follows that the equation of the $\dot{k} = 0$ nullcline is $\lambda = S^{-\gamma}k^{-(\upsilon+\gamma)}$. Thus, the nullcline behaves asymptotically as $\lambda = k^{-(\upsilon+\gamma)}$, which is a strictly decreasing and strictly convex curve asymptotically approaching zero. This line separates the plane into two regions. In the region above the nullcline, we have $\dot{k} > 0$, while there is no relevant case under it as there is no mechanism for capital depreciation; hence, $\dot{k} < 0$ is ruled out. The competitive equilibrium thus stays above the $\dot{k} = 0$ nullcline. On the other hand, the $\dot{\lambda} = 0$ locus also tends toward zero but stays above $\dot{k} = 0$ over the whole domain. Any non-optimal trajectory starting between the lines either crosses $\dot{k} = 0$ from above or $\dot{\lambda} = 0$ from below, so the trajectory of the competitive equilibrium lies in the constantly

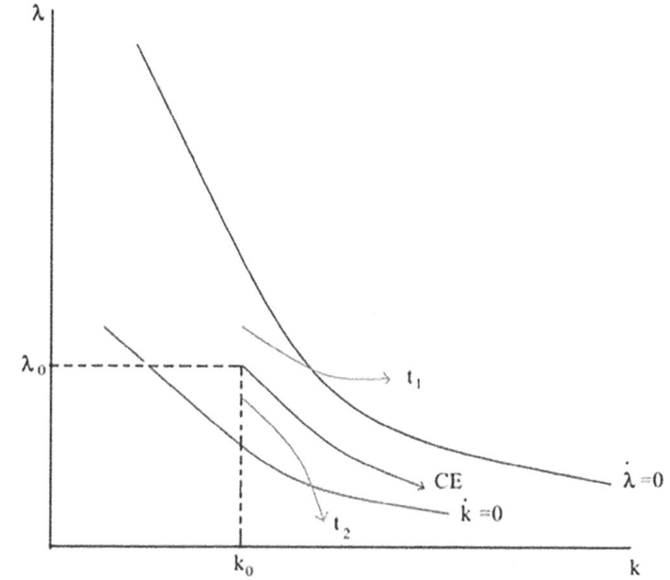

Fig. 2. Dynamics of the Competitive Equilibrium in Romer (1986a).

narrowing area between the loci $\dot{k}=0$ and $\dot{\lambda}=0$. Along this trajectory $k\to\infty, \lambda\to 0$, and as $c=\lambda^{-1}$, $c\to\infty$. (see Fig. 2).

With linear utility $U(c)=c$, we have similar results with both $k\to\infty$ and $c\to\infty$, while Romer's mathematics, partly because of the extensive use of Brock and Gale's results, becomes more exciting. First, Brock and Gale (1969, p. 234) claim that in growth theory applications, where states like capital may grow toward infinity, we may want to know as closely as possible how our functions behave at the far end. For this purpose, they introduce the exponential of a function $f(x)$ defined as

$$\log_x|f(x)|=e_f(x),$$

the limit of which at infinity is the *asymptotic exponential* given as

$$\lim_{x\to\infty}\log_x|f(x)|=e_f.$$

This means that when $x\to\infty$, the function $f(x)$ behaves like x^{e_f}. Then as a useful result, they show that e_f can be reduced to the asymptotic elasticity E_f of the function. To see this, note that

$$e_f=\lim_{x\to\infty}e_f(x)=\lim_{x\to\infty}\frac{\ln f(x)}{\ln x}=\lim_{x\to\infty}\frac{\frac{1}{f(x)}f'(x)}{\frac{1}{x}}=\lim_{x\to\infty}\frac{x}{f(x)}$$

$$f'(x)=\lim_{x\to\infty}E_f(x)=E_f,$$

where the second equality comes from the basic logarithmic identities, the third comes from the application of L'Hôpital's rule, and in the fifth, we realize that what we have is the elasticity of $f(x)$ the limit of which is asymptotic elasticity E_f. This means that the asymptotic exponential of any function $f(x)$ is identical with its asymptotic elasticity. This is the result that Romer (1986a, p. 1030) applies when claiming that the equation of the $\dot{\lambda}=0$ nullcline is $\lambda = Bk^{\upsilon+\gamma-1}$ for an appropriate $B>0$ constant and that the trajectory of the competitive equilibrium is trapped by this line and another graph given as $\lambda = Ak^{\upsilon+\gamma-1}$ with $A>B$. Then, the trajectory of the competitive equilibrium is $\lambda = Ck^{\upsilon+\gamma-1}$ for $A>C>B$ so that the path does not cross either of the trapping lines. Then, by the results of Brock and Gale regarding $e_f = E_f$, we can say that when $k \to \infty$ along the equilibrium path λ behaves like $k^{\upsilon+\gamma-1}$. This is a useful result as from the Hamiltonian of the problem,

$$\hat{H}(k;\lambda;K;c) = c + \lambda k g\left(\frac{f(k;K)-c}{k}\right),$$

we know that the first-order condition for c implies that $c = f - \alpha k\left(\lambda^{0.5}-1\right)$. Then, we can characterize the asymptotic behavior of c by characterizing the asymptotic behavior of the three separate functions in its equation. As for the first part, $f = S^{\gamma}k^{\upsilon+\gamma}$, hence $e_f = E_f = \upsilon+\gamma$, and f behaves asymptotically like $k^{\upsilon+\gamma}$. As for the second part, the asymptotic exponent of k is $e_f = E_f = 1$, so the asymptotic behavior of αk is described by αk. And as for the third component, $\lambda^{0.5}-1$, by combining it with the asymptotic behavior of λ, we get $k^{0.5(\upsilon+\gamma-1)}-1$. At this point, Brock and Gale's (1969, p. 234) rule that $e_{f+g} = \max\left(e_f;e_g\right)$ applies, and as the elasticity of (-1) with respect to k is zero, we have $e_f = E_f = 0.5(\upsilon+\gamma-1)$, which is strictly positive, so this part behaves like $k^{0.5(\upsilon+\gamma-1)}$ when $k \to \infty$. Combining these results, we have that the asymptotic behavior of c is described by $k^{\upsilon+\gamma} - \alpha k^{1+0.5(\upsilon+\gamma-1)}$, from which it follows that c goes to infinity as $\upsilon+\gamma > 1+0.5(\upsilon+\gamma-1)$ as $\upsilon+\gamma>1$ by the convexity assumption.

Most importantly, in this example, investment also goes to infinity; hence, $g(I/k) \to \alpha$, so the rate of growth of knowledge is increasing until the upper bound α is reached. It means that the growth is bounded from above, so poor countries cannot converge to rich countries starting from a better position with higher initial value k_0.

Having discussed Romer (1986)'s paper in detail, we need to note that Romer (2015) himself considered this approach to be flawed. The flaw stems from the twin assumptions on the way knowledge affects production. On one hand, Romer assumes that firms own the knowledge they create, which presumably means that the private returns generated from this accumulation process is returned to the households as profits. Since it is household savings that finance the creation of new knowledge, these households will presumably take the returns into account in their consumption-saving decisions.

At the same time, though, the aggregate accumulation of knowledge is treated as a positive externality. The reason for this is straightforward: if the returns generated by the aggregate effect were internalized, then Euler's theorem on homogeneous functions would imply that at any competitive equilibrium, the factor payments for inputs would exceed total output. To retain the competitive equilibrium solution concept, then, Romer is forced to assume that the aggregate effect is freely available. But this is not conceptually different from treating technical progress in the Solow model as a simple, exogenous consequence of capital accumulation. Somehow, improvements in technology just happen as a result of using technology. This, of course, is Arrow's famous learning-by-doing approach, which we discuss next. But, to conclude our discussion of Romer's initial approach to endogenous growth, we note that if households recognized the value of the external effects of knowledge creation and demanded a share of the value from such creation, the competitive equilibrium solution concept would not be viable. One can make it viable by changing the interpretation of investment in knowledge creation from an activity that households fund directly to one in which they pay taxes to a "national science foundation" that then funds the research that generates the external effects. This was the approach taken by Shell (1973). The alternative to this is to abandon the competitive paradigm and work directly with models of imperfect competition. Shell (1973) also examined a version of the increasing returns model with a monopoly firm whose profits funded research. The innovation in Romer (1990a, 1990b) was to introduce intangible ideas as inputs in a monopolistically competition framework in which the Euler theorem problem doesn't arise. We will discuss this in more detail in a later chapter.

ARROW'S MODEL OF GROWTH WITH TECHNOLOGICAL CHANGE FROM LEARNING BY DOING

As Lucas (1988, p. 17) argues, Arrow's (1962) learning by doing paper is as an immediate predecessor of his idea of describing technical progress with human capital accumulation. As we point out below, however, behind the basic idea of boiling technological change down to learning and the growing of knowledge, there are differences of fundamental importance.

Arrow (1962) understands knowledge as resulting from a special form of experience when people respond to some stimuli steadily evolving. In contrast with the perfection of repetitive tasks that can hardly be regarded as *development* or *change*, Arrow's conception is one of learning which generates steadily increasing performance and which can be identified with the growth of knowledge. Arrow chooses cumulative gross investment or, in other words, cumulative production of capital goods, $G(t)$, as a proxy variable for experience. As a by-product of investment, then, there is a change in knowledge that is incorporated in newly produced capital goods at any moment of time. As we can numerically describe the path of $G(t)$, Arrow understands it as a serial number, so a machine produced at time t, when cumulative gross investment was $G(t)$, has the serial number $G(t)$. Serial numbers thus describe the technological level of capital goods. Then, we have the following system of four variables:

- $\lambda(G)$: amount of labor used in production with a capital good having the serial number *G*;
- $\gamma(G)$: output capacity of a capital good having the serial number *G*;
- x: total output;
- L: labor employed.

Note that $\lambda(G)$ and $\gamma(G)$are functions of the technological level embedded in a piece of equipment. Assuming that $\lambda(G)$is non-increasing in *G*, and $\gamma(G)$ is non-decreasing in *G*, Arrow draws a sharp picture of his idea of technological progress. As technology improves, society has more developed capital goods, and a more modern unit *never needs more labor* and *never produces less* than a piece of equipment embodying a previous technological level. Specifically, Arrow assumes $\lambda(G)=bG^{-n}$ with some $n>0$ and $\gamma(G)=a$ with $a>0$. Arrow also assumes that capital goods in the economy have a fixed lifetime $\bar{T}$ at which they must be withdrawn from production in the increasing order of their serial numbers. At any moment of time, $G'(t)$ is the serial number that ceases to take part in the production process. This typically happens when a machine reaches the end of its lifetime. If this was the only source of equipment withdrawal, then $G'(t)=G(t-\bar{T})$. We follow Arrow's notation using $G'(t)$ to denote the serial numbers of machines withdrawn from service, so the reader should note that this is not a derivative. Of course, machines might also be put out of production *before* their time, so it follows that $G'(t)\geq G(t-\bar{T})$. By using the fact that the serial numbers of equipment currently in use ranges from *G* to *G'*, output and employment are

$$x=\int_{G'}^{G}\gamma(G)dG=\Gamma(G)-\Gamma(G'), \tag{3.3.1}$$

$$L=\int_{G'}^{G}\lambda(G)dG=\Lambda(G)-\Lambda(G'). \tag{3.3.2}$$

Since population follows an exogenous path and $G(t)$ is given at any moment of time, under the equilibrium condition, equation (3.3.2) can be solved for $G'(t)$; hence, (3.3.1) gives $x(t)$ for any t. With $\lambda(G)=bG^{-n}$ and $\gamma(G)=a$ with $0<n<1$, we have $\Lambda(G)=cG^{1-n}$ with $c=b/(1-n)$, and $\Gamma(G)=aG$. Then, solving (3.3.2) for *G'* yields

$$G'=\Lambda^{-1}\left[\Lambda(G)-L\right], \tag{3.3.3}$$

and finally, (3.3.1) becomes

$$x=\Gamma(G)-\Gamma\left\{\Lambda^{-1}\left[\Lambda(G)-L\right]\right\}\equiv aG\left[1-\left(1-\frac{L}{cG^{1-n}}\right)^{\frac{1}{1-n}}\right], \tag{3.3.4}$$

with $n \neq 1$, which is a production function with increasing returns to scale in G and L. As compared to Romer's (1986a, pp. 1015-1021) and Lucas (1988, p. 18) production functions, (3.3.4) is strictly concave (for fixed L) as clearly shown by the sign of its second derivative in G:

$$\frac{\partial^2 x(G)}{\partial G^2} = -\frac{2G^{n-2} La}{c\left(1-\frac{G^{n-1} L}{c}\right)^{\frac{1}{n-1}+1}} - \frac{G^{n-2} La(n-2)}{c\left(1-\frac{G^{n-1} L}{c}\right)^{\frac{1}{n-1}+1}} - \frac{G^{2n-3} L^2 a\left(\frac{1}{n-1}+1\right)(n-1)}{c^2\left(1-\frac{G^{n-1} L}{c}\right)^{\frac{1}{n-1}+2}}.$$

First, denominators are positive, as due to (3.3.2) $cG^{1-n} > L$, from which it follows that

$$1 > \frac{G^{n-1}L}{c} > 0.$$

Note that the numerators of the first two terms give $G^{n-2} L\, an > 0$. After expanding the third term, we have $G^{2n-3} L^2 an > 0$, so the second derivative of $x(G)$ is strictly negative; hence, it is strictly concave. When $n = 1$, we have $x(G)$ as a linear function of G.

There is a second aspect in which Lucas (1988, p. 20) regards Arrow's paper as a predecessor. Following Muth's (1961) definition, Arrow describes a rational expectation equilibrium as a state where agents have perfect foresight of the deterministic future values of the model's endogenous variables. As Arrow argues, firms deciding upon investment consider the future profitability of the planned capital good. Given the parameters of the system and especially the fact that after completion a machine shows no technical improvement and operates at a given output rate and labor requirement, profitability depends on the expected path of wages that the firms regard as exogenously given. Arrow shows that output x and cumulated gross investment G grow and, consequently, technological progress evolves at a unique and common constant rate. As his main result at this point, Arrow emphasizes that adjusting to the exogenous paths of wage and labor force dynamics firms can find an optimal rate of capital accumulation that implies an optimal rate of technological change.

As with Romer (1986a, 1986b, 1986c)'s model, Arrow needs to assume that the learning effects in his model are uncompensated, that is, the firm is not engaging in costly R&D to improve the operation of its technology. Workers in Arrow's model simply (and freely) find ways to make the machines they work with better over time.

LUCAS (1988) MODEL OF GROWTH WITH HUMAN CAPITAL ACCUMULATION FROM TIME INVESTMENT

Lucas' main drive that led him to his 1988 endogenous growth theory paper was his dissatisfaction with the theoretical foundations and the empirical performance of the basic neoclassical growth model. When looking at the data, Lucas realized that there is a large diversity in the levels and growth rates of per-capita income across countries, while there was no meaningful correlation between growth rates and levels – both rich and poor countries can grow at both high and low rates. Nothing in the neoclassical growth model explains these differences; indeed, the model suggests that given access to the same technology, countries' growth performance should converge to the same steady state. In view of this, Lucas suggested a model that can help economists understand what factors are *necessary* for growth and what factors are *possibilities* that lead to higher growth rates and levels of per-capita income only if a country, its government, population, and other agents take actions to realize this potential.

As a first step, he showed the limited capabilities of the basic neoclassical growth model including the case of technological change. He assumed technological progress to be exogenous. There is one commodity in the economy the production of which is shared between consumption and net investment $\dot{K}(t)$ according to a first-order homogenous Cobb–Douglas production function with $0<\beta<1$. With this assumption, the economy-wide resource constraint is given by

$$c(t)N(t)+\dot{K}(t)=A(t)K(t)^{\beta}N(t)^{1-\beta}, \tag{3.4.1}$$

where $c(t)$ is per-capita consumption, $N(t)$ is labor force measured in manhours and growing at rate λ, and $A(t)$ is the exogenously given technology parameter growing at rate μ. Allocation is perfectly competitive and there are no market distortions, so we can let the social planner solve the problem of maximizing lifetime utility from consumption expressed as

$$\int_0^{\infty} e^{-\rho t}\frac{1}{1-\sigma}\left[c(t)^{1-\sigma}-1\right]N(t)dt, \tag{3.4.2}$$

where $\rho>0$ is the discount rate and $\sigma>0$ is the risk-aversion parameter. This is a strictly concave utility function, as compared to the linear utility Uzawa (1965) used where he simply identified utility from consumption with the level of consumption. Note that $K(t)$ is the endogenous state, $N(t)$ and $A(t)$ are exogenous states, so $c(t)$ is the only control variable that completely determines $\dot{K}(t)$, given the states, through (3.4.1). On this basis, the current value Hamiltonian of the social planner is

$$H(K;\theta;c;t)=\frac{N}{1-\sigma}\left(c^{1-\sigma}-1\right)+\theta\left(AK^{\beta}N^{1-\beta}-Nc\right), \tag{3.4.3}$$

where θ is the costate variable for K. The necessary and sufficient conditions are standard and yield the following system of equations:

$$c(t)^{-\sigma}=\theta(t), \tag{3.4.4}$$

$$\dot{\theta}(t)=\theta(t)\left[\rho-\beta A(t)N(t)^{1-\beta}K(t)^{\beta-1}\right], \tag{3.4.5}$$

$$\dot{K}(t)=A(t)K(t)^{\beta}N(t)^{1-\beta}-c(t)N(t), \tag{3.4.6}$$

$$\lim_{t\to\infty} e^{-\rho t}\theta(t)K(t)=0. \tag{3.4.7}$$

Equation (3.4.4) is the requirement that the marginal utility of the single commodity must be equal whether it is used in consumption or capital accumulation. The same equation links the dynamics of $c(t)$ to the dynamics of $\theta(t)$, so the path of $c(t)$ is optimal only if $\theta(t)$ follows (3.4.5). The dynamics of $K(t)$ simply follows its law of motion, and (3.4.7) is the usual transversality condition. By substituting (4) into (6), we have a system of two interrelated differential equations:

$$\dot{\theta}(t)=\theta(t)\left[\rho-\beta A(t)N(t)^{1-\beta}K(t)^{\beta-1}\right], \tag{3.4.8}$$

$$\dot{K}(t)=A(t)K(t)^{\beta}N(t)^{1-\beta}-N(t)\theta(t)^{-\frac{1}{\sigma}}. \tag{3.4.9}$$

By definition, along the balanced growth path, $K(t)$, $\theta(t)$, and $c(t)$ grow at constants rates. Let $\dot{c}(t)/c(t)=\kappa$ be the constant growth rate for consumption. By using (3.4.4), through the time derivative of $c(t)=\theta(t)^{-\frac{1}{\sigma}}$, we can easily establish that $\dot{\theta}(t)/\theta(t)=-\sigma\kappa$. Using this latter result in (3.4.8) implies that

$$\beta A(t)N(t)^{1-\beta}K(t)^{\beta-1}=\rho+\sigma\kappa, \tag{3.4.10}$$

so along the balanced growth path, given the exogenous processes of $A(t)$ and $N(t)$, the path of $K(t)$ must be such that the marginal product of capital is constant. By dividing (3.4.6) with $K(t)$, we have $\frac{\dot{K}(t)}{K(t)}=\frac{A(t)K(t)^{\beta}N(t)^{1-\beta}}{K(t)}-\frac{c(t)N(t)}{K(t)}$, which must also be constant along the balanced growth path. Given (3.4.10), the first term on the right is also constant, so the second term must also be constant. Given the growth rates of $c(t)$ and $N(t)$, capital stock $K(t)$ must grow at rate $\kappa+\lambda$. From this, the per-capita capital stock grows at rate $\dot{k}(t)/k(t)=\kappa$.

Given these growth rates, the final step to take is to describe κ, on which all other growth rates are based, as the function of the parameters of the system. According to (3.4.10), by realizing that $A(t)=A_0e^{\mu t}$, $N(t)=N_0e^{\lambda t}$, and $K(t)=K_0e^{(\kappa+\lambda)t}$, the marginal product remains constant all along the balanced growth path only if the time derivative of the corresponding process,

$$\beta A_0N_0^{1-\beta}K_0^{\beta-1}\,e^{\left[\mu+(1-\beta)\lambda-(1-\beta)(\kappa+\lambda)\right]t}=\rho+\sigma\kappa,$$

is zero, that is, $\mu+(1-\beta)\lambda-(1-\beta)(\kappa+\lambda)=0$. From this, it follows that

$$\kappa=\frac{\mu}{1-\beta}. \tag{3.4.11}$$

Lucas shows that the model also implies a constant savings rate s and concludes that s has no effect on the rate of growth. In the model, all growth rates are expressed in terms of κ, while κ hinges upon the growth rate of technical progress and β. From these peculiarities, Lucas infers that the neoclassical growth model places too much emphasis on the role of technological progress while neglecting the contributions of other factors – changes in any of the other parameters of the system do not affect the balanced growth rate of an economy. To make his point, Lucas underlines that the theory assumes technology to be diffused across countries and the rate of technological change to be uniform everywhere, so on the basis of (3.4.1), the *actual* growth rates of per-capita income y and per-capita capital k should follow the equation

$$\frac{\dot{y}}{y}-\beta\frac{\dot{k}}{k}=\frac{\dot{A}}{A}, \tag{3.4.12}$$

while the differences by (3.4.12) for actual economies do not imply a constant ratio $\dot{A}(t)/A(t)$ in the data. Hence, the growth patterns of actual economies cannot be driven by uniform technological progress – if technology is uniform for all economies, and if technology is the core factor underlying economic growth, then where do the differences of growth patterns of actual economies come from? To answer this question, Lucas suggests that a more meaningful and practically useful theory of economic growth must be able to explain the differences in growth rates in terms of the differences in parameter values for those economies. It may be true that technological progress is the main force behind economic growth, but behind the diversity of the growth patterns across countries, there must exist a diversity of patterns of technological progress. Then, in contrast with the basic model, technological change can no longer be assumed to follow a uniform and exogenous growth process. Instead, by realizing that knowledge is the driver of technological progress, and that knowledge is always the knowledge of someone, Lucas regards knowledge as a form of human capital and attempts to explain technological progress in terms of individual decisions. He thus creates a channel through which parameter differences for countries might imply different patterns of technological change.

In this version of his model, Lucas adopts a version of the Uzawa (1965) production function in which workers must allocate their time between production activities and the accumulation of skills, that is, human capital. The specific form of this production function is similar to the first-order homogenous Cobb–Douglas production function of the previous model, but now specified as

$$AK(t)^{\beta}\left[u(t)N(t)h(t)\right]^{1-\beta}h_a(t)^{\gamma}, \tag{3.4.13}$$

in which $A>0$ is a constant term, $u(t)$ is time allocated to production, $h(t)$ is the skill level or technological knowledge boosting the effectiveness of labor force, and $h_a(t)$ is the average level of knowledge exerting an *external* effect on production governed by the parameter $\gamma \geq 0$. When $\gamma = 0$, we have the same production function Uzawa (1965) postulated. Note that (3.4.13) is also equivalent to Romer's (1986a, p. 1015) production function which was first-order homogenous in the variables other than the variable capturing the external effect of knowledge. As in Uzawa or Romer's models, this assumption means that with the human capital level fixed, production exhibits constant returns to scale. When human capital is variable, however, production exhibits increasing returns.

The term $u(t)N(t)h(t)$ is skill-weighted manhours that expresses how knowledge $h(t)$, taken as the stock of human capital, affects productivity *internally*. As agents are assumed to be identical, $h(t)$ is uniform for the whole population and $h(t)=h_a(t)$. Individual decisions have negligible impact on $h_a(t)$, so optimizing agents do not take this effect into account when deciding on $u(t)$ and $1-u(t)$, the latter being the time allocated to learning to increase future productivity. Given the states $K(t)$, $N(t)$, and $h(t)$, the dynamics of $K(t)$ then depends on current consumption $c(t)$ and time allocation $u(t)$ as controls, and the economy-wide resource allocation constraint becomes

$$c(t)N(t)+\dot{K}(t)=AK(t)^{\beta}\left[u(t)N(t)h(t)\right]^{1-\beta}h_a(t)^{\gamma}. \tag{3.4.14}$$

A second equation describes the dynamics of human capital as

$$\frac{\dot{h}(t)}{h(t)}=\delta\left[1-u(t)\right], \tag{3.4.15}$$

where $\delta>0$ is a constant parameter expressing the maximum rate of human capital accumulation when $u(t)=0$ and all available time is allocated to learning. The technology responsible for human capital accumulation is thus linear with a constant marginal product of time $\left[1-u(t)\right]$ devoted to learning. This is compatible with the weakly increasing and weakly concave production function ϕ of Uzawa (1965) but differs from the production function Romer assumed for knowledge accumulation. Obviously, at any given level of $h(t)$ doubling the time $\left[1-u(t)\right]$ doubles $\dot{h}(t)$, while Romer assumed diminishing returns. However, there is an upper bound on the growth rate of human capital in both models, so knowledge cannot grow too fast.[6] Lucas also assumed that knowledge increases uninterruptedly, so the transition from one generation to the next causes no loss in the overall level of human capital. This setting is compatible with the implicit assumption that a certain portion of human capital is carried over between generations, without which the social level of knowledge $h(t)$ could increase only at the rate of population growth. So, the dynamics embedded in (3.4.15) can be regarded as describing "net" or actual human capital accumulation where the intergenerational setback is incorporated in $\delta>0$. Note that as a first attempt, Lucas suggested the function

$$\dot{h}(t)=h(t)^{\xi}G\left[1-u(t)\right], \tag{3.4.16}$$

[6]As both Romer (1986a) and Lucas (1988) specify their functions of production of knowledge in different forms, it may be beneficial to have a closer look at both. For Romer, $\dot{k}=G(I;k)$, where G shows constant returns to scale in the two variables, while at any given k, the growth effect of increasing I is diminishing. Consequently, the marginal product of I/k is decreasing in the corresponding function $\dot{k}/k=g(I/k)$. For Lucas, by contrast, at any given h in $\dot{h}=h\delta(1-u)$, the effect of $(1-u)$ is linear, mapping an increase in learning time into a proportional increase in h. When written as $\dot{h}/h=\delta(1-u)$, the marginal product of $(1-u)$ is the constant δ.

instead of (3.4.15) with $0 < \xi < 1$ and $G(\cdot)$ as an increasing function such that $G(0) = 0$. In this formulation, human capital has diminishing marginal product that seems to be a good explanation to why knowledge is accumulated at lower rates later in life. However, as Lucas noted, then

$$\frac{\dot{h}(t)}{h(t)} = h(t)^{\xi-1} \; G\left[1 - u(t)\right] \leq h(t)^{\xi-1} \; G(1),$$

so eventually, $\dot{h}(t) / h(t) \to 0$ as $h(t)$ increases. This implies that human capital accumulation eventually comes to an end under (3.4.16), so with this production function, technological progress could not serve as an engine of sustained economic growth. Lucas rejects the assumption of diminishing marginal returns in human capital accumulation. Although the observation that human capital accumulation continuously slows down along an individual life cycle seems to corroborate diminishing marginal returns, this pattern is due to the fact that returns to human capital falls with time. It is thus not diminishing marginal returns of knowledge but the shortening of time available for the profitable use of human capital that causes the rate of human capital accumulation to decrease (Lucas, 1988, p. 19).

The external effect in (3.4.13) drives a wedge between optimal and competitive allocations. The former is the solution provided by the social planner, which, however, does not coincide with the competitive equilibrium. Lucas thus solves the problem for both cases to compare the results. Along the optimal plan, the social planner chooses optimal paths for $K(t)$, $h(t)$, $h_a(t)$ as endogenous states, and for $c(t)$ and $u(t)$ as controls, subject to the constrains in (3.4.14) and (3.4.15) to maximize (3.4.2) so that $h_a(t) = h(t)$. This problem is easy to study with the previous Hamiltonian approach as the social planner takes h_a as a variable to manipulate. Along the equilibrium path, by contrast, the population takes $h_a(t)$ as exogenously given and agents, solving their own individual optimization problems of maximizing (3.4.2) by responding and adjusting to this process, choose optimal paths for $K(t)$, $h(t)$, $c(t)$, and $u(t)$ constrained by (3.4.14) and (3.4.15). As a result of individual optimization, the path of average human capital accumulation will satisfy $h_a(t) = h(t)$ in equilibrium. Note that this equilibrium condition is imposed only after the individual problem is solved with respect to the exogenous process of $h_a(t)$. Here, Lucas applies the same *rational expectations equilibrium* that Stokey and Lucas (1989, pp. 479-480) outlined and Ljungqvist and Sargent (2018, p. 231) promoted in which an aggregate-level path implies itself through individual optimization – what agents do in response to the exogenous path becomes the path they adjust to.

The current-value Hamiltonian for the social planner's optimization problem is

$$H(K;h;\theta_1;\theta_2;c;u;t) = \frac{N}{1-\sigma}\left(c^{1-\sigma} - 1\right) + \theta_1\left[AK^{\beta}(uNh)^{1-\beta} h_a^{\gamma} - Nc\right] + \theta_2\left[\delta h(1-u)\right], \tag{3.4.17}$$

where θ_1 and θ_2 are the costate variables of K and h, respectively. Again, describing the necessary and sufficient conditions is standard and yields the following system of equations:

$$c(t)^{-\sigma} = \theta_1(t), \tag{3.4.18}$$

$$\theta_1(t)(1-\beta)AK(t)^{\beta}\left[u(t)N(t)h(t)\right]^{-\beta} N(t)h(t)^{1+\gamma} = \theta_2(t)\delta\, h(t), \tag{3.4.19}$$

$$\dot{\theta}_1(t) = \theta_1(t)\left\{\rho - \beta AK(t)^{\beta-1}\left[u(t)N(t)h(t)\right]^{1-\beta} h(t)^{\gamma}\right\}, \tag{3.4.20}$$

$$\dot{\theta}_2(t) = \rho\theta_2(t) - \theta_1(t)(1-\beta+\gamma)AK(t)^{\beta}\left[u(t)N(t)\right]^{1-\beta} h(t)^{\gamma-\beta} - \theta_2(t)\delta\left[1-u(t)\right], \tag{3.4.21}$$

$$\dot{K}(t) = AK(t)^{\beta}\left[u(t)N(t)h(t)\right]^{1-\beta} h_a(t)^{\gamma} - c(t)N(t), \tag{3.4.22}$$

$$\dot{h}(t) = h(t)\delta\left[1-u(t)\right], \tag{3.4.23}$$

$$\lim_{t\to\infty} e^{-\rho t}\theta_1(t)K(t) = 0 \text{ and } \lim_{t\to\infty} e^{-\rho t}\theta_2(t)h(t) = 0. \tag{3.4.24}$$

According to (3.4.18) and (3.4.19), optimal values of K and u must be equal in their two alternative uses. Note that the social planner chooses $h(t)$ by taking its external effect into account. There is thus no distinction between $h(t)$ and $h_a(t)$, and we derive (3.4.21) accordingly. By the same token, in (3.4.19), the internal and external effects are drawn together. Note that Lucas (1988, p. 26) provided estimates of $1-\beta = 0.75$ and $\gamma = 0.417$, so the social planner, just like in Romer (1986a, p. 1020), faces a production function which is strictly convex in human capital implying increasing returns to scale. This is unlike the production function of Arrow (1962), where convexity does not accompany increasing returns to scale. Equations (3.4.22) and (3.4.23) are the laws of motions for the endogenous states, while (3.4.24) gives the two transversality conditions.

Under competitive equilibrium, households solve the same maximization problem, so we still have (3.4.18), (3.4.19), and (3.4.20). However, unlike the social planner problem, the individual household when choosing the optimal path for $h(t)$ does not take its external effect into account, so in the Hamiltonian, we distinguish $h(t)$ and $h_a(t)$. In place of (3.4.21), we now have

$$\dot{\theta}_2(t) = \rho\theta_2(t) - \theta_1(t)(1-\beta)AK(t)^{\beta}\left[u(t)N(t)\right]^{1-\beta} h(t)^{-\beta} h_a(t)^{\gamma} - \theta_2(t)\delta\left[1-u(t)\right], \tag{3.4.25}$$

to which we impose the equilibrium condition $h_a(t)=h(t)$ only at this stage, that is, once the optimum problem of the individual market agent is solved. With the equilibrium condition, (3.4.25) becomes

$$\dot{\theta}_2(t)=\rho\theta_2(t)-\theta_1(t)(1-\beta)AK(t)^{\beta}\left[u(t)N(t)\right]^{1-\beta}h(t)^{\gamma-\beta}-\theta_2(t)\delta\left[1-u(t)\right] \tag{3.4.26}$$

With no external effect when $\gamma=0$, equations (3.4.21) and (3.4.26) are equivalent.

To solve these separate cases, Lucas assumes that $c(t)$, $K(t)$, and $h(t)$ grow, while costates θ_1 and θ_2 decline at some constant rates. As far as the latter is concerned, the optimal choice for $u(t)$ is some constant $\bar{u}$ by (3.4.23). Their paths of course abide by the conditions in (3.4.18)–(3.4.24) and (3.4.26).

Applying the previous procedure, it is easy to establish that $\dot{K}(t)/K(t)=\kappa+\lambda$. By assuming that $\dot{h}(t)/h(t)=v$ and using the condition of the constant marginal product of capital, we can express the connection between these two key growth rates as

$$\kappa=\frac{1-\beta+\gamma}{1-\beta}v, \tag{3.4.27}$$

which applies in both the social planner case and the competitive equilibrium setting.[7] At the end of a very technical part where Lucas utilizes the connections between the dynamics of θ_1 and θ_2, he gets the final results for the growth rates of human capital as

$$v^*=\sigma^{-1}\left[\delta-\frac{1-\beta}{1+\gamma-\beta}(\rho-\lambda)\right] \text{ and } v=\frac{(1-\beta)(\delta+\lambda-\rho)}{\sigma(1-\beta+\gamma)-\gamma}, \tag{3.4.28}$$

where v^* is the *optimum* rate and v is the *equilibrium* rate of human capital accumulation – due to the external effect the competitive allocation cannot thus be optimal. Both rates are positively related to the parameter of human capital accumulation δ, and negatively to ρ. This latter result is interesting in comparison to the basic model, where s being also affected by ρ had no effects on the growth rates. This is one of the aspects of the variants of the basic neoclassical growth model, including Arrow's (1962) endogenous growth paper, that Lucas heavily criticized: savings behavior has no effects on the growth rates, only on the level of variables like income or capital stock. Here by (3.4.28), however, savings also affect growth rates. Lucas also shows that $v^*>v$ and the difference is positively dependent upon γ, so with the external effect taken into account, an economy has higher human capital stocks when growing along the balanced path. As an additional consequence, a stronger external effect causes wages (interpreted as the marginal product of the effective labor unit) to grow at a higher rate.

[7]Note that assuming a constant rate of growth of human capital is in line with Romer's (1986a, p. 1031) result that intangible capital asymptotically grows at a constant rate.

We note that while Lucas' results are quite appealing and have been quite influential (getting more than 45,000 Google Scholar cites), the basic model suffers from the same flaw as Romer (1986a, 1986b, 1986c)'s model. As Romer has noted in the "Mathiness" paper (Romer, 2015), the obvious question one must ask about this model is why (and how) the average level of human capital leads to increasing returns. As a matter of simple correlation, it is obvious from the data that more educated economies grow faster, and we can interpret Lucas' specification of the external effect as a reduced form way to capture this correlation. But if the generation and application of new knowledge to economic activities is costly and subject to economic decision processes above and beyond the allocation of time, then the Euler theorem critique we outlined in discussing Romer (1986b) is applicable here. Even though knowledge is valuable, no one owns it, so it goes uncompensated. If this value is somehow internalized in the model, then the Euler theorem critique implies that competitive compensation will not be viable. It is a matter of speculation as to why Lucas never acknowledged this issue despite his student Paul Romer's subsequent breakthrough work addressing the problem, and despite a contentious American Economic Association panel discussion at the 2015 Winter Meetings in Boston (which culminated in Romer's "Mathiness" paper). Romer himself has suggested that political views on the role of government came into play, while Lucas' University of Chicago affiliation suggests a long-held affinity for competitive equilibrium. Lucas himself never answered the question, and with his passing, speculation is all that remains for us.

In private communication (email of 08-05-2025), Romer has told us that a primary impetus for the "Mathiness" paper was Lucas and Moll (2014). This paper, published in the University of Chicago's flagship *Journal of Political Economy*, was Lucas' last attempt to convince the economics profession that the drivers of growth, even taking account of the costs of research and development, were fundamentally external to the operations of the rest of the economy, which could, therefore, be taken to be perfectly competitive.

Lucas and Moll (2014) posit a search process for the accumulation of knowledge based on Newton's parable of "standing on the shoulders of giants." In Lucas–Moll, a continuum of agents are endowed with different degrees of knowledge and engage in costly bilateral search for other agents who may have better knowledge that they can appropriate. At any point in time, the aggregate distribution of knowledge among the agents determines the productivity of the economy's output sector. The equilibrium dynamics of the model entail tracking how the distribution of knowledge changes over time since this determines how output changes.

The math in Lucas–Moll is not easy, so we don't pursue it in detail here. The evolution of the knowledge distribution depends on the average state of the economy at the beginning of any period and the way in which pairwise random meetings generate knowledge improvements. The analytic structure Lucas–Moll use is that of a mean field game. These games have been studied extensively and applied productively in areas as diverse as epidemiology with behavioral feedback, physical system phase transition mechanics, and intrafirm corruption behavior. In

Lucas–Moll, the key result is that under the assumption that the knowledge distribution has its support on $[0,\infty]$, the knowledge distribution density function evolves as a "traveling wave," with the average level of knowledge increasing continuously. This increase in knowledge then drives endogenous growth.

It should be clear, though, that it is the assumption on the support of the knowledge distribution that drives the result. If there were an upper bound on knowledge, then the distribution would ultimately converge to a spike at the upper bound, at which point the economy would enter a non-growing steady state. More damning of the result, though, is the fact that it must assume that all possible knowledge pre-exists: there is always some measure of agents far out in the upper tail of the knowledge distribution who can pass on what they know to agents below them. This is no different from the basic assumption in Lucas' earlier human capital work, or, ultimately, in the assumption in the early Solovian models that technological progress just happened. That Lucas–Moll build in a search cost at best captures the idea that diffusing new knowledge out into the economy can be costly, but it in no way explains how economic agents themselves might drive the economy's growth.

Despite Romer's objections in the "Mathiness" paper that Lucas was using clever and complex mathematics to hide the fact that his models assumed the result they were trying to prove, Lucas–Moll have been cited 606 times on Google Scholar as of this writing. So, it seems that the old Freshwater–Saltwater split in macroeconomics continues apace. In the context of endogenous growth, we also note that it was Chicago economists who consistently led the attack against deviations from perfect competition or the adoption of models of monopolistic competition from the 1930s onward. In this sense, Lucas was maintaining the old school tradition.

With this framing, we turn next to look at how Romer's post-thesis work led both naturally and necessarily to the introduction of imperfect competition in models of endogenous growth.

CHAPTER 4

ROMER AND THE "NEW GROWTH THEORY"

ORIGINS OF ROMER'S MODELS

Models and theories that bring about change in economic discourse do not fall from trees, as the proverbial apple of Newton. Rather, as we have shown in the previous chapters, they are usually the outcome of *synchronic* or *diachronic* processes such as seminar and conference presentations; working and discussion papers and subsequent publication; interaction between doctoral students and supervisors and between students themselves; cross-fertilization of ideas within and between individuals and groups; all these culminating in research programs – informal or formal. The case of Romer's approach and the "new growth" research program that developed from the mid-1980s onward exemplify these processes. In Chapter 1 on the *first wave* in endogenous growth theory, we dealt with the period from the early 1950s to the mid-1970s, including the contributions of Uzawa and Shell, among others, based upon "inventive activity," "technical change," and what Shell termed "Uzawa-like human capital" (Spear and Wright, 2001, p. 706). Here, we examine the *transformation* that the endogenous approach underwent to also take account of the effects of scale, competition, education, information, and knowledge, in addition to technology and human capital, on possible growth paths. In his *MD* 2001 interview (Spear & Wright, 2001), Shell referred to the relationship between his early work and other endogenous and "technological evolution" models. As he put it (Shell, 2001, p. 706):

> I love the new growth theory. I applaud the focus on technological evolution. I like the emphasis on empirical facts. Romer's three most important papers draw heavily on my work. Paul very clearly cites my three papers. I don't think that Lucas has cited this work much. One always likes a cite from Bob [Lucas], but there are substantial differences between his stuff and mine. His models are based on Uzawa-like "human capital" as opposed to "technological knowledge." So, Bob's focus was on education broadly defined, while mine was on invention. External effects are important in both the education and invention models. For Romer and me, issues about appropriability, excludability, and nonrivalry of technological knowledge are basic.

Endogenous Growth: Theory, Methods and Morphology
International Symposia in Economic Theory and Econometrics, Volume 35, 91–126

Published under exclusive licence by Emerald Publishing Limited
ISSN: 1571-0386/doi:10.1108/S1571-038620260000035014

> The effects of technology on industrial organization and the effects of industrial organization on technology are also central for Paul and me. Bob's problem is simpler: There can be positive spillovers from private human capital formation. There are no deep increasing-returns problems. Industrial organization is not central .... The Romer 1990 model is based on patents. My 1973 model is driven by the short-run technological advantages enjoyed by advanced technologies. Most students of technological evolution do not think that patents are the basis for the lion's share of technological improvements. On the other hand, Romer combines patents and vintages to make a fully Walrasian theory. My early work on monopolistic competition is a bit too "Marshallian" at the edges. Romer was not alone in this period. Phillipe Aghion and Peter Howitt, Gene Grossman and Elhanan Helpman, and others also did very important work that refers back to my stuff from the sixties and seventies. I do believe I was doing new growth theory before new growth theory.

The *transition* to Romer's "New Growth Theory" involved, first, his utilization of *increasing returns to scale*. The second was his application of what can be called *New Growth Mathematics*. The third was his application of *monopolistic competition* to his "New Growth" models. In this context, we try to provide the answer to the question as to why post-Solow (1956) growth models took so long to adopt Solow (1956)'s *own suggestion* regarding "introducing monopolistic competition into aggregative [growth] models ... with greater realism the reward" (pp. 79–80, note7). Indeed, while monopolistic competition approaches were applied in other areas of economics from the late 1970s and early 1980s onward, it took some time for a *tractable non-competitive approach to be applied to growth*.

One factor that enabled the *transition* from "Old" (Solow-vintage) to "New" Growth (Romer-vintage) models followed from the *dissemination and extended* application of mathematical techniques of the *New Growth Mathematics* (NGM) including variational calculus in the form of Hamiltonian methods, and the application of the Kuhn–Tucker approach.

The contributions of Shell, Cass, and Arrow to the dissemination and application of the NGM *from 1967 onwards* were discussed in Chapter 1, as was the *catalytic* role of the three Mathematical Social Science Board (MSSB) sponsored meetings organized by Cass and Shell, 1975–1977, at which the *Hamiltonian* approach to growth and dynamic systems was essentially *standardized*, when papers presented at the respective meetings were disseminated via the February 1976 issue of *JET* and afterwards. The *pedagogical* utilization of the new growth mathematics is illustrated here by recollections regarding the *Fall 1977 lectures on growth given by David Cass at the University of Pennsylvania*, as recounted by Stephen Spear, one of the authors of the present volume. As he recalled:

> [The] last part of the course was devoted to dynamic analysis. We started first with consideration of discrete time versus continuous time models, looked briefly at the classic Solow model results, then tracked back to programming to examine duality and pricing. The culmination of the course was an introduction to Hamiltonian dynamics and the maximum principle.

Romer (1983)'s Ph.D. thesis was entitled "Dynamic Competitive Equilibria with Externalities, Increasing Returns and Unbounded Growth." It focused on optimizing growth models in economics. The dissertation aimed at developing a *generalized* optimal growth model based on the original approaches of Ramsey, Cass, and Koopmans, by applying the Hamiltonian algebra of thermodynamics.[1]

Romer first discussed naïve growth models and their related necessary conditions, the optimal control form of the social planning problem focusing on a single factor of production and a representative consumer. In the dissertation, he first showed that even when welfare theorems did not apply, competitive equilibrium could be considered solutions to problems of optimization. Romer went on to establish, in a general setting, the formal approach needed for defining equilibrium prices and quantities and provided proofs for theorems related to the existence of social optima and competitive equilibria, by focusing on the implications of externalities and increasing returns. In the dissertation, he provided three examples of the behavior of the models he proposed. The first used a logarithmic utility function to demonstrate the existence of unbounded growth trajectories. In the second example, he contrasted his proposed utility function against a linear function, to illustrate the differences in behaviors along paths of equilibrium. Romer's third example used a two-country model to assess the impact on growth of capital mobility and externalities. Romer's findings showed that economic growth is closely related to *increasing returns*, externalities, and endogenous technical change, as against the Solow approach based upon diminishing returns and exogenous technical change.

In private communication with us, Romer outlined his approach and contrasted it with that of his thesis advisor, Robert Lucas:

> When I started thinking about growth, there were serious concerns about when and if one could prove the two required existence results for any well-posed equilibrium model:
>
> 1. A robust proof of the existence of a competitive equilibrium;
>
> 2. A robust proof of the existence of a social optimum.
>
> By robust, I mean that the proofs apply on an open set of parameter values. A result that holds only on a knife-edge is not robust.
>
> The type of model based on a knife-edge that Lucas proposed can be taken seriously if one can generalize it in a way that leaves the qualitative features of the knife-edge result intact but which makes sure that nearby parameters also lead to a well behaved equilibrium and social optimum. This type of generalized structure was what I set out to create in my thesis. (Email of 8/5/2025)

---

[1]In private communication, Romer indicated that his application of the Hamiltonian approach came not as a result of exposure to the work of Cass and Shell, but rather from his prior experience with the Hamiltonian method. To quote from this communication:

> When I arrived at Chicago, I had learned continuous time Hamiltonians from a physicist turned economist named Russel Davidson during my year at Queen's University (after two years at MIT and before my two years at Chicago). Then when I went to Chicago, everyone was including uncertainty and doing Dynamic Programming, which did make things simpler in the presence of uncertainty. My view was that to understand the most basic issues in growth, we had to get a firm understanding of the existence issues in the perfect certainty case before we brought in any additional complications. (Email of 8/5/2025).

The knife-edge results Romer refers to are based on the fact that one can have increasing returns to scale technologies that generate endogenous growth and still obtain classical competitive equilibrium results as long as the returns to capital are neither increasing nor decreasing – which is to say they are constant. This was explained succinctly in Solow (1994):

> Suppose that the production function is $f(K,L)$, with non-decreasing returns to capital. Treat L as constant for the moment, so we can think of this as just $f(K)$. Let net investment be the fraction s of output so that the time path of K is determined by $dK/dt = sf(K)$. It is obvious on the face that there is potential for fairly explosive behavior if $f(K)$ increases more and more rapidly with K. For instance, if $f(K)/K$ increases with K, the rate of growth of K gets faster as K gets larger. Then the time path for this growth model has the property that the stock of capital becomes infinite in finite time. (It is one thing to say that a quantity will eventually exceed any bound. It is quite another to say that it will exceed any stated bound before Christmas.) It takes a little calculus to show that "fairly explosive" puts it mildly.

> In his own words, Romer's approach his thesis work from the perspective that [T]he type of model based on a knife edge that Lucas proposed can be taken seriously if one can generalize it in a way that leaves the qualitative features of the knife edge result intact but which makes sure that nearby parameters also lead to a well behaved equilibrium and social optimum. This type of generalized structure was what I set out to create in my thesis.

Ultimately, though, the knife-edge requirement of Lucas' approach, together with what we have called the Euler theorem problem led to a divergence of Romer's views on endogenous growth and those of Lucas, culminating in the 2015 AEA session confrontation and Romer's "mathiness" critique.

After completing his Chicago Ph.D. thesis, Romer moved to the University of Rochester and put out working papers (WP) for the Department of Economics and Rochester center for economic research (RCER). There, parallel to the emerging work on growth of Barro, Romer developed his approach, focusing initially on growth and increasing returns over the period 1984–1986. The first of these was a 1984 Rochester Department of Economics WP entitled "Externalities and Increasing Returns in Dynamic Competitive Analysis." Interestingly enough, in their April 1986 Federal reserve Bank of Minneapolis WP entitled "Dynamic Coalitions, Growth and the Firm," Prescott and Boyd cited this Romer WP and noted the difference between the approaches of Lucas as against Romer in the following terms (Prescott & Boyd, 1986, p. 22, note 1):

> Romer (1984) assumes individuals' productivities depend on the average human capital of other members of society as well as their own.

> Lucas (1985) obtains sustained growth by assuming a standard neoclassical production function for the production of goods and an individual-specific technology for production of that individual's human capital. The latter technology has constant returns to scale, with an individual's human capital as the input and increments to that individual's human capital as the output. Unlike Romer's (1984) economy, but like ours, there is constant rather than accelerating growth.

The next was RCER WP 27 dated October 1985, entitled "Increasing Returns and Long Run Growth" (Romer, 1985). According to Romer, "this work" was based on his 1983 dissertation, and "an early version was circulated" as "Externalities and increasing returns in dynamic competitive analysis" mentioned above. The October

1985 RCER WP 27 version of the paper was published in the October 1986 issue of *Journal of Political Economy*. There, Romer again noted that an "early version of this paper circulated" as his 1984 Rochester WP; however, for some reason, Romer *did not cite* the October 1985 RCER WP 27 version in his 1986 JPE paper.

But it was the application of *monopolistic competition* to growth models that brought the "New Growth" research program to fruition. Romer, for his part, recognized the tractability of a *conflation* of the *Dixit and Stiglitz* (1977) and *Ethier* (1982) monopolistic competition approaches (*DSE*) thereby making the breakthrough others had missed, that is, applying monopolistic competition to growth theory. He did this as early as December 1986 in his RCER Working Paper 70. He presented the text of the WP at the *AEA* session "New Theories of Economic Growth" in December 1986. It was subsequently published in the *AER* as "Growth based on increasing returns due to specialization" (Romer, 1987a, 1987b). Below, by reference to his 1987 *AER* paper, we will present Romer (1990a, 1990b)'s method of integrating the *DSE* approach and illustrate his results, which provided the basis for his subsequent working and published papers in 1988 and 1989, and his now famous *JPE* paper "Endogenous Technical Change." But before doing this, we must briefly deal with the *enigmatic* utilization of monopolistic competition in growth theory, as compared to macroeconomic theory, and trade theory from the late 1970s onward.

We start with a brief historical digression in order to understand how the monopolistic competition (*DSE*) approach came to "rule the roost" in two key areas of modern economic analysis, that is, trade theory and growth theory. The modern approaches emanate from two works: Chamberlin (1933)'s *Monopolistic Competition* and Robinson's *Imperfect Competition*. Samuelson (1967) conflated the approaches, writing:

> the time has come when we may permit ourselves to use the terms monopolistic competition and imperfect competition interchangeably, emancipating them from their first associations with the different conceptions of Chamberlin and Mrs. Robinson. *using them as convenient names for the best current models of price theory* (our emphasis).

Regarding the Dixit–Stiglitz (DS) model of monopolistic competition, it first appeared as a Stanford University *Technical Report* with the title "Monopolistic Competition and Optimum Product Diversity," in 1974 (Dixit & Stiglitz, 1974). It appeared under the same title as a Warwick University *Research Paper* (Dixit & Stiglitz, 1975). It was published as "Monopolistic Competition and Optimum Product Diversity" in the *AER* (Dixit & Stiglitz, 1977). In his 1982 *AER* paper "National and International Returns to Scale in the Modern Theory of International Trade," Ethier (1982) proposed utilizing the D-S "formalization of Chamberlinian monopolistic competition" in production function form (p. 391). And it is the application of *tractable* monopolistic competition approaches such as *DSE* to economic theory that characterizes the period of the 1980s that brought about New Trade theory and New Growth theory; "New" being the operational term for the application of the DSEJ Monopolistic Competition approach. The approaches of Dixit–Stiglitz *and* Ethier will be discussed in more detail below.

In "new trade theory," increasing returns not only brings about trade and specialization and trade beyond comparative advantage, but it can bring about trade even where comparative advantage is a negligible influence, for example, between countries with similar technology and resources. Regarding monopolistic competition, according to Krugman, he first learned about it as a doctoral student at MIT, in a course given by Solow. Krugman later integrated monopolistic competition and comparative advantage with trade theory in his 1979 *JIE* and 1980 *AER* papers and by 1985 had published (with Helpman) a volume entitled *Market Structure and Foreign Trade: Increasing Returns, Imperfect Competition, and International Economy*, which brought "new trade theory" into the mainstream of economic discourse.

ROMER'S ENDOGENOUS GROWTH WPs AND MODELS

RCER WP 64 (December 1986)

In his December 1986 RCER WP 64 entitled "Increasing Returns, Specialization, and External Economies: Growth as Described by Allyn Young" (Romer, 1986b), Romer recognized the Euler theorem problem earlier recognized by Shell (1965, 1966, 1973), that is, that competitive equilibrium is *not viable* with increasing returns and, for first time, applied a conflation of the Dixit and Stiglitz (1977) and Ethier (1982) monopolistic competition approaches to a growth model. Romer starts by discussing a growth model with increasing returns from external economies and specialization. By conflating the Dixit–Stiglitz utility function with Either's re-interpretation of it as a production function, Romer linked increasing returns and specialization and showed how, as the range of specialized inputs increased, final goods output exhibited unbounded growth. This model was characterized by (a) total input being held constant, with an indefinite increase in output; (b) profit maximization, with the economy consisting of a continuum of intermediate goods producers and many final output firms, where each firm in the final goods sector is a price-taker, for a given amount of intermediate inputs; (c) fixed costs bring about non-convexities and prevent a competitive equilibrium. Producers of intermediate goods receive zero profits, and prices of final goods influence derived demands. A competitive equilibrium cannot be achieved due to the nature of production of inputs and fixed costs, resulting in a monopolistically competitive equilibrium accordingly.

As we noted above, Romer viewed the Euler theorem problem with his 1986 model as a fatal flaw and came to recognize that any internalization of the increasing returns to scale needed to drive endogenous growth would require introducing imperfect competition. This subsequently became an important difference between the Lucas and Romer approaches to modeling and explaining endogenous growth. Romer (1990a, 1990b) effectively described why it is necessary to switch from perfect competition to some imperfect competition frameworks. As he argues, the key question of growth is what powers the engine of technological progress. We have seen above that saying only that economic growth stems from technological change without specifying the source of this change is just a form of ignorance.

However, Solow's idea of regarding technological progress as manna from heaven can be replaced in various ways. Increasing returns to scale can be inherent in technology itself. The best-known example of this is the so called square–cube law, in which the benefits of a construction activity scale with the volume of space being enclosed, while the costs scale with the area. In economic activities subject to this law, the largest feasible (in engineering terms) structures are the most efficient. Moore's law in semi-conductor manufacturing is another different example. Shell (1973) examined a model with internalized increasing returns to scale using a monopoly framework to get around the Euler theorem problem.

Romer's approach was one based on his previous notion that ideas (and the generation of new ideas) were the driver of growth, in the form of commercial R&D and basic research. In this setting if a market agent creates and reveals new knowledge, it becomes a public good since ideas, once revealed, can be freely used by all. Hence, for the production of useful ideas to be economically viable, they must be excludable, that is, fully internalized, as without efficient legal protections, no agent would undertake the trouble and cost of the investment. But this option is not compatible with perfect competition. Romer takes it as a fact of life that the increasing returns associated with the development of new technology give firms market power. The question he then faced was how to model this market power. At the time Shell was looking at these issues, there were no good general equilibrium models of imperfect competition. By the time Romer took up the question, there were two key models of imperfect competition in general equilibrium available. One was the Shapley and Shubik (1977) strategic market game, and the other was the Dixit and Stiglitz (1977) model of monopolistic competition. The Shapley–Shubik model provides a framework for doing general equilibrium with small numbers of large firms. Dixit–Stiglitz, on the other hand, models general equilibrium settings with large numbers of small firms selling diversified products. Of the two models, Dixit–Stiglitz is the easiest to work with, and, in Romer's case, it was also the most appropriate since ideas come in all shapes, forms, and configurations. Furthermore, it is generally the combination of ideas that make given technical processes better, again pointing toward monopolistic competition as the best way to model returns to scale generated by the costly private accumulation of human capital that then conferred general benefits to all firms (the external effect in Romer's 1986 *JPE* paper or Lucas' 1988 paper). We will argue later that when increasing returns to scale or scope are better modeled using the Shapley–Shubik framework since firms using these kinds of technologies have significant market power and tend to exist as either natural monopolies or large-scale oligopolies.

THE DIXIT AND STIGLITZ FRAMEWORK

Dixit and Stiglitz (1977) invented the utility function, later transformed by Ethier (1982) into a production function, that served as the basis for Romer's (1987b) growth model. The model of monopolistic competition was thus the framework by which he distanced himself from the perfect competition assumption of Romer (1986a).

The basic question for Dixit and Stiglitz is the trade-off between product variety and output. They define an economy with a possibly infinite range of products[2] produced by firms on distinct markets, with each firm producing a single product. In addition, there is a competitive sector producing quantity x_0 of a single product serving as the numéraire, and in which the economy's total endowment is stored. Dixit–Stiglitz assume that utilities from consuming different products are additively separable, with differentiated products have constant elasticity of substitution:

$$u = U\left[x_0; \left(\sum_i x_i^{\rho}\right)^{\frac{1}{\rho}}\right]. \tag{4.1.1}$$

Since all of the differentiated products are substitutes, while each is produced by a monopoly, they are still in competition through the preferences of the consumers. We assume that $0 < \rho < 1$, so utility functions x_i^{ρ} related to distinct products are concave, and it is possible to have zero quantities for some products. As for the shape of U, we assume first-order homogeneity in its two variables. Optimization of (4.1.1) is done subject to a budget constraint of the form

$$I = x_0 + \sum_i p_i x_i, \tag{4.1.2}$$

where I is income in terms of the numéraire and p_i is the price of differentiated good i, and the summation on the right-hand side of (4.1.2) is the profits of firms distributed to consumers that might have either sign (if firms receive lump sum transfers, the sum $\sum_i p_i x_i$ is negative). If this part is zero, then $I = 1$. Following Dixit and Stiglitz, maximizing utility subject to the budget constraint is done in two steps. In the first step of optimization, income defined in (4.1.2) is spent to maximize $U(x_0; y)$, where y is the quantity index:

$$y = \left(\sum_i x_i^{\rho}\right)^{\frac{1}{\rho}}, \tag{4.1.3}$$

based on the price index,

$$q = \left(\sum_i p_i^{-\frac{1}{\beta}}\right)^{-\beta}, \tag{4.1.4}$$

[2]Although in the original version of the model Dixit and Stiglitz assumed a countable range, there are continuum versions as well.

out of the income so that $I = x_0 + qy$, where $\beta = (1-\rho)/\rho$. To see where the price index comes from, start with the first-order conditions for the utility maximization with respect to the differentiated goods:

$$u_2 \frac{1}{\rho}\left(\sum_i x_i^\rho\right)^{\frac{1}{\rho-1}} \rho x_i^{\rho-1} - \lambda p_i = 0 \text{ for all } i.$$

Moving λp_i to the right-hand side and taking ratios over goods i and j and simplifying gives us

$$\frac{x_i^{\rho-1}}{x_j^{\rho-1}} = \frac{p_i}{p_j}.$$

From this, we obtain

$$p_i x_i = x_j p_j^{\frac{1}{1-\rho}} p_i^{\frac{\rho}{\rho-1}}.$$

Summing this over i then yields

$$\Sigma p_i x_i = I - x_0 = x_j p_j^{\frac{1}{1-\rho}} q,$$

where q is as defined in (4.1.4).

If $s(q)$ depending on the preferences is the budget share of y in I (i.e., $I - x_0$), then we have $Is(q) = qy$ and $I[1-s(q)] = x_0$, from which it follows that the ratio of the products from the two sectors is

$$\frac{x_0}{y} = \frac{q}{s(q)} - q. \tag{4.1.5}$$

The ratio thus depends on q, the price index of the monopolistically competitive sector alone. The elasticity of the ratio with respect to q, called the intersectoral elasticity of substitution, is

$$\sigma(q) = \frac{s(q)[1-s(q)] - qs'(q)}{s(q)[1-s(q)]},$$

which is expected to be positive, so the higher q is, the higher the ratio in (4.1.5) is, that is, the more consumption is biased toward x_0.

After the first step then, the income share devoted to the products by the competitive sector of x_0 is determined, so in the second step we maximize (4.1.3) out of the remaining part of I. Here, we can follow the usual consumption optimization process where the ratio of marginal utilities of any pair of products must be equal to the price ratio, that is, with (4.1.1) we have (as above)

$$\frac{x_i}{x_j} = \frac{p_i^{\frac{1}{\rho-1}}}{p_j^{\frac{1}{\rho-1}}}, \tag{4.1.6}$$

as the optimum ratios of pairs of products as functions of their prices. Consumption must abide by the budget constraint, so

$$\sum_i p_i x_i = qy,$$

from which eventually we have

$$x_i = y\left(\frac{q}{p_i}\right)^{\frac{1}{1-\rho}}, \tag{4.1.7}$$

which is a demand function for each x_i in terms of its own price, provided variety in the monopolistically competitive sector is large enough to disregard the effect that a change in p_i exerts on q through (4.1.4). If so, then the elasticity of x_i with respect to p_i, that is, the elasticity of the individual demand function of each monopoly is $-(1+\beta)/\beta$.

At this point, Dixit and Stiglitz suggest using the basic symmetry of (4.1.1), namely, that all products from the monopolistically competitive sector are expected to be produced in the same quantity and sold at the same price. If we have n types of products, then (4.1.1) becomes

$$u = U\left[x_0; \left(n x_i^{\rho}\right)^{\frac{1}{\rho}}\right],$$

where diversity n is an argument and (4.1.3) and (4.1.4) become $y = xn^{1+\beta}$ and $q = pn^{-\beta}$, and in place of (4.1.7) through $Is(q) = qy$, we have

$$x = \frac{Is(q)}{pn}, \tag{4.1.8}$$

which is a demand function for x where the effect of a change in p no longer has a negligible effect on q. The slope of x in terms of p can easily be characterized through the elasticity of (4.1.8) with respect to p, according to which the demand function is negatively sloped.

Using this symmetry, Dixit and Stiglitz perform three distinct analyses for the cases of monopolistically competitive equilibrium; where marginal cost (assumed to be constant from the uniform cost function $a + cx$) and marginal revenue are equal; and where firm profits are zero. From the first condition, a unique supply price p_e is established upon which the number of firms and hence the number of kinds of products emerges by the twofold criterion:

$$p_n x_n - a - cx_n \geq 0,$$

$$p_{n+1} x_{n+1} - a - cx_{n+1} < 0,$$

meaning that firms enter until the next entrant would make a loss, so n is determined by $p_n x_n - a - cx_n = 0$. For comparison, we can also find the optimum price and supply of firms in the monopolistic sector under two alternative assumptions. First, in the case of a constrained optimum where the social planner insists on the condition, acting as the constraint, that firms make no losses; and second, in the case of an unconstrained or first-best optimum, where potential losses by firms are compensated by the government with lump-sum transfers. In the first of these additional cases, Dixit and Stiglitz show that the same results regarding prices and the number of firms emerge. Not surprisingly, when government subsidies are available, firms can apply a lower supply price, but each product is demanded in the same quantity as in the previous two cases, so variety n must be higher. When price is lower, consumers have higher real income and instead of buying higher quantities from the same variety of products, they prefer to disperse their incomes across more kinds of products.

ETHIER ON MONOPOLISTIC COMPETITION

Ethier (1982) applied the monopolistic competition framework to international production and trade. His goal was to use the model to explain the empirical fact of intensifying exchange of manufactured goods between industrialized economies. As Ethier underlines, trade intensification happened without considerable specialization as countries increased exports of all sorts of manufactures leading to extensive intra-industrial trade, and consequently, specialization declined. A viable explanation is product differentiation and the monopolistic competition it implies, the latter having technologies with increasing returns to scale as a rationale. Increasing returns to scale, in turn, might result from various sources. Ethier suggested an explanation in the monopolistic competition framework of Dixit and Stiglitz (1977) in which scale economies stem from an increased division of labor.

In Ethier's model, there are two factors of production, capital and labor, that are used to produce two products, wheat (W) and manufactures (M). Wheat is produced with a constant-returns-to-scale technology, while the production of M takes place along the production function $M = km$, where k is an index of scale economies to be determined by the parameters of the model, and m is and index of the scale of factor utilization. The production of M might be subject to increasing returns to scale arising from the degree of the division of labor, so the transformation curve of the economy describes the trade-off between W and m as $W = T(m)$, and not between W and M. Any drop in the production of W releases some quantity of m which can then be devoted to the production of manufactures. Although Ethier neglects to make it explicit, the usual assumptions of $T(m)$ being strictly concave, strictly decreasing and continuously differentiable with $\lim_{m \to 0} T'(m) = 0$ and $\lim_{m \to m_0} T'(m) = -\infty$ all apply, where there is a unique m_0 such that $T(m_0) = 0$. Of course, $T(0)$ is finite. Any unit of M (which can be viewed as a finished product) is assembled from intermediate components free of costs. The number n of the variety of components is also to be determined endogenously. Their production from the same primary factors takes place via identical production functions, and all sorts of intermediate parts enter the production of finished manufactures symmetrically. Under these assumptions, all intermediate products are produced in the same quantity x, so the total quantity of components is nx. From the side of components, production of manufactures at the firm level can be described with the function

$$M = n^{\alpha}\left[\sum_{i=1}^{n}\frac{x_i^{\beta}}{n}\right]^{\frac{1}{\beta}}, \tag{4.2.1}$$

where x_i is the quantity of the ith component, and $\alpha > 1$. With the symmetry assumption $x_i = x$ above, however, the production function in (4.2.1) boils down to

$$M = n^{\alpha}x. \tag{4.2.2}$$

The parameter β determines how easily a component can be substituted for any other. Higher values of β make it easier for the economy to use a given component in place of another which in turn implies lower levels of product differentiation. All components have the same production function $ax+b$ with $a,b>0$ that offers an index of the primary factors needed to produce a quantity of x, so with n sorts of components the index of total factors devoted to manufacturing is

$$m = n(ax+b). \tag{4.2.3}$$

Note n in (4.2.2) implies increasing returns to scale at any given x, while constant returns to scale in x at any given n. This means that M can be increased by an increase in n or x to different extents. Ethier assumes that the production of components, described by the individual component production functions $ax+b$, is subject to scale returns in the form that Balassa (1967) termed the "traditional sense" and that makes firms to realize that more of a given product can be produced cheaper. This idea comes from the fact that $ax+b$ is the total amount of production factors needed for producing any x_i, and by $(ax+b)/x = a + b/x$, the production of higher quantities of x implies lower average cost in terms of primary factors. This, in turn, creates an incentive for firms to concentrate geographically, each kind of component is thus provided by a single firm at a single location. By contrast, Ethier also assumes that scale economies provided by (4.2.2) are dependent upon the size of the market for finished manufactures, so they cannot be realized by geographical concentration alone but require an increase in variety n of components leading to an increased division of labor. Individual competitive producers of M thus take n as a parameter dependent upon the world economy and operate under (4.2.2) with constant returns to scale.

Having laid down the basics, Ethier examines two distinct settings – autarkic equilibrium and international equilibrium. In the first case, he starts the analysis with the problem of the individual M-producer. Ethier cuts the problem into two parts. While the individual producer decides on the quantities of n components, Ethier imposes the earlier symmetry assumption and distinguishes only two: one is x_0 and the other is x standing for all other, non-x_0 components. Respective prices are q_0 and q. Now, the profit of the individual M-producer is

$$n^{\alpha}\left(\frac{x_0^{\beta}}{n}+\frac{x^{\beta}}{n}\right)^{\frac{1}{\beta}}-qx-q_0x_0.$$

To maximize profit, we have the usual first-order conditions by differentiating the profit function with respect to x_0 and x. After some simple algebra, we have

$$x_0 = x\left(\frac{q}{q_0}\right)^{\frac{1}{1-\beta}}, \tag{4.2.4}$$

which is the demand curve faced by the producer of x_0, with given x and q. To find the price q_0, we must recall that to produce x_0, a quantity $ax_0 + b$ of factors is to be used, and it is measured in the same units as m. The function $-T'(m)$ showing how much wheat must be sacrificed to have an additional unit of m that can be used in component production is the unit price of m in terms of W. Therefore, the total cost of the producer of x_0 is $-T'(m)(ax_0 + b)$. Note that the producer of x_0 is a monopoly, so its supply price is to be determined accordingly. From (4.2.4), it is straightforward to obtain the inverse demand function and show that the total revenue of the monopoly is

$$q_0x_0 = x_0^{\beta}x^{1-\beta}q,$$

given x and q, leading to the marginal revenue function $\beta qx^{1-\beta}x_0^{\beta-1}$. Marginal cost is $-aT'(m)$, and the maximum profit of the monopoly is where

$$\beta q\frac{x^{1-\beta}}{x_0^{1-\beta}} = -aT'(m),$$

in which the ratio on the is familiar from (4.2.4). Substituting from (4.2.4) yields

$$q_0 = -\frac{aT'(m)}{\beta}. \tag{4.2.5}$$

By substituting q_0 into the profit function of the component producer, we have

$$T'(m)(ax_0 + b) - \frac{T'(m)}{\beta}x_0, \tag{4.2.6}$$

which must be zero in equilibrium set by entering and exiting firms that varies n. After simplification, it turns out that

$$x_0 = \frac{\beta b}{a(1-\beta)}, \tag{4.2.7}$$

which, due to the previous symmetry assumption, also gives the equilibrium quantity of each component that is supplied at the price of $q_0 = q$. Most importantly, the equilibrium production x of components is independent of m and is determined by the parameters of the system, which implies that M in (4.2.2) can only be increased by increasing n, and that any reallocation of primary factors from agriculture into manufacturing (i.e., any increase in m) triggers an increase in n, not in x. The next step is thus to find the equilibrium extent of the division of labor described by n. By substituting (4.2.7) into (4.2.3), we have

$$n = \frac{m(1-\beta)}{b}, \tag{4.2.8}$$

which shows that an increase in m increases n linearly. Next, substituting (4.2.7) into (4.2.2) gives

$$M = \frac{(1-\beta)^{\alpha-1}}{b^{\alpha-1}} \frac{\beta}{a} m^{\alpha}, \tag{4.2.9}$$

from which

$$k = \frac{(1-\beta)^{\alpha-1}}{b^{\alpha-1}} \frac{\beta}{a} m^{\alpha-1}, \tag{4.2.10}$$

follows. Note that the equilibrium value of m, the quantity of factors devoted to manufacturing is still undetermined. If we had both a demand curve and a supply curve for M, then we would have an equilibrium value of manufactures and through (4.2.9) and (4.2.10) a unique value for m. Ethier's plan is thus to establish a Marshallian cross for the market for manufactured products. As M is produced on a competitive market, profits are zero, so at the supply price P_S for M, we have

$$P_S M = P_S n^{\alpha} x = q_0 n x,$$

from which $P_S = q_0 n^{1-\alpha}$, and eventually,

$$P_S = -T'(m) \frac{ab^{\alpha-1}}{\beta(1-\beta)^{\alpha-1}} \frac{1}{m^{\alpha-1}} = -\frac{T'(m)}{k}. \tag{4.2.11}$$

This equation describes a function in the $P_S \times m$ plane, and by (4.2.9), the demand curve in the $P_S \times M$ plane. As x is determined by parameters, and the production of M exhibits increasing returns in terms of n,[3] the demand curve must be downward sloping. However, Ethier's assumption of the negative slope of the inverse supply

[3]This case is to be distinguished from the increasing-returns production function of Lucas (1988). Note that Lucas assumed a constant-returns-to-scale technology in which output at any fixed level of investment could be increased by increasing labor and capital utilization with increasing returns. However, Lucas ensured that the only way of increasing the capital stock is intensifying investment, so the firm cannot in fact exploit increasing returns. In Ethier's model, by contrast, x in $M = n^{\alpha}x$ is pinned down by the parameters of the system, so any change in n indeed affects the producers with increasing returns, even if n is not their decision variable.

function $P_S(M)$ is problematic. Obviously, P_S is a function of m in (4.2.11), but using the strict monotonicity and invertibility of M on m in (4.2.9), we have

$$m = \left[\frac{ab^{\alpha-1}}{\beta(1-\beta)^{\alpha-1}}\right]^{\frac{1}{\alpha}} M^{\frac{1}{\alpha}}$$

that we can readily use in (4.2.11) to describe P_S as the function of M. Substitution yields

$$P_S = -\frac{ab^{\alpha-1}}{\beta(1-\beta)^{\alpha-1}} \frac{T'\left[\left[\frac{ab^{\alpha-1}}{\beta(1-\beta)^{\alpha-1}}\right]^{\frac{1}{\alpha}} M^{\frac{1}{\alpha}}\right]}{\left[\frac{ab^{\alpha-1}}{\beta(1-\beta)^{\alpha-1}}\right]^{\frac{\alpha-1}{\alpha}} M^{\frac{\alpha-1}{\alpha}}} = -\frac{A}{B^{\alpha-1}} \frac{T'\left(BM^{\frac{1}{\alpha}}\right)}{M^{\frac{\alpha-1}{\alpha}}}, \tag{4.2.12}$$

where

$$A = \frac{ab^{\alpha-1}}{\beta(1-\beta)^{\alpha-1}} > 0 \text{ and } B = \left[\frac{ab^{\alpha-1}}{\beta(1-\beta)^{\alpha-1}}\right]^{\frac{1}{\alpha}} = A^{\frac{1}{\alpha}} > 0.$$

By differentiating (4.2.12) with respect to M, we have the slope of P_S as

$$P'_{SM} = -\frac{A}{B^{\alpha-1}}\left[\frac{\frac{B}{\alpha}T'' - \frac{\alpha-1}{\alpha}T'M^{-\frac{1}{\alpha}}}{M^{2\frac{\alpha-1}{\alpha}}}\right].$$

Given that $-A/B^{\alpha-1} < 0$, $P'_{SM} < 0$ if and only if

$$\frac{B}{\alpha}T'' > \frac{\alpha-1}{\alpha}T'M^{-\frac{1}{\alpha}}, \tag{4.2.13}$$

for all $M \in (0; M_0)$ where M_0 is the maximum quantity of manufactures appertaining to m_0 through (4.2.9). As (9) is strictly increasing in m, M_0 exists and it is unique. Condition (4.2.13) boils down to

$$\frac{B}{\alpha-1} < \frac{T'\left(BM^{\frac{1}{\alpha}}\right)}{T''\left(BM^{\frac{1}{\alpha}}\right)} M^{-\frac{1}{\alpha}},$$

where

$$\lim_{M \to 0} T'\left(BM^{\frac{1}{\alpha}}\right) = 0,$$

therefore, in the neighborhood of $M = 0$, the supply function need not be negatively sloped.

Ethier applies a similar strategy to derive the demand function. Total income of a household is $W + P_D M$, where P_D is the demand price of manufactures expressed in wheat. Ethier assumes that a household spends a constant fraction γ on manufactures, so in equilibrium $P_D M = \gamma(W + P_D M)$, from which

$$P_D = \frac{\gamma}{1-\gamma}\frac{W}{M} = \frac{\gamma}{1-\gamma}\frac{T(m)}{km}.$$

In equilibrium, $P_S = P_D$ implying

$$\frac{\gamma}{1-\gamma}\frac{T(m)}{km} = -\frac{T'(m)}{k},$$

and finally,

$$-\frac{\gamma}{1-\gamma} = \frac{m}{T(m)}T'(m).$$

It is straightforward to see that the right-hand side is strictly decreasing in m; hence, we have an equilibrium solution $m \in [0; m_0]$. Corner solutions emerge in cases where $\gamma \to 0$ or $\gamma \to 1$.

To examine international equilibrium, Ethier obtains many of the same results he does in the autarkic case. In the international setting, monopolies producing the components are located in two countries. Trade is free, so international equilibrium looks as if one had divided the previous closed economy into two parts. Optimum production of a component in (4.2.7) remains valid. From the previous results, it also follows that

$$n_F = (1-\beta)\frac{m^*}{b} \text{ and } n_H = (1-\beta)\frac{m}{b},$$

where n_F and n_H are the component diversities of the foreign economy and the home economy, and m^* and m are the scales of manufacturing operations for the two economies, respectively. From this, total manufacturing at home and in the foreign economy is

$$M + M^* = \frac{\beta}{a}\frac{(1-\beta)^{\alpha-1}}{b^{\alpha-1}}(m + m^*)^{\alpha}.$$

Demand price on the market of the two economies is given by $P_D\left(M+M^*\right)=\gamma\left[W+W^*+P_D\left(M+M^*\right)\right]$, where W^* is wheat consumption in the foreign economy. From this,

$$P_D=\frac{\gamma}{1-\gamma}\frac{a}{\beta}\frac{b^{\alpha-1}}{(1-\beta)^{\alpha-1}}\frac{T(m)+S\left(m^*\right)}{\left(m+m^*\right)^{\alpha}},$$

where $S\left(m^*\right)$ is the transformation curve of the foreign economy. Ethier assumes that the economies differ only in terms of factor endowments m and m^*, so the transformation curves are identical, that is, $T(m)=S(m)$ for any $m\in[0;m_0]$, but $T(m)=S\left(m^*\right)$ if and only if $m=m^*$. Claiming that the price in (4.2.5) remains valid, Ethier implicitly assumes that primary factors are immobile, so home monopolies buy factors from the home economy the cost of which is still given by the slope of the home transformation curve. Supply price for the home economy is $P_S^H=q_0n^{1-\alpha}$, as previously, from which

$$P_S^H=-\left[\frac{(1-\beta)\left(m+m^*\right)}{b}\right]^{1-\alpha}\frac{aT'(m)}{\beta}, \tag{4.2.14}$$

follows and is built on the implicit assumption that manufactures are traded internationally as their price is calculated from $n=n^F+n^H$. In home equilibrium, $P_D=P_S^H$ that implies the equation Ethier calls the home allocation curve

$$\gamma\left[T(m)+S\left(m^*\right)\right]+(1-\gamma)\left(m+m^*\right)T'(m)=0, \tag{4.2.15}$$

determining such pairs of m and m^*. that preserves the equilibrium. This gives m^* as an implicit function of m. By the same procedure,

$$\gamma\left[T(m)+S\left(m^*\right)\right]+(1-\gamma)\left(m+m^*\right)S'\left(m^*\right)=0 \tag{4.2.16}$$

is the foreign allocation curve, which determines the analog of (4.2.15), giving a second implicit function of m^* in m for the equilibria of the foreign economy. Both (4.2.15) and (4.2.16) are negatively sloped, shown by the implicit differentiation of m^* with respect to m:

$${}_Hm_m^*=\frac{T'(m)+(1-\gamma)\left(m+m^*\right)T''(m)}{(\gamma-1)T'(m)-\gamma S'\left(m^*\right)}<0,$$

and

$${}_Fm_m^*=\frac{(\gamma-1)S'\left(m^*\right)-\gamma T'(m)}{S'\left(m^*\right)+(1-\gamma)\left(m+m^*\right)S''\left(m^*\right)}<0.$$

Ethier, however, assumes this without providing formal proofs. As the implicit functions in (4.2.15) and (4.2.16) describe the equilibrium of each economy, their intersection would be an allocation $\left(m; m^*\right)$ where both economies are in simultaneous equilibrium. By finding this allocation, the price of manufactures is determined by (4.2.14), and we have n from the sum $n^F + n^H$. Ethier also assumes that the home allocation curve at any m is steeper than the foreign allocation curve, but this assumption cannot generally be underpinned by formal arguments. Ethier argues that any change in m in the home economy affects both the world price P_D and the home supply price P_S^H. To keep the home economy in equilibrium, the trade-off between m and m^* is needed as ${}_H m_m^* < 0$. While ${}_F m_m^*$ is also negative, from the viewpoint of the foreign economy, an increase in m of the home country only affects P_D the compensation of which requires smaller changes in m^* of the foreign economy, so ${}_H m_m^* < {}_F m_m^* < 0$. However, it is not too difficult to find cases where this inequality does not hold. When $\gamma \to 1$, for instance, from (4.2.15), we have

$$ {}_H m_m^* \to -\frac{T'(m)}{T'\left(m^*\right)} < 0, \tag{4.2.17} $$

in which we utilize the fact that the transformation curves are the same for the two economies. Note that for any given m, m^* in (4.2.17) is read off the home allocation curve. The case where $\gamma \to 1$ implies from (4.2.16) that

$$ {}_F m_m^* \to -\frac{T'(m)}{T'\left(m^*\right)} < 0, \tag{4.2.18} $$

in which m^* is read off the foreign allocation curve. If at any given m we have a point of intersection, then the two curves are equally sloped. But if at any m the foreign allocation curve is under the home allocation curve, then m^* in (4.2.18) is lower than m^* in (4.2.17), and ${}_F m_m^* < {}_H m_m^* < 0$ which contradicts Ethier's assumption.

ROMER'S 1987 GROWTH MODEL WITH IMPERFECT COMPETITION

RCER WP 70 (December 1986) and AER 1987

In his second WP dated December 1986, RCER 70 entitled "Growth Based on Increasing Returns Due to Specialization" (Romer 1986c), later published in the May 1987 *AEA Papers and Proceedings* (Romer 1987b), Romer presented a model that explored how increasing returns in production could result from specialized inputs in a monopolistically competitive equilibria setting. Once again Romer applies the Ethier production function reinterpretation of the Dixit–Stiglitz utility function and shows how it is dependent on intermediate inputs that are specialized. The approach proposed is based on a monopolistically competitive market with decentralized equilibrium, with firms producing inputs that are specialized.

The paper then describes the implications of this type of market structure on pricing and production. The first model Romer proposed was *static* in nature, with the following characteristics: (i) there is a continuum of firms producing intermediate goods, each with *market power*; (ii) the price of the primary resource Z is denoted as R, with firms maximizing profits based on derived demand curves; and (iii) in equilibrium, some goods are produced while others are not, something that leads to zero profits for all firms in intermediate goods industries; (iv) the equilibrium values of input quantities and the range of inputs that are produced are determined by the price of the primary resource.

Romer then moved from a static to a *dynamic* model and allowed for the accumulation of the primary resource Z, durable capital. Labor was taken as exogenous, with conventional intertemporal preferences. This model incorporated consumer behavior and investment decisions over time as follows: (i) consumers maximize utility by allocating output between consumption and investment in capital Z; (ii) the instantaneous rate of return on investments in capital is 100% per unit time, with consumption and capital growing at an exponential rate; and (iii) the equilibrium condition requires that the range of inputs produced at time t equals the stock of capital Z. Romer's analysis revealed that the decentralized equilibrium is suboptimal compared to a social planner's solution, which accounted for the positive externalities of specialization. According to Romer, in this case: (a) a social planner would optimize the production of inputs and investment levels, leading to higher growth rates; (b) the decentralized equilibrium results in lower investment and growth rates due to individual agents' decisions; and (c) the model suggested that a binding agreement to increase savings and production of a wider range of goods could improve overall welfare.

Following Dixit and Stiglitz (1977) and Ethier (1982), the production function Romer (1987b) assumed can be written in the discrete case as

$$Y(L;x) = L^{1-\alpha}\sum_{i=1}^{N} x_i^{\alpha} = L\sum_{i=1}^{N}\left(\frac{x_i}{L}\right)^{\alpha}, \tag{4.3.1}$$

where L is labor input, and inputs x_i are intermediate goods used in production and sorted into a finite list. In a continuum version of the function, (4.3.1) becomes

$$Y(L;x) = L\int_{\mathbb{R}_+} g\left[\frac{x(i)}{L}\right]di, \tag{4.3.2}$$

where $x(i)$ denotes the amount of the ith intermediate input used in production, $i \in \mathbb{R}_+$. Since intermediate inputs are additively separable in the production function their marginal products are independent of each other, and since all of them have the same exponential α, in a static equilibrium they are used in the same quantities. If this quantity is taken to be $x(i) = N / M = \bar{x}$, where $i \in [0, M]$, so M is the number of intermediate goods, then the total quantity used is N. If we use the same power function for g in the production function, then (4.3.1) becomes

$$Y\left(L;\{N;M\}\right)=L^{1-\alpha}\underbrace{\left[\left(\frac{N}{M}\right)^{\alpha}+\left(\frac{N}{M}\right)^{\alpha}+\dots\right]}_{M \text{ times}}=\left[M\left(\frac{N}{M}\right)^{\alpha}\right]L^{1-\alpha}=L^{1-\alpha}M^{1-\alpha}N^{\alpha}. \tag{4.3.3}$$

Romer underlines that the variety of intermediate goods M is a variable in the production function, of which output is an increasing function, *ceteris paribus*. As was the case in Ethier's model, production in Romer's model exhibits (internalized) increasing returns to scale. If available resources are limited, then M should be determined optimally.

To show this optimization in terms of the range of intermediate inputs, Romer creates a static problem in which the production of any x_i requires the use of intermediate inputs given by a U-shaped cost function,

$$h(x)=\frac{1+x^2}{2}, \tag{4.3.4}$$

and the total production cost of the whole variety must not exceed the resource constraint Z, which is the available stock of a primary input (e.g., a raw material). So,

$$M\frac{1+x^2}{2}\leq Z. \tag{4.3.5}$$

The economy consists of two sectors, a primary sector producing the intermediate goods, and a secondary one responsible for the production of final output goods. In the primary sector, each firm is a monopoly on its own market, so that overall, the model is one of monopolistic competition since intermediate goods are substitutes in the production function (4.3.3). Hence, the production of any firm in the primary sector follows two basic rules: in equilibrium, marginal revenue equals marginal cost, and the firm has zero profit, so total revenue equals total cost. Because Romer assumes a continuum of intermediate good firms, the price of the intermediate good is equal to its marginal product, so $p_i=g'(x_i)$. The price R of the primary input Z is calculated so that the zero profit requirements should hold. For simplicity, following Romer (1986b, p. 6), we take $L=1$. The problem of the decentralized economy and the social planner is the same: to find the number of intermediate goods M, and the symmetric output of intermediate goods $\overline{x}$ for each producer. In the analysis, we maintain the assumption that $g(x)=x^{\alpha}$; hence, $p_i=\alpha x^{\alpha-1}$.

In the decentralized equilibrium, we use the two criteria simultaneously so that marginal revenue of any firm is $\alpha^2x^{\alpha-1}$ and marginal cost is x; hence, $\alpha^2x^{\alpha}=x^2$. On the other hand, the zero-profit condition requires

$$\alpha x^{\alpha}=\frac{1+x^2}{2}.$$

Combining the two, we find the optimal production of intermediate goods as

$$\bar{x} = \left(\frac{\alpha}{2-\alpha}\right)^{\frac{1}{2}}, \tag{4.3.6}$$

and the equilibrium value for *M* is calculated from (4.3.5) after substituting (4.3.6) into the cost function. Doing so, we have $M = Z(2-\alpha)$. Interestingly, by using the last two results, the dynamic version of (4.3.3), $Y(t) = M(t)^{1-\alpha} L^{1-\alpha} N(t)^{\alpha}$, is

$$Y(t) = (2-\alpha)Z(t)L^{1-\alpha}\left[\frac{N(t)}{M(t)}\right]^{\alpha} \equiv AZ(t)L^{1-\alpha},$$

which looks like a process with exogenous technical change, now fed by increases in product diversity.

The problem of the social planner is to maximize utility by maximizing total output from (4.3.3) and to find the optimal value for *M*. Output-maximization and utility-maximization are the same as neither the intermediate good nor the primary input has alternative uses in consumption. The Lagrangian of the benevolent social planner is simply

$$\mathcal{L}(M; x) = Mx^{\alpha} - \lambda\left(M\frac{1+x^2}{2} - Z\right), \tag{4.3.7}$$

where the production function Mx^{α} preserves the basic symmetry, so the social planner is to find a unique optimal value $\bar{x}$ for all kinds of intermediate goods. From (4.3.7), we have the first-order conditions for *M* and *x*, respectively:

$$x^{\alpha} = \lambda\frac{1+x^2}{2} \tag{4.3.8}$$

$$M\alpha x^{\alpha-1} = \lambda Mx. \tag{4.3.9}$$

Note that the optimal value of *M* is not part of the problem after this point as it immediately drops from (4.3.9). The social planner, thus, optimizes in terms of *x*, and on the basis of the optimal value *x*, it determines *M* from the resource constraint and the cost function. From (4.3.9), $\lambda = \alpha x^{\alpha-2}$ follows, and substituting into (4.3.8) yields

$$\bar{x} = \left(\frac{\alpha}{2-\alpha}\right)^{\frac{1}{2}},$$

so in the optimum, we must also have $M = Z(2-\alpha)$. Note that the social planner does not care if firms in the primary sector have positive profit or loss, so this solution is the first-best optimum as well. We know from the decentralized equilibrium that firms have zero profit at (4.3.6), so the first-best and the constrained optima coincide for Romer, unlike Dixit and Stiglitz (1977).

In the equilibrium, total cost expressed in quantities of Z is

$$\frac{1+\left[\left(\frac{\alpha}{2-\alpha}\right)^{\frac{1}{2}}\right]^2}{2}=\frac{1}{2-\alpha},$$

meaning that total expenditure is $R/(2-\alpha)$. On the other hand, total revenue is

$$\alpha\left(\frac{\alpha}{2-\alpha}\right)^{\frac{\alpha}{2}}.$$

Zero profit in terms of R means

$$\frac{R}{2-\alpha}=\alpha\left(\frac{\alpha}{2-\alpha}\right)^{\frac{\alpha}{2}},$$

from which $R=\alpha(2-\alpha)\left(\frac{\alpha}{2-\alpha}\right)^{\frac{\alpha}{2}}$ follows, which is the equilibrium and optimal unit price for the primary input. Romer asks if this is the appropriate price for Z.

To see the answer, we have to measure the marginal utility of Z in the optimum (and the equilibrium). Utility at the optimum is simply the total quantity of final goods produced,

$$M\bar{x}^{\alpha}=M\left(\frac{\alpha}{2-\alpha}\right)^{\frac{\alpha}{2}}=Z(2-\alpha)\left(\frac{\alpha}{2-\alpha}\right)^{\frac{\alpha}{2}},$$

from which the marginal utility of Z is

$$(2-\alpha)\left(\frac{\alpha}{2-\alpha}\right)^{\frac{\alpha}{2}}=\frac{R}{\alpha}>R,$$

so Z is undervalued at price R.

In the subsequent static and dynamic analysis, Romer uses a general production function g which generates a general demand function for the intermediate input. The underlying motivation is, as he argues, the fact that the downward sloping demand curve for the intermediate good creates a tendency toward lower values of $\bar{x}$ and hence higher values for M, while an additional unit of the intermediate good generates a surplus for the producers of the final product greater than the price they pay for it, and this generates a tendency to increase $\bar{x}$ and decrease M. Equilibrium is where these tendencies are offset. Regarding the former, note that the steeper the demand curve, the steeper the marginal revenue curve of the monopoly, and its intersection with a fixed marginal cost function is closer to the origin. To see the latter of the two tendencies, note that, on the one hand, the marginal utility of an additional unit of x is $\alpha x^{\alpha-1}$ realized by the producers of the final consumption good (as the derivative of the production function x^{α} with respect to x), while the producer of this additional x receives the marginal revenue $\alpha^2 x^{\alpha-1}$, and for $\alpha \in (0,1)$, marginal utility is always higher than marginal revenue of the firm.

Instead of $g(x) = x^{\alpha}$, in this second part of the analysis, Romer suggests using a production function having two separate sections. First, when $x \in [0, x_0]$, it is strictly concave, strictly increasing with $g(0) = 0$ and $g'(x_0) = 1$. Second, in cases where $x \in [x_0, \infty)$ $g'(x) = 1$ all along, so overall, the production function is weakly concave. The description of the function involves another constant G, which is the intersection along the vertical axis of the linear extension of the second, linear phase of the function (see Fig. 3)

Note that G defines a secondary horizontal axis with the line that contains the linear segment of $g(x)$ starting from the secondary origin, so for $x \in [x_0, \infty)$, we have $g(x) = G + x$. As the analog of (4.3.3), we have total output as

$$Y(L;\{N;M\}) = ML\left(G + \frac{N}{ML}\right) = MLG + N. \qquad (4.3.10)$$

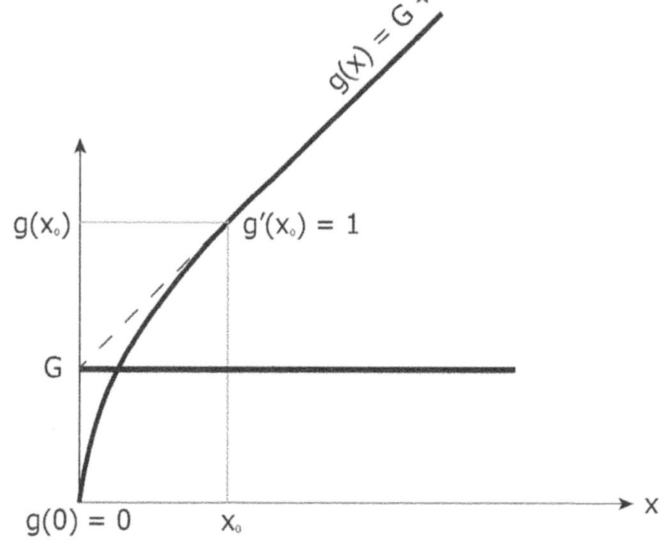

Fig. 3. Romer's Production Function of Input x.

As before, $L=1$ and (4.3.4) applies. For additional simplicity, $R=1$. In this case, the marginal cost of producing x is $Rh'(x)=Rx=x$. To obtain the demand function for x from the production function, it is easy to realize that there is an initial segment in the positive neighborhood of zero where the inverse demand function is strictly decreasing, while along the second segment, where $g(x)$ is linear, $p_i=1$ for $x\in[x_0,\infty)$ (see Fig. 4).

Along the linear phase of the demand function, which is the relevant segment if x_0 is sufficiently small, $p(x)=1$; hence, total revenue is $x\,p(x)=x$ and marginal revenue is 1. As marginal cost is x, at the monopoly pricing, the coordinates of the equilibrium are $[x,p]=[1,1]$. Under simple conditions like setting x_0 to a small value and ensuring that under x_0 the demand function is below the U-shaped average cost curve (so that it will have a non-empty intersection with the marginal cost curve), the monopolistically competitive equilibrium is unique. Note that at $\bar{x}=1$, the firm's total cost is 1, so from the resource constraint of the economy, it follows that $M=Z$, and the production function becomes $Y=Z(G+1)$. From this, the marginal value of M is $(G+1)>1=R$, so at $R=1$,. the primary factor Z is undervalued. The most important lesson of this part of the analysis is that the utility gain from an additional unit of x is 1 (as in the previous case, since the derivative of the production function $G+x$ with respect to x is one), and marginal revenue is also 1, as we have already seen. So, unlike the previous model, the demand function is horizontal in the relevant segment, and there is no distinction between private and social utility gains from the introduction of an additional unit of x.

The constrained objective of the social planner is given by the Lagrangian

$$\mathcal{L}(M;x)=M(G+x)-\lambda\left(M\frac{1+x^2}{2}-Z\right), \tag{4.3.11}$$

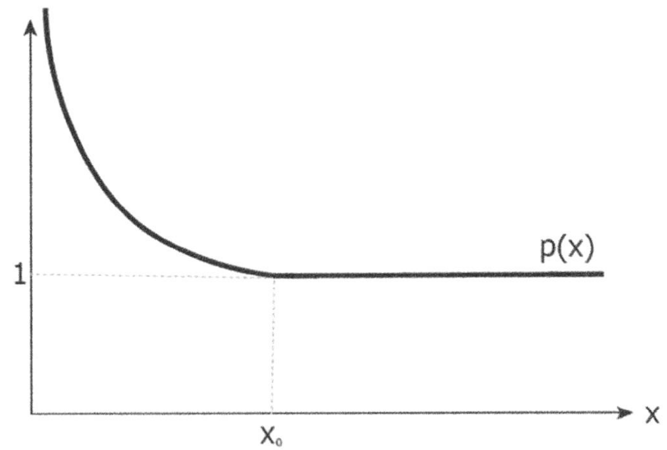

Fig. 4. Romer's Inverse Demand Function for x Stemming from the Production Function.

from which the first-order conditions for M and x, respectively, are

$$G + x = \lambda \frac{1 + x^2}{2}, \tag{4.3.12}$$

$$M = \lambda M x. \tag{4.3.13}$$

From (4.3.13), after the elimination of M, we have $\lambda = 1/x$. Taking ratios of the two conditions, we have

$$G + x = \frac{1 + x^2}{2x},$$

so that $2Gx + x^2 - 1 = 0$. This equation has only one positive root as $\bar{x} = \sqrt{G^2 + 1} - G = \bar{x}(G)$, so the symmetric solution for all x_i is dependent on G. To compare this result to the monopolistically competitive equilibrium above, we should characterize this dependence. It is easy to see that the slope of the function $\bar{x}(G)$ is

$$\bar{x}'(G) = \frac{G}{\sqrt{G^2 + 1}} - 1.$$

As $\sqrt{G^2 + 1} > G$, $\bar{x}(G)$ is strictly decreasing and has its highest value at $G = 0$, which would imply $\bar{x} = 1$. However, for any $G > 0$, which is the relevant range, in the first-best optimum of the social planner $\bar{x} < 1$, which is smaller than in the equilibrium, hence M in the optimum must be higher than it was in the previous case.

In the final part of the paper, Romer uses the same production function in a dynamic problem. As a major difference from the previous static analysis, the stock of Z, now interpreted as a form of capital, can be modified by savings out of current production. There is a continuum of identical households, and a continuum of identical firms in the secondary sector. Their numbers are the same, so per capita and per firm quantities coincide. Households own the capital and rent it to firms in the primary sector (i.e., the producers of the intermediate input). Technology of the primary sector is described by the cost function in (4.3.4), to which the resource constraint in (4.3.5) still applies. For simplicity, $L = 1$ so that the dynamics of the capital stock is described by

$$\dot{Z} = Y(1, x) - c, \tag{4.3.14}$$

which is the usual neoclassical law of motion, where specifically $Y(1; x) = M(G + x)$. As is standard in one sector models, the output good can be either consumed or used as capital, so that consumption and capital will have the same price. Following the usual practice, Romer takes output as the numeraire so that the price of both capital and consumption is 1. As the same demand and cost conditions hold as in the previous static case, $\bar{x} = 1$ still holds, and the production function becomes $Y(t) = Z(t)(G + 1)$, where $M = Z$ due to the resource constraint. Now, the current value Hamiltonian for the representative household with the usual objective function

$$\int_0^\infty U[c(t)]\, e^{-\rho t}\, dt,$$

where

$$U(c)=\frac{c^{1-\sigma}-1}{1-\sigma} \text{ and } \sigma \in (0;\infty),$$

is

$$\hat{H}(Z;c;\Lambda)=\frac{c^{1-\sigma}-1}{1-\sigma}+\Lambda\left[Z(G+1)-c\right].$$

The first-order condition for c is $c^{-\sigma}=\Lambda$, from which $\dot{\Lambda}=-\sigma c^{-\sigma-1}\dot{c}$, and finally,

$$\frac{\dot{\Lambda}}{\Lambda}=-\sigma\frac{\dot{c}}{c}. \tag{4.3.15}$$

Note that as a necessary condition

$$\dot{\Lambda}-\rho\Lambda=-\Lambda(G+1), \tag{4.3.16}$$

also applies, where $(G+1)$ is the derivative of the law of motion with respect to the state (Z). By following Romer's suggestion that the problem should be solved by the same method as was applied in his 1986 paper (Romer, 1986a), we are supposed to use the asymptotic exponentials by Brock and Gale (1969) to characterize the behavior of variables at infinity. As the asymptotic exponential of a function is its elasticity, we have

$$\lim_{Z\to\infty} \log_Z \left|Z(G+1)\right|=1,$$

since the elasticity of the production function is simply

$$\frac{Z}{Z(G+1)}(G+1)=1,$$

therefore, when $Z\to\infty$, the production function $Z(G+1)$ becomes linear in Z. Its derivative in (4.3.16) is 1, instead of $(G+1)$, so in place of (16), we have

$$\frac{\dot{\Lambda}}{\Lambda}=\rho-1,$$

from which (4.3.15) implies that

$$\frac{\dot{c}}{c}=\frac{1-\rho}{\sigma},$$

so consumption grows at a constant rate toward infinity. The derivative of the Hamiltonian with respect to the costate yields the law of motion for the state, which asymptotically behaves as $\dot{Z}=Z-c$, also implying that

$$\frac{\dot{Z}}{Z}=1-\frac{c}{Z}.$$

Along the balanced growth path, Z is supposed to grow at a constant rate (both a declining or increasing rate would be suboptimal), which is possible only if Z grows at the same constant rate as c, therefore,

$$\frac{\dot{Z}}{Z}=\frac{1-\rho}{\sigma},$$

which is the desired result. Given that the household is representative, so its counterparts make the same decision, aggregate capital stock follows the same growth rate.

RCER WP 123 (March 1988) and Romer in Barro, ed. (1989)

Romer's RCER WP 123 "Capital Accumulation in the Theory of Long Run Growth" (Romer, 1988a) was written for publication in Barro's edited volume *Modern Business Cycle Theory*. It highlighted the renewed interest in growth theory with a focus on the accumulation of capital, after what Romer described as a period of "quiescence" (1988a, 1988b, 1988c, p. 1; 1989a, 1989b, 1989c, 1989d, 1989e, p. 51). In it, Romer first addressed classical questions regarding the reconciliation of rising income per capita with growth in population and diminishing returns. He noted that the literature of the 1960s had focused on exogenous explanations; however since then, it had moved from exogenous to endogenous factors to explain growth. According to Romer, models of 1960s vintage, such as those of Shell, Phelps, and von Weizsacker (see Chapter 1), were limited, in their explanatory power because of increasing returns. Moreover, Arrow (1962)'s "learning-by-doing" model which was based upon the assumptions of exogenous population, and the existence of a steady-state, was also limited in its efficacy. The model of endogenous technological change Romer first presented was based on his work from 1983 and 1986. In it, technology (A) was treated as a public good, influenced by investments in physical capital (K) and labor (L), with increasing returns to scale resulting when all three factors (K, L, A) were considered together. Romer noted that the previous models, mentioned above, were problematic due to increasing returns, as they assumed technology was exogenous. He maintained that empirical studies showed a correlation between physical capital investment and the extent of patenting; something that indicated a two-way relationship between them. By allowing technology (A) to vary, Romer maintained that all factors could not be compensated at their marginal products due to increasing returns, that a doubling of inputs could lead to more than a doubling of output, and that the investment rate and growth in population could affect the growth in income per capita.

In the RCER WP and the published version in Barro's volume, Romer then explained why, in his view, the Kuhn–Tucker approach was so important in dealing with dynamic equilibrium models, since it related maximization and saddle points in both suboptimal and optimal equilibrium, being a method that provided a unifying result based upon convex analysis, such that as he saw it, *the*

Kuhn-Tucker theorem was at the core of not only all equilibrium growth models, but of general equilibrium theory overall. As Romer (1988a, p. 17; 1989e, p. 70) put it:

> Growth is a general equilibrium process. All markets and all participants in an economy influence growth and are influenced by it. A growth theorist must therefore construct a dynamic general equilibrium model, starting with a specification of preferences and the technology, and specifying an equilibrium concept. To be able to say anything about the properties of the model beyond an assurance that some equilibrium exists, the theorist must be able to explicitly solve the model or at least give a qualitative description of the solution.

He went on to say:

> Either explicitly or implicitly, the central tool that is used in the characterization of dynamic competitive equilibrium models is the Kuhn-Tucker theorem. It offers a general procedure for reducing the problem of calculating a competitive equilibrium to the problem of solving a maximization problem. All of the theory of growth can be understood in terms of the application of this theorem to models with tractable functional forms for preferences and the technology.

Romer (1988a, p. 57; 1989e, p. 97) then set out a *taxonomy* of what he termed "recent models of growth." He identified *five* model types (Romer, 1988a, 1988b, 1988c, pp. 57–76; 1989a, 1989b, 1989c, 1989d, 1989e, pp. 97–113): (i) Arrow–Romer model, which incorporated endogenous technological change and increasing returns; (ii) Uzawa–Lucas model, which emphasized human capital and its role in economic growth; (iii) Linear (King & Rebelo, 1990); (iv) Krugman–Lucas model, which focused on trade and its implications for growth; (v) Marshall–Young–Romer model, which introduced monopolistic competition and the importance of new goods in growth. It shows similar behavior, in dynamic form, to models of competitive equilibrium with externalities.

The "Arrow-Romer" model explained how allowing technology to vary brings about increasing returns, which, in turn, impacts the distribution of both income and growth rates across countries. Moreover, allowing technology (A) to vary leads to the conclusion that all factors cannot be compensated at their marginal products due to increasing returns. The models suggest that doubling inputs can lead to more than double the output without changing the qualitative nature of technology. According to Romer, the "Uzawa-Lucas" model emphasizes human capital and its role in economic growth. Romer wrote that it incorporates human capital (H) alongside physical capital (K) and suggests they are good substitutes, allowing for increasing returns through direct human capital interactions, such as knowledge sharing and collaboration. Romer noted that in the "Uzawa-Lucas" model, unbounded growth could occur without sole reliance on increasing returns and that due to the higher ratio of K to H, wages would be higher in countries that were developed.

Romer then provided his interpretation of Krugman's model linking trade, increasing returns and growth. He noted that according to this model, increasing returns could overturn the conventional view on the impact of trade, such that countries could specialize in industries having slow rather than high learning rates, given the existence of multiple goods and trade dynamics that bring this about. Romer described what he called the "Marshall-Young-Romer" model, based on "monopolistic competition," which focused on the introduction of "new goods" as one of the drivers of growth. According to Romer, the model relied on fixed costs associated with producing new goods, that led, in turn, to external economies of scale, with the variety of goods available enhancing both productivity and growth. Romer (1989e, p. 97) wrote:

> The models of growth that have been proposed in the last few years, like all general equilibrium models, can be characterized in terms of the assumptions they make on preferences, the technology, and the equilibrium concept. In all but one case, the equilibrium concept for the model described here is a complete markets competitive equilibrium or a complete markets competitive equilibrium with externalities. The exception, the Marshall-Young-Romer model, *uses a notion of monopolistic competition*, but its dynamic behaviour is identical with that of a model of competitive equilibrium with externalities.

ROMER'S 1988 PAPERS AND CONFERENCE PRESENTATIONS

In several places, including papers presented at conference over the period 1988–1990, Romer referred to "Romer. P. 1988. 'Endogenous technological change' University of Chicago Working Paper." In May 1988, Romer presented a paper entitled "Endogenous Technological Change" (Romer, 1988b, 1988c), at a conference at the State University of New York at Buffalo on "The Problem of Development: Exploring Economic Development Through Free Enterprise," which appeared in Proceedings of the Institute's First International Conference, May 27–29, 1988, Part II, Institute for the Study of Free Enterprise Systems, State University of New York at Buffalo.

The reason for dealing with this presentation here is that it has been problematically represented by David Warsh (2006) in his book, *Knowledge and the Wealth of Nations*. According to Warsh (2006, p. 290),

> Among the papers presented in Buffalo … was Romer's "Micro Foundations for Aggregate Technological Change." The other papers swiftly faded into the background – Becker and Murphy's perfectly competitive model of the demographic transition, Krugman's attempt to link trade and growth, Jorgenson's study of the effects of tax policy on growth, another AK model in the spirit of Von Neumann. But "Micro Foundations" was the article that in due course would be retitled "Endogenous Technological Change" – that is, it would become Romer '90.

But an examination of the Buffalo Conference list of presentations and *subsequent publication in the same special issue* of *JPE* where Romer's paper appeared – and their citations – shows that other papers *were also widely cited*, such as those by Barro (1990), Becker et al. (1990), and King and Rebelo (1990) (see Appendix 2).

ROMER MAY 1988 BUFFALO CONFERENCE PAPER: A ROMERIAN *"FLOW DIAGRAM"*

In the Buffalo Conference version of his approach, Romer again linked up endogenous technical change, research, and human capital. What is interesting to note is that the little-known *Conference Volume* in which it appeared also contained a summary of the paper in which there appeared a four sector *Flow Diagram*: (i) Research and Design Sector; (ii) Household Sector; (iii) Intermediate Goods Sector; (iv) Final Goods Sector. This is, to our knowledge, *the only diagrammatic representation* of Romer's approach extant. It is important as it illustrates the *Stock-Flow* nature of his system, that is, the inter-relationship between the *Stock* of Knowledge and Designs, *and* the *Flows* of (i) inputs and outputs and *payments* for them and (ii) *new* designs increasing the stock of designs to produce new designs.

ROMER'S JULY 1988 NBER CONFERENCE PAPER AND 1989 NBER WPs

In July 1988, Romer presented his paper "Endogenous Technological Change" at the NBER's *Program in Economic Fluctuations* organized by Barro and Mankiw. The paper was discussed by Jorgenson. According to the NBER *Reporter* account of the meeting (Romer, 1988a, 1988b, 1988c, pp. 24–26):

> Romer presents a growth model that is driven by an endogenous process of discovery, innovation, invention, and refinement. Human capital is the key to producing these components of technological change. In equilibrium, the model has monopolistic competition; firms must charge a price higher than marginal cost to recoup their fixed investments in research. Romer concludes that the stock of human capital determines the rate of growth, that the employment of more human capital in research would raise growth, that integration into world markets increases growth rates, and that having a large population is not sufficient to generate growth.

In 1989, three NBER WPs by Romer appeared. The *first*, NBER WP 3098, dated September 1989 (Romer, 1989b), was entitled "Increasing Returns and New Developments in the Theory of Growth" (subsequently published in Barnett et al., 1991). In it, Romer stressed the importance of his utilization of the imperfect competition approach in his model. As he put it (Romer, 1989b, p. 6):

> The tools for undertaking the analysis of this kind of market and equilibrium were introduced by another of Allyn Young's students, Edward Chamberlain (1933), and independently by Joan Robinson (1933). These tools have only begun to be used for aggregate analysis of issues in trade and growth. It is sometimes supposed that a predisposition against government intervention explains the preference that economists have for models with perfect competition, but this does not explain why they should prefer models with externalities to ones with imperfect competition. A far more likely determinant of modelling strategy is technical difficulty. Perfect competition is the first pass model for many questions simply because it is the easiest model to describe and understand. Allowing for external effects in the next pass removes the presumption in favor of optimality but preserves price-taking behavior. The formal tools used in the analysis remain largely the same. Imperfect competition is naturally a last resort because it forces a more drastic change in the formal analysis of equilibrium and is associated with a much higher level of analytical difficulty than competition with external effects.
>
> Until the specification of the additively separable functional form for preferences over many goods (Dixit & Stiglitz, 1977) an aggregate analysis of a model with monopolistic competition was completely infeasible. With the interpretation of this functional as a production functional depending on a large number of intermediate inputs instead of a preference functional (Ethier,

> 1982), a dynamic aggregate analysis of a model with imperfect competition comparable to the Solow-Swan analysis of the competitive model can now be undertaken.

In November 1989, Romer's NBER WP 3173 with the title "Human Capital and Growth: Theory and Evidence" appeared (Romer, 1989c). It was subsequently published in the *Carnegie-Rochester Conference Series on Public Policy* (1990). Romer (1989c, p. 12) wrote:

> There have been repeated acknowledgments that the production of knowledge or technological change seems to conflict with the assumption of price-taking. Schumpeter (1942) gives one of the classic statements of the conflict between innovation and perfect competition. Arrow (1962), Shell (1966), and Wilson (1977) do so as well. Despite the central role played by knowledge or technology in models of growth, growth theory has tended not to dwell on this issue. The neoclassical model of exogenous technological change (as presented by Solow, 1956) implicitly acknowledges the nonrival aspects of knowledge – improvements in the technology can be exploited simultaneously by all firms – but it does not consider the possibility that knowledge is privately provided. Arrow (1962) allows for nonrival knowledge that is privately produced, but only as an unintended side effect of other activities. (Romer, 1986a, 1986b, 1986c) and Lucas (1988) introduces forms of knowledge that are partly excludable and rival, and partly nonexcludable and nonrival. As in the Arrow model, non-rival knowledge is produced only as a side effect of some other activity. All three of these models allow for spillovers, that is, problems relating to excludability of knowledge, but they do not address the conflict between nonrivalry and private creation of a good in competitive markets.

The *third* 1989 NBER paper circulated by Romer (1989d), NBER WP 3210, was dated December 1989 and entitled "Endogenous Technological Change." On the title page, Romer noted the following:

> [P]repared for the conference "The Problem of Economic Development," SUNY Buffalo, May 1988. I have benefited from the comments of many seminar and conference participants and two discussants (Rob Vishny, Buffalo May 1988, and Dale Jorgenson, NBER Economic Fluctuations meeting, July 1988) ... Discussions with Gary Becker, Karl Shell, Robert Lucas, Gene Grossman, and Elhanan Helpman were especially helpful.

In concise and lucid terms, Romer summed up his work from his 1987 AER paper to his 1989–1990 model that subsequently appeared in the JPE special issue based on the 1988 Buffalo Conference papers. He wrote (Romer, 1989d, p. 1):

> The argument presented in this paper is based on three premises. The first is that technological change – improvement in the instructions for mixing together raw materials – lies at the heart of economic growth ... The second premise is that technological change arises in large part because of intentional actions taken by people who respond to market incentives. Thus, the model is one of endogenous rather than exogenous technological change ... The third and most fundamental premise is that instructions for working with raw materials are inherently different from other economic goods. Once the cost of creating a new set of instructions has been incurred, the instructions can be used over and over again at no additional cost. Developing new and better instructions is equivalent to incurring a fixed cost. This property is taken to be the defining characteristic of technology.

Romer (1989d, p. 10) then said:

> The only way to accept all three of the premises ... is to return to the suggestion of Schumpeter (1942) and explicitly introduce market power. Shell (1973) described a model with a single monopolist who invests in technological change, but as he recognizes, it is difficult to give an

aggregate interpretation to a model dominated by a single firm. In a recent paper (Romer, 1987a, 1987b) presented a model with market power but also with free entry and many firms. It builds on the model of monopolistic competition in consumption goods formulated by Dixit and Stiglitz (1977), applied in a dynamic setting by Judd (1985), and extended to differentiated inputs in production by Ethier (1982). Like the present model, this model has the property that the size of the market affects the rate of growth, but the motivation for the presence of the fixed cost is not well articulated, and a separate role for human capital in the production of technological innovation is not emphasized. The extension of this model presented here tries to remedy these defects.

ROMER'S 1990 *JPE* PAPER

From what we have examined so far, it is clear that Romer was addressing three distinct problems in his analysis of the problem of endogenous growth. The first was the mathematical problem of how to ensure the existence of solutions to the private and public Ramsey optimizations when technology was allowed to exhibit increasing returns to scale. The second was the problem of separating the intertwined effects of human capital accumulation from knowledge creation. The third was how to model the impact of non-rival factors of production – the knowledge creation part of the second problem, which is to say, ideas – that gave rise to the increasing returns that drive growth.

The solutions to these three problems come together in Romer's 1990 "Endogenous Technological Change" (Romer, 1990c) paper published in the *Journal of Political Economy*. While we have covered most of the technical aspects of what is in this paper above, the intellectual impact of this paper lies in its clear identification of personal human capital accumulation as a finite-lived rival good specific to individuals, whether line workers, executives, or scientists. This is in contrast to research in the Lucas tradition which conflated human capital as a set of personal skills with the knowledge embedded in human capital and thus treated the accumulation of human capital as equivalent to the creation of new knowledge. Romer says most forcefully in this paper that ideas are non-rival. Once loose in the wild, they cannot be made proprietary. Hence, to capitalize on the value of new ideas, they must be kept secret or provided some form of intellectual property protection. Earlier work on spillover models, going back to Arrow (1962), made the non-rival benefits of new ideas immediately and publicly available as an external benefit to the economy. As we've noted before, though, the problem with this approach is that if there is any cost to producing new ideas, they won't be produced under this market structure. As Shell (1966) showed, when the cost of producing new ideas was compensated, and the ideas generated increasing returns, then the market structure would not be competitive. Romer (1987c) gave this idea new life by making use of the Dixit–Stiglitz model of monopolistic competition, and he borrowed from this earlier work in the 1990 paper to give the producers of new ideas monopoly control over ideas, now protected by appropriate intellectual property laws.

So, in summary, the reason the 1990 *JPE* paper gets more than 43,000 citations on Google Scholar while his 1987 *AER* paper gets only 3,000, and his 1986

Econometrica paper on the mathematical foundations of these models get 124 is due to the way the *JPE* paper pulls together the various strands of Romer's research into a single overarching model. This is, of course, also the reason this is the paper cited by the Nobel Committee in their awarding the 2018 prize in Economics to him.

ROMER'S POST-*JPE* PAPERS, 1990–1994

Most accounts of the Romer story end in 1990. But Romer's contributions to "New Growth" theory continued. In the period immediately following his 1990 *JPE* paper, Romer published several papers that extended his approach to human capital and productivity, economic integration, and introduced the notion of "idea gaps" and "object gaps."

CAPITAL, LABOR, AND PRODUCTIVITY (1990) *BPEA*

In this paper, Romer (1990b) discussed the relationship between growth in the labor force, accumulation of capital, and the impact of technological change on *productivity*. He first dealt with growth in Total Factor Productivity (TFP), comparing variations in cross-country TFP growth. He suggested that technological change may be slowed down by increases in the labor force, while on the other hand, technological change may be potentially speeded up by increases in capital; all this given that *educated* human capital is employed in applied R&D activities.

The theoretical model Romer presented in this paper linked technological change to *educated* human capital. It showed that, under certain conditions, an increase in labor force could actually impact negatively on technological change, while technological change may not be impacted by an increase in capital accumulation. This result contrasted with previous models that had indicated that capital and technological innovation were strongly complementary.

Romer found a positive correlation between growth rates and investment over the century, suggesting that an increase in investment did not necessarily lead to a proportional increase in technological change, indicating that an increase in investment correlated with a lower marginal product of capital. Regarding the relationship between productivity and growth in the labor force, Romer presented data that showed a negative correlation between them, suggesting that rapid growth in the labor force could result in a reduction in growth in productivity as a result of changes in the allocation of human capital, something which highlighted trends that indicated a negative impact on growth in labor productivity, as an outcome of the increase in the labor supply. He went on to discuss the link between per capita growth in GDP and investment and found that higher income levels were associated with higher rates of investment and saving, suggesting that an increase in the accumulation of capital did not necessarily result in a higher rate of technological change. Romer concluded that technological change and the growth in productivity may be positively influenced by the scarcity of labor.

ECONOMIC INTEGRATION AND GROWTH DYNAMICS (1991) *QJE*

In this paper (written jointly with Rivera-Batiz), Romer discussed the relationship between endogenous growth and economic integration, investigating how an increased flow of trade and ideas between similar developed economies could potentially result in an increase in the global growth rate. In the paper, models of R&D were specified and studied to determine how long-run growth was influenced by integration, arguing that *economic integration* would encourage the exploitation of increasing returns to scale in R&D sectors, significantly enhancing growth rates. The paper presented two models of R&D technology illustrating how different aspects economic integration could affect long-run economic growth. The first model, which was called "knowledge-driven" R&D, emphasized existing knowledge and human capital as inputs for producing *new designs*. The second model, which was termed "lab equipment" R&D, utilized the same inputs as manufacturing and allowed for a more integrated approach to research and production. The figure we now develop provides the gist of the "knowledge-driven" model.

In Fig. 5, based on Rivera-Batiz and Romer (1991), we can specify pairs of balanced growth paths on the production side based on a negative relationship between the interest rate and growth rate (r, g), which can be called the *Technology Curve*. The reason for specifying such a relationship follows from the fact that the return to an investment of labor in research is the stream of future net revenue

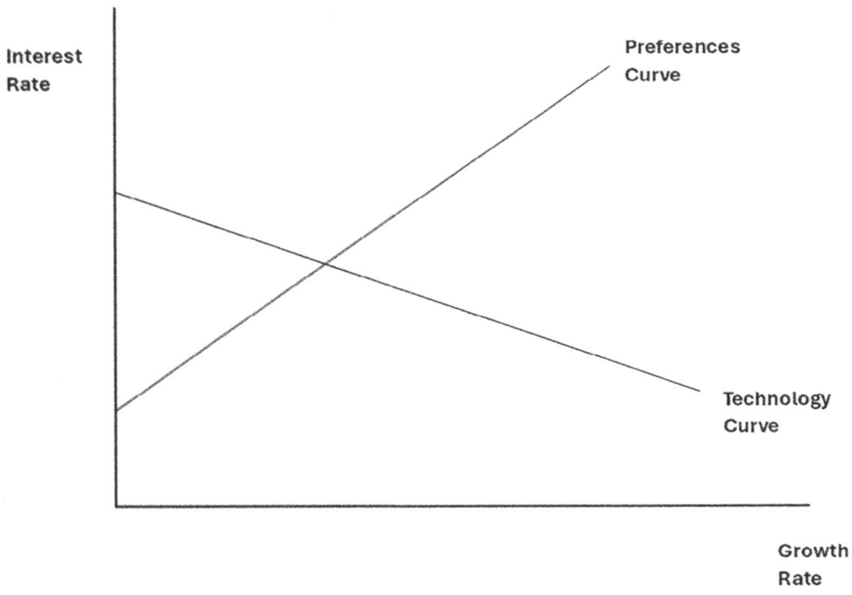

Fig. 5. Preferences and Technology Curves. *Source*: Adapted from Rivera-Batiz and Romer (1991).

that a design generates. The opportunity cost is then the wage rate received in the final goods sector. If there is a rise in the rate of interest, the present discounted value of the revenue stream will be lower than previously, bringing about a shift of labor into the final goods sector from the research sector, decreasing, in turn, the growth rate. On the consumption side, we can specify pairs of balanced growth paths illustrating a positive relationship between the growth rate and interest rate, which they call the *Preferences Curve*. As shown in the diagram below, the balanced growth path in this model is where the two curves intersect, which is a state of general equilibrium. They conclude that the balanced growth rate increases in *both* models after integration, indicating that integration is welfare-improving; however, the rate of growth under the condition of free trade may not reach that in the case of complete integration of economies, a result that highlights the importance of both ideas and goods in the growth process.

IDEA GAPS AND OBJECT GAPS IN ECONOMIC DEVELOPMENT (1993) *JME*

This paper deals with the *distinction* between *object gaps* and *idea gaps* in economic development and its implications for policy and growth. According to Romer, there are two types of "gaps" faced by developing nations, object gaps (lack of physical capital) and idea gaps (lack of knowledge), that may be concurrent and must be dealt with by means of differential policies. He maintained that to reduce both gaps, some conditions were required, among these supports for the educational system, a functioning legal system, and monetary policy stability. Romer observed that in the case of object gaps, countries lacking factories and infrastructure, human capital was an essential element, as it impacted on economic growth and productivity. He said that dealing with this gap involved long-term investment with accompanying high costs, which meant a pessimistic outlook for their future. Turning to idea gaps, Romer observed that this involved a lack of access to innovative processes and the knowledge that drove growth. He said that the scope of ideas included, beyond technology, a range of elements that included management, distribution, and marketing. Moreover, he noted that as ideas could be shared without incurring opportunity costs, the closing of idea gaps could be attained with relatively low costs. Turning to the role that could be played in this process by what he termed "Multinational Corporations," Romer said that they could bring about the flow of ideas between countries, thereby facilitating development. These corporations could assist developing countries to access technologies and knowledge via joint ventures and direct investment. Romer asserted that the available evidence showed that developing countries that had better access to foreign technologies and ideas had higher rates of economic growth.

Regarding implications for policy, Romer said that effective policies should create an environment encouraging foreign investment and the flow of ideas, and that governments in developing countries should not implement strategies of self-sufficiency by limiting interactions with other countries and the global

Table 1. Morphology of Romer's Models, 1983–1993.

Year	Model and Place of Publication	Returns	Competition	Extensions
1983	*Thesis*	*IRS*	*Perfect*	
1986	*RCER WP 64*		*Imperfect*	
1990	*JPE*			
1990	*BPEA*			*Productivity*
1991	*QJE*			*Trade and integration*
1993	*JME*			*Development*

Source: Compiled from Romer's publications 1983–1993.

economy. He noted that investments in infrastructure, legal systems, and education were necessary to improve the capacity of absorption of new ideas.

Table 1 provides what can be described as a morphological insight into the characteristics and development of Romer's models over the decade 1983–1993.

CHAPTER 5

AUGMENTED AK, POST-LUCAS, AND POST-ROMER MODELS AND RESEARCH PROGRAMS

In 1995, Charles Jones (1995) made a crucial observation about one of the implications of the new endogenous growth models developed five years earlier by Romer (1990a), Grossman and Helpman (1991), and Aghion and Howitt (1992)[1]: all of the models in these papers exhibited "scale effects" in the sense that doubling the number of workers dedicated to R&D doubled the growth rate of GDP. This is significantly at odds with the data, as shown in Fig. 6 (taken from Bloom et al., 2020). What the data show is what might be called (after Lewis Carroll) a "red queen" effect, where keeping the growth rate of the economy constant at a positive level requires devoting ever-increasing amounts of resources to research and development.

One can show the problems associated with scale effects in Romerian models by considering[2] a simple toy model in which the production of new ideas gives rise to an increasing returns to scale technology of the form

$$Y = A^{\sigma} L_Y,$$

where A is the stock of ideas and L_Y is the labor input to production. The stock of new ideas evolves as

$$\frac{\dot{A}}{A} = \delta L_A,$$

where L_A is the labor input to R&D. Finally, close the model by assuming that there is a constant fraction s of total labor devoted to production, and a fraction

[1]Both of these papers were circulated in working paper form in 1990 prior to their publication dates.
[2]This analysis is borrowed from Jones (1999).

Endogenous Growth: Theory, Methods and Morphology
International Symposia in Economic Theory and Econometrics, Volume 35, 127–140

Published under exclusive licence by Emerald Publishing Limited
ISSN: 1571-0386/doi:10.1108/S1571-038620260000035016

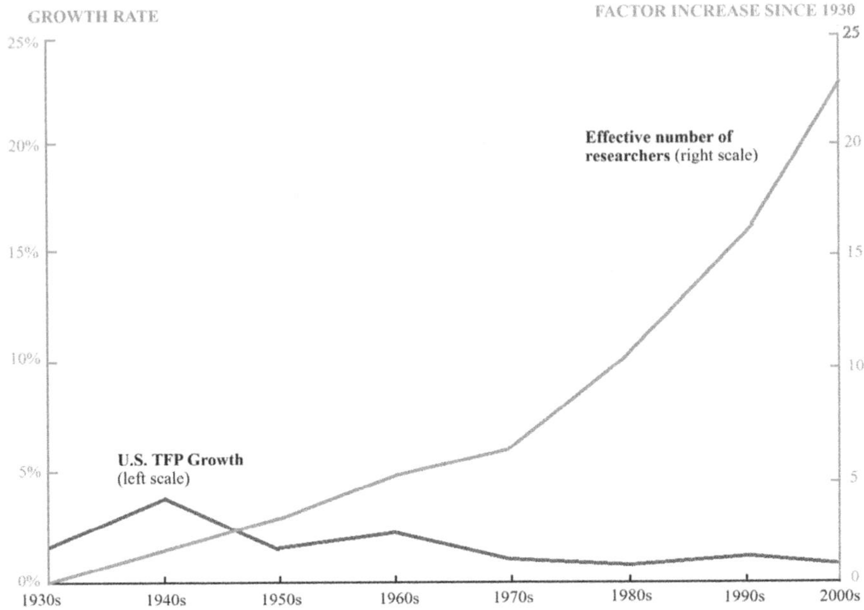

Fig. 6. Red Queen Effect.

(1–*s*) devoted to research. Taking logs and differentiating with respect to time then gives

$$\frac{\dot{Y}}{Y} = \sigma\frac{\dot{A}}{A} + \frac{\dot{L}}{L},$$

so that the per capita GDP growth rate is

$$g_y = \frac{\dot{Y}}{Y} - \frac{\dot{L}}{L} = \sigma\frac{\dot{A}}{A} = \sigma\delta sL.$$

This immediately implies that if populations L is growing exponentially, the growth rate of per capita GDP must also be growing exponentially. This is clearly contradicted by the data.

Having made this observation, Jones introduced a modification of the canonical endogenous growth model, which he dubbed semi-endogenous growth, by allowing for diminishing returns to scale in R&D activity. To illustrate Jones' model, we start with the basic Romerian endogenous growth framework. In this framework, the relationship between GDP growth and knowledge is captured by two equations:

$$Y = (K)^{1-\alpha}(AL_Y)^{\alpha},$$

$$\frac{\dot{A}}{A} = \delta L_A \tag{5.1}$$

where Y is output, K is capital, A is a measure of knowledge, and $L_i, i = Y, A$ is the labor input to production or the creation of new knowledge. The scale effect Jones identified is apparent here, since if the growth rate of GDP is proportional to the growth rate of knowledge, then both of these variables scale with L_A.

To address this problem, Jones develops an alternative model, which he calls semi-endogenous growth, by starting with the assumption that the creation of new knowledge is just proportional to the labor resources put into R&D:

$$\dot{A} = \bar{\delta} L_A.$$

To capture the fact that new knowledge builds on existing knowledge – Isaac Newton's invention of calculus (once he published it) allowed other scientists to extend this new mathematics in new and useful ways – by letting $\bar{\delta} = \delta A^{\phi}$ so that

$$\dot{A} = \delta A^{\phi} L_A. \tag{5.2}$$

As Jones notes, the parameter ϕ captures the possibility of external effects of existing knowledge on the creation of new knowledge. If $\phi < 0$, then the stock of knowledge is limited and can be depleted (or the process associated with research is constrained to consider only a fixed set of possible ideas), while $\phi > 0$, there are external increasing returns to knowledge creation. The borderline case of $\phi = 0$ is the original benchmark case where the creation of new ideas only depends on the labor input into R&D.

Finally, Jones also allows for the possibility of individual diminishing returns to the research input, so that

$$\dot{A} = \delta A^{\phi} L_A^{\gamma}, \tag{5.3}$$

with $0<\gamma\leq 1$. To then capture the fact that individual firms don't take account of what other firms are spending on R&D in their own R&D efforts, Jones rewrites equation 5.3 as

$$\dot{A} = \delta L_A A^{\phi} \ell_A^{\gamma-1},$$

where ℓ_A is the specific firm's input of labor to R&D. Of course, in equilibrium $L_A = \ell_A$, and if $\phi, \gamma = 1$, then we are back in the simple Romerian framework. In Jones' semi-endogenous setting, the growth rate of the knowledge in equilibrium is

$$\frac{\dot{A}}{A} = \delta L_A^{\gamma} A^{\phi-1}. \tag{5.4}$$

In a balanced growth steady state with the labor supply increasing, we need the right side of 5.4 to be constant. To determine the parameter values of ϕ and γ for which this will hold when the rate of growth of population is n, we log differentiate 5.4 with respect to time to get

$$0 = \gamma \frac{d}{dt} \ln L_A - (1-\phi) \ln A,$$

$$\Leftrightarrow 0 = \gamma g_L - (1-\phi) g_A,$$

where g_x is the growth rate of the variable x=L, A. From this, when the labor force is growing at rate n, we have

$$g_A = \frac{\gamma n}{1-\phi},$$

so that the growth rate of knowledge (and output; see Jones' appendix for derivations) depends on the parameters γ and ϕ and the exogenously give rate of population growth. This is what eliminates the scale effect and makes Jones' model semi-endogenous. In this model, the rate of growth of population determines the level of the growth rate of output, without generating exponential growth in the growth rate itself. Note also that in the Romerian case with $\phi = 1$, the steady state doesn't exist.[3]

After developing a full growth model (which we do not pursue here), Jones asks the obvious question of whether the semi-endogenous growth restrictions implied by the model have any testable implications. Cross-country comparisons of population growth and GDP growth show no consistent correlations, which is easily explained given the non-rival properties of ideas and the comparatively free flow of ideas and technology across international boundaries. Jones points out that there is a testable implication in the fact that the model predicts that growth in research intensity is what determines the rate of growth of knowledge and that this fact can be taken to data. He cites work by Kremer (1993) on the effects of sea-level rise after the ice ages in cutting off the Americas and Oceania from the technological developments in Europe and Asia over the following millennia. Kremer argues that the observed technological differences are consistent with the predictions of semi-endogenous growth models in terms of the differing degrees of resources devoted to the accumulation of technological knowledge. We will also argue below that the theory of recombinant growth developed by Martin Weitzman (1998) provides an important microfoundation for the semi-endogeneity of growth.

As Jones notes in his 1999 *American Economic Review* paper, the semi-endogenous growth model that he and others developed in the mid-1990s[4] generated a new conundrum even as they resolved the old one about scale effects. Looking back at Jones' formula for the growth rate of ideas,

$$g_A = \frac{\gamma n}{1-\phi}$$

it is apparent that without population growth, that is, $n > 0$, there can be no growth in output. As Jones himself notes

[3]Jones notes that in a model with capital accumulation (as well as knowledge accumulation) and labor force growth, the condition for the existence of a balanced growth steady state is that the returns to scale for both accumulable inputs must be less than unity.
[4]The other papers addressing the issue of scale affects that came out during this period were Kortum (1997) and Segerstrom (1998).

> [E]liminating the scale effects induces a return to Solow-like implications for long-run growth. In the extended model, long-run per capita growth depends only on parameters that are usually taken to be exogenous and is therefore independent of policy changes such as subsidies to R & D or subsidies to capital accumulation. (Jones, 1995, p. 760)

Since the original intent in the first endogenous growth models of Romer, Grossman and Helpman, and Aghion and Howitt was to provide an explanation of economic growth that wasn't dependent on population growth, the semi-endogenous approach seems like something of a throwback. As Jones notes, however, the model does show that growth rate of per capita income can exceed the growth rate of population, which was one of the key observations that led economists to explore the possibilities of endogenous growth in the first place. Nevertheless, the implication of the semi-endogenous approach that growth would halt as population growth did was troubling, and it led to a number of new papers that attempted to merge the original results of the Romerian approach with the kinds of mitigating factors that Jones and others explored for removing scale effects.

Jones (1999) identifies a set of follow-on papers by Dinopoulos and Thompson (1999), Peretto (1998), Young (1998) which deal with the problem of pure semi-endogeneity by including sectoral growth in response to population increase while R&D accumulations to knowledge occur within sectors. This eliminates the scale effects of the Romerian models but retains the purely endogenous growth response to the creation of new knowledge.

These new models introduce sectoral growth via a Dixit–Stiglitz preference for variety. Following Jones' analysis, aggregate consumption is given by a CES aggregator over a large variety of goods (as in Romer's original model):

$$C = \left[\int_0^B Y_i^{1/\theta} di \right]^\theta,$$

where the parameter B measures the variety of goods available, Y_i is the amount of good i produced, and θ determines the elasticity of substitution between the various goods.

Along a balanced growth path, we can assume that $B = L^\beta$, where L is the labor input and β is any real number. To illustrate the operation of the model, assume that all goods i are produced in the same amount Y. Then,

$$C = B^\theta Y.$$

Per capita consumption will then be given by $c = B^\theta y$ so that

$$\ln c = \theta \ln B + \ln y.$$

With production per capital dependent on the usual inputs plus the accumulation of new knowledge, as in the original Romerian models, the steady-state balanced rate of growth for per capita consumption will be

$$g_c = \theta g_B + g_{A.}$$

From the specification that the variety grows as population does, $g_B = \beta g_L = \beta n$, so that

$$g_c = \theta\beta n + g_A.$$

The growth rate of ideas in these models now depends on research effort per variety

$$g_A = \frac{\delta s L}{B} = \delta s L^{1-\beta},$$

where δ is the relevant proportionality factor for the balanced growth path and s is the fraction of labor devoted to R&D. Under the assumption that $\beta = 1$, g_A will be independent of population growth. So, with the Dixit–Stiglitz mechanism in place, and dependence of production on new ideas as in the Romerian models, overall growth in per capita consumption now depends both on population

Table 2. Equations of Models by "Generation."

"First Generation" R/GH/AH models

$$Y = A^{\sigma} L_Y. \qquad (1)$$

$$\frac{\dot{A}}{A} = \delta L_A. \qquad (2)$$

$$g_y \equiv \frac{\dot{Y}}{Y} - \frac{\dot{L}}{L} = \sigma\delta s L. \qquad (3)$$

"Second Generation" J/K/S models

Equation (2) "production function" for new ideas is replaced in these types of models by

$$\dot{A} = \delta L_A A^{\phi} \qquad (4)$$

$$g_y = \sigma g_A = \frac{\sigma n}{1-\phi}$$

"Third Generation" Y/P/AH/DT models

$$g_c = \theta\beta n + \sigma\delta s L^{1-\beta 1}$$

Jones; "General Model" (1999)

$$g_c = \theta\beta n + \sigma\delta s \frac{L^{1-\beta}}{A^{1-\phi}}$$

Where

Y = output
A = stock of ideas
L = total labor force
L_Y = L not engaged in research
L_A = L engaged in research
g_y = growth rate of output per worker
g_c = per capita output growth
n = growth rate of total labor force
g_A = growth rate of knowledge

σ = degree of increasing returns
δ = *parameter* of proportionality
s = fraction of labor force in research
ϕ = "research intensity"
θ = product elasticity of substitution
β = variety of consumption goods
g_y = growth rate of output per worker
n = growth rate of total labor force

Source: Adapted from Jones (1995, 1999).

Table 3. Research Intensity Parameters.

	Research Intensity (ϕ), Consumption Goods Variety (β), Model/Stability			
Values of ϕ and β	$\phi = 1$ $\beta < 1$	$\phi > 1$ and $\beta > 1$ $\phi < 1$ and $\beta < 1$ $\phi < 1$ and $\beta > 1$	ϕ and $\beta = 1$	$\phi > 1$ and $\beta < 1$
Model type/stability	R/GH/A	J/K/S or unstable	Y/P/AH/DT	Unstable

Source: Diagram and table adapted from Jones (1999).

growth and on the growth of new ideas (independent of population growth). As Jones notes, though, if $\beta \neq 1$, then the model again exhibits scale effects so that these results are very much a knife-edge case.

Tables 2 and 3 and Fig. 7 are adapted from Jones' papers (1995, pp. 761–769; 1999, pp. 140–143). Together, they provide a comparative perspective on what Jones called "generations" of Post-Romer Models of growth.

The fact that semi-endogenous growth leaves no room for any useful policies for determining long-run rates of economic growth stimulated additional follow-on work by Peretto and Smulders (1998) and Howitt (1999) using multi-sector R&D models to show that the scale effects of population growth could be removed by combining growth in variety with growth in quality (as in the modeling framework just analyzed), while allowing for endogenous policy actions to have an effect in determining the mix of variety and quality produced along a balanced growth path. This approach was subsequently reexamined by Li (2000) who made the observation that in the Peretto-Smulders and Howitt papers, spillovers between sectors were not permitted, when in fact such spillovers are well-documented in the empirical literature. Li demonstrates that this makes a significant difference. While Li's model is complex, his result is fairly easy to show (as Li himself does

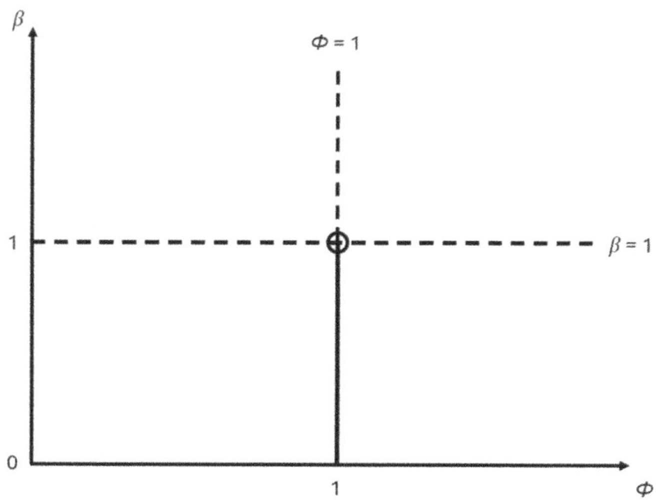

Fig. 7. "Generations" of Models – Stability.

at the start of the paper). Like Howitt's model, Li assumes there are two R&D sectors, one which increases the variety N of inputs to the production of the final consumption good, and the other which increases the quality Q of these inputs. Li specifies the change in each of these quantities by

$$\dot{N} = \frac{R_N}{Q} Q^{\delta_N} N^{\varphi_N},$$

and

$$\dot{Q} = \frac{R_Q}{N} Q^{\delta_Q} N^{\varphi_Q},$$

where $R_i, i = N, Q$ is the number of workers in sector i. The ratios of workers to sectoral knowledge levels reflect a fundamental diminishing returns assumption: as varieties or quality increase, the fixed number of workers must be spread more thinly across the production processes for each type of knowledge. The exponents $\delta_Q, \delta_N, \varphi_Q$, and φ_N reflect the within sector spillover effects that are assumed away in the earlier multi-sector models.[5] From these specifications, it is straightforward to derive the growth rates for quality and variety as

$$g_N = \frac{R_N}{N^{1-\delta_N} Q^{1-\varphi_N}},$$

$$g_Q = \frac{R_Q}{N^{1-\delta_Q} Q^{1-\varphi_Q}}.$$

To avoid the scale effects problem here, we need these two growth rates to be constant on a long-run balanced growth path. Log differentiating these expressions with respect to time, letting the growth rate of population (and hence workers) be γ, we will get

$$0 = \dot{g}_N = \gamma - (1-\varphi_N) g_N - (1-\delta_N) g_Q,$$

and

$$0 = \dot{g}_Q = \gamma - (1-\varphi_Q) g_N - (1-\delta_Q) g_Q$$

This gives us two equations in two unknowns

$$\begin{bmatrix} \gamma \\ \gamma \end{bmatrix} = \begin{bmatrix} 1-\varphi_N & 1-\delta_N \\ 1-\varphi_Q & 1-\delta_Q \end{bmatrix} \begin{bmatrix} G_N \\ G_Q \end{bmatrix}.$$

As long as the coefficient matrix here is non-singular, we will find that the two knowledge growth rates are functions of the population growth, that is, we have semi-endogenous growth. As Li points out, if $\gamma = 0$ and $\delta_N = \delta_Q = \varphi_N = \varphi_Q = 1$, then we have $g_N = R_N$ and $g_Q = R_Q$ and the model exhibits scale effects. If the spillover coefficients are all less than one, then long-run growth without population

[5]See Li's references for empirical evidence in favor of including these spillover effects.

increase is impossible, since the denominators in the two growth expressions go to infinity as the two knowledge sectors grow. The case where some coefficients are bigger than one leads to explosive growth, which we can rule out for the same empirical reasons that lead us to reject scale effects. One can obtain endogenous growth by, for example, taking $\delta_N = \delta_Q = 1$ and $\varphi_N = \varphi_Q = 0$ (which, as Li notes, captures features of the previously cited two-sector models). In this case, we have $\gamma = g_N$ and g_Q is indeterminate. These knife-edge results then indicate that semi-endogenous growth will be generic.

The next argument in the endogenous versus semi-endogenous growth debate appears in Cozzi (2017). The model proposed in this paper is a hybrid of the one-sector semi-endogenous growth model of Jones and a fully endogenous growth model along the lines of Peretto–Smulders–Howitt. Cozzi proposes that the actual growth in knowledge is a convex combination of the semi-endogenous and fully endogenous processes

$$\frac{\dot{A}(t)}{A(t)} = \alpha\gamma\frac{L_A(t)^{\lambda}}{A(t)^{1-\phi}} + (1-\alpha)\gamma\left[\frac{L_A(t)}{L(t)}\right]^{\lambda}, 0 < \alpha < 1. \tag{5.5}$$

Here, the first term is the semi-endogenous knowledge accumulation process of Jones, and the second term is the fully endogenous process of PSH.[6] Cozzi notes that while it is tempting to then assume that the growth rate of knowledge will then be a convex combination of the rates generated by these two processes, this is in fact wrong.

To show this, consider what happens if the growth rate of population goes to zero. Then in the first term in equation (5.5) will go to zero since $L_A(t)$ is constant while $A(t)$ is going to infinity. Hence, in the limit we have

$$g_A = (1-\alpha)\gamma s_A(t),$$

where $s_A(t)$ is the share of labor devoted to knowledge creation. Cozzi then identifies a cut-off population growth level

$$\bar{n} = (1-\alpha)\gamma s_A\frac{(1-\phi)}{\lambda},$$

such that if the actual rate of population growth is less than $\bar{n}$, then the overall growth rate of knowledge will approach $(1-\alpha)\gamma s_A$. To see this, note that when $n < \bar{n}$, the rate of growth of knowledge will be no smaller than the rate of growth due to the fully endogenous component. This then implies that knowledge is growing faster than what could be sustained by semi-endogenous population effects so that the left-hand term of equation (5.5) is going to zero. When $n \geq \bar{n}$, we will have

[6]One can relate the specification of the fully endogenous process back to the varieties model by noting that the number of varieties grows as population grows so that it is the ratio of the labor input to knowledge production to total labor that determines the endogenous growth rate.

$$g_A = \alpha\gamma \lim_{t\to\infty} \frac{L_A(t)^{\lambda}}{A(t)^{1-\phi}} + (1-\alpha)\gamma s_A.$$

This will be a finite constant if and only if the asymptotic growth rate is

$$g_A = \frac{\gamma n}{1-\phi}.$$

Hence, in this case, semi-endogenous growth dominates.

While the 2017 publication date for Cozzi's paper would seem to be the most recent word on the semi-endogenous versus fully endogenous growth debate, there is an additional contribution worth examining. Weitzman (1998) introduced the idea of recombinant growth as a way of microfounding how new ideas come into being. The essence of Weitzman's argument is that new ideas are based on combining existing ideas in ways that produce new and useful outcomes. Because of the way the possible number of combinations grows, Weitzman's model is capable of generating growth that exceeds the conventional exponential mechanisms. Mathematically, Weitzman uses the number of combinations of k ideas out of a pool of N total ideas,

$$C_k(N) = \binom{N}{k} = \frac{N!}{k!(N-k)!},$$

Table 4. Combinatorial, Factorial, and Geometric Growth.

X	2^x	x_Factorial	Combinatoric			
1	2	1				
2	4	2	$N(t+1)$	$N(t)$	$N(t-1)$	Psi
3	8	6	2.4	2	1	0.4
4	16	24	2.672	2.4	2	0.272
5	32	120	2.893517	2.672	2.4	0.221517
6	64	720	3.095785	2.893517	2.672	0.202268
7	128	5,040	3.297619	3.095785	2.893517	0.201835
8	256	40,320	3.515335	3.297619	3.095785	0.217715
9	512	362,880	3.768449	3.515335	3.297619	0.253114
10	1,024	3,628,800	4.086552	3.768449	3.515335	0.318103
11	2,048	39,916,800	4.522671	4.086552	3.768449	0.436119
12	4,096	479,001,600	5.186376	4.522671	4.086552	0.663705
13	8,192	6,227,020,800	6.342424	5.186376	4.522671	1.156048
14	16,384	8.7178E+10	8.776783	6.342424	5.186376	2.434359
15	32,768	1.3077E+12	15.65103	8.776783	6.342424	6.874244
16	65,536	2.0923E+13	47.86072	15.65103	8.776783	32.2097
17	131,072	3.5569E+14	450.5576	47.86072	15.65103	402.6969
18	262144	6.4024E+15	40,512.32	450.5576	47.86072	40,061.77
19	524,288	1.2165E+17	3.28E+08	40,512.32	450.5576	3.28E+08
20	1,048,576	2.4329E+18	2.15E+16	3.28E+08	40,512.32	2.15E+16
21	2,097,152	5.1091E+19				
22	4,194,304	1.124E+21				

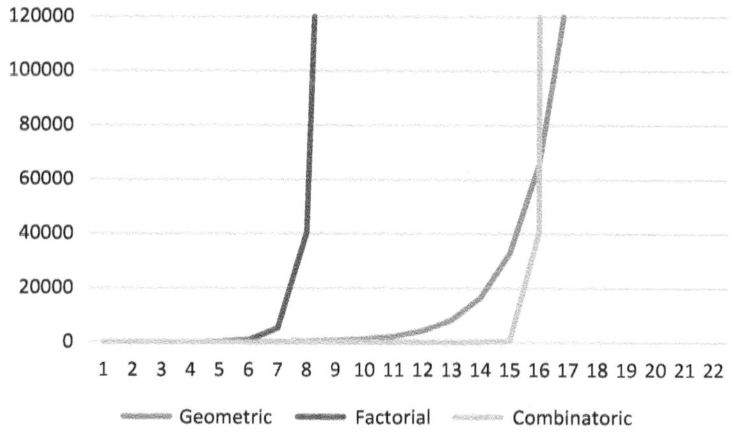

Fig. 8. Combinatorial Versus Exponential Growth.

as the basis for his model of newly produced ideas. If the economy starts with some number N_t of existing ideas, then at time *t+1*, we will have $N_{t+1} = C_k(N_t)$ potentially useful new ideas. Hence, the growth in the number of potential ideas at any given time will be

$$C_k(N_t) - C_k(N_{t-1}).$$

Weitzman then assumes that some proportion α of these new ideas will actually be useful, leading to his fundamental growth relationship for ideas

$$N_{t+1} - N_t = \alpha\left[C_k(N_t) - C_k(N_{t-1})\right]. \tag{5.6}$$

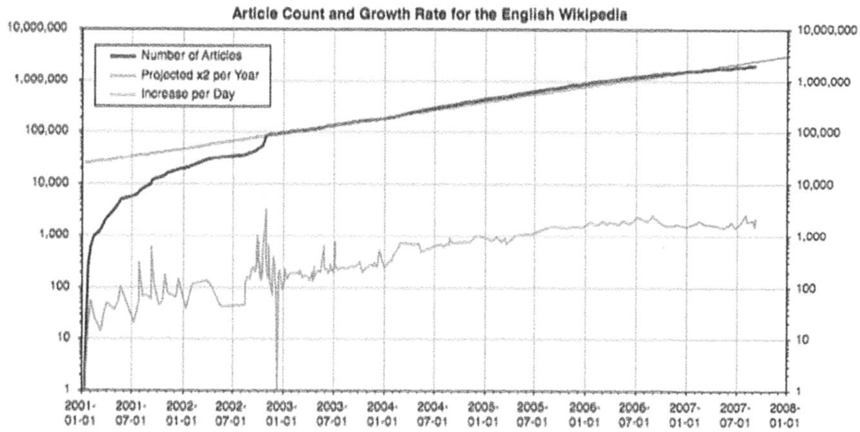

Fig. 9. Wikipedia Growth Experience.

Weitzman then shows in his first lemma that for the case where $k = 2$, the growth process generated by equation (5.6) exceeds that of a geometric growth process. We can illustrate this result with some simple calculations. In Table 4, we show the growth of an integer variable x for geometric, factorial, and combinatoric processes. For the combinatoric process, we set Weitzman's $\alpha = 0.2$.

Fig. 8 plots the graphs of these three growth processes.

From the graphs, it is clear that the combinatoric process eventually becomes explosive. So, a natural question is do we see this in the real world? Fig. 9 shows the growth (in log scale) for the number of articles in Wikipedia after its initial launch.[7]

In the figure, the orange line indicates exponential growth, while the solid blue line is the actual number of articles. In the period from the beginning of 2001 until 2003, the growth is clearly explosive, though it eventually settles down to simple exponential growth after 2003.

Weitzman then constructs a formal model of endogenous growth based on the recombinant growth of ideas. In the interests of brevity, we forgo a full exposition of Weitzman's model but refer the interested reader to the paper. But we do note two key features. First, as Weitzman notes, the ultimate limiting factor that determines the actual growth rate of GDP in his model is the availability of resources devoted to the creation of new knowledge. Second, in the limit along a balanced growth path, Weitzman shows that the growth rate is constant (and hence exponential), and that the long-run ratio of the stock of capital to the stock of ideas is given by

$$\frac{K^*}{A^*} = \frac{s_1 c^*}{s_2}.$$

Here, c^* is the average real resource expected to be spent per successful new idea, under the assumption that seed ideas are so abundant that their availability is not the operative constraint in determining this cost. The parameter s_1 is the asymptotical savings rate of the economy, s_2. is the fraction of total resources devoted to the creation of new ideas, and $s_1 + s_2 = 1$. If we interpret s_2 as the fraction of the labor force devoted to ideas production, then we obtain a standard endogenous growth interpretation of Weitzman's model.

Weitzman also examines an extension of the model in which the labor input is allowed to grow and notes that if the fraction of labor devoted to ideas production is held constant, but the actual amount of labor in the knowledge sector is growing, then the model exhibits the same scale effects as the original Romerian models. Weitzman shows that one can accommodate labor force growth without scale effects by assuming that the effect of population growth on ideas enters linearly rather than multiplicatively, but, as he notes, it is hard to come up with a compelling story as to why this should be the case.

It is also possible that there is some version of the diminishing returns to the production of ideas modification in the combinatorial growth setting that would

---

[7]Figure used under GNU Free Documentation License.

render the equilibrium semi-endogenous. What form this might take is hard to make out without detailed analysis, but it is surely the case that Weitzman's formulation, in which simple recombination of ideas leads to new productive ideas, oversimplifies what researchers actually do. Pursuing this idea further, connecting two ideas in a way that makes the combination useful requires the effort of discerning the connection, as well as insight into why the connection makes the

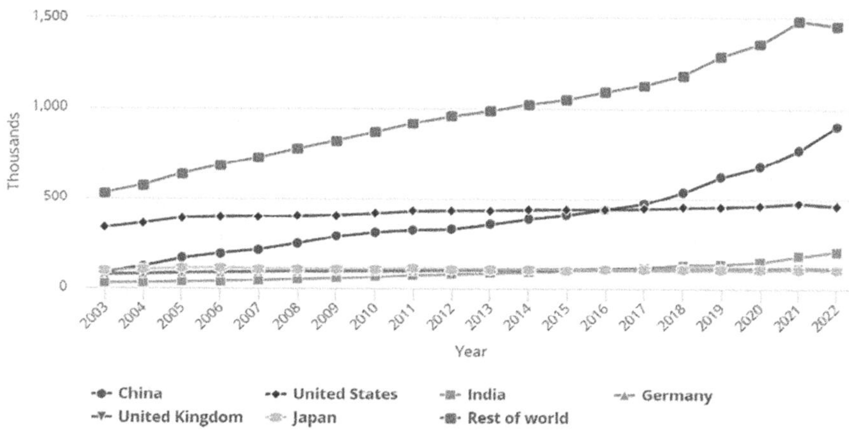

Fig. 10. International Employment in Science and Engineering.

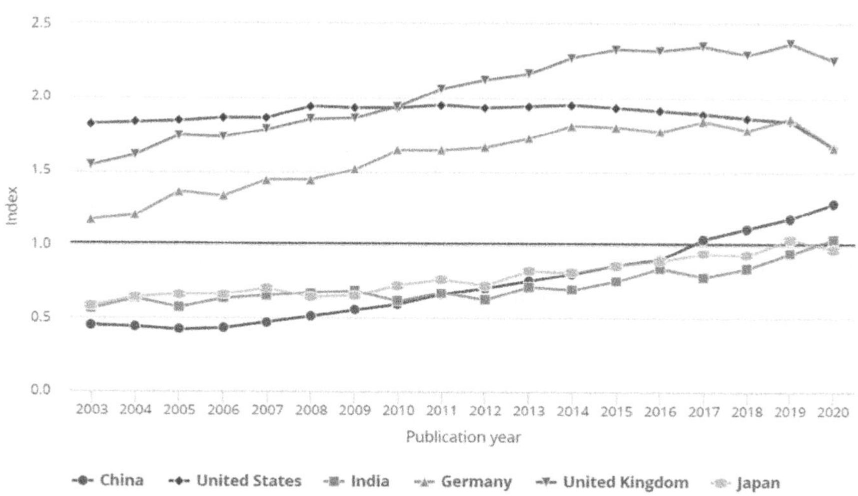

Fig. 11. International Citations.[8]

[8]Source for both graphs: "The State of U.S. Science and Engineering," National Science Board, NSB-2024-3.

combination useful. This is likely a hugely time-consuming process. For example, think of the time between Fermat's famous "last theorem" conjecture in 1637 and Andrew Wiles proof of the result in 1993. The process of developing new ideas into new technologies and then incorporating these in production is also a time-consuming process, and at each step, a different kind of expertise and training is required for success. So, clearly, modeling these processes requires detailed consideration of the human capital accumulation process as well.

If we view human capital as putty when it is undertaken but clay once it is put in place, then population dynamics – not necessarily growth, but the turnover of the lifecycle – become important in allowing new ideas to be embodied in new forms of human capital that are then allocated to the various processes of idea discovery, development, and deployment as technology. It is entirely conceivable that in this process, the amount of actual human labor allocated to the process of recombinant discovery remains constant, even as the ideas discovered become more complex. There is some empirical support for this conjecture. Fig. 10 shows science and engineering employment between 2003 and 2022 for various regions of the world. For all of the countries listed, with the exception of China, the employment levels are effectively constant.

Fig. 11 shows an index of highly cited science and engineering articles for 2003 to 2020. The U.S. citation rate is high and virtually constant. The increasing rates for the other listed countries likely reflect "catching up" with U.S. dominance in STEM fields.

Putting this evidence together with Cozzi's hybrid model of semi-endogenous and fully endogenous growth, the fact of low population growth rates in developed countries suggests that a model in which basic research is carried out by a small and relatively fixed proportion of the country's population does explain the initial data anomaly identified by Jones.

Before we leave the topic of post-Romerian growth theory, we should note that there is another distinct branch of endogenous growth theory, that of Schumpeterian growth, that has also had a substantial impact on the way economists think about growth. As the Schumpeterian characterization implies, this branch of theory develops the ideas of Joseph Schumpeter (1942) about the role of "creative destruction," market organization, and firm dynamics in driving growth as new ideas and technologies drive old forms of industrial organization out of the market in favor of the new forms. We do not delve into this branch of endogenous growth theory given our focus on the Lucas–Romer nexus in the initial development of endogenous growth but refer the reader to the excellent summary by Aghion et al. (2015). We do note that both the Romerian and Schumpeterian approaches emphasize the role of basic and applied research as drivers of new technologies (what Shell referred to as "inventive activity") and so turn next to an examination of the economics of research.

CHAPTER 6

UNDERSTANDING RESEARCH

As we have seen from earlier chapters, the mainstream economic approach to incorporating the creation of scientific knowledge in models of endogenous economic growth has followed two distinct paths. One, the Schumpeterian approach assumes that new ideas find their way into and are expressed by the firms in the economy through their investments in research and development (R&D). In this approach, firms invest in knowledge creation to improve the productivity of their workers, which in turn yields higher profit. The other, the human capital approach (which we will call Lucasian after Bob Lucas' work on these models), assumes that new ideas (created by some other non-economic process) are embedded in the skills of the firms' workers who then bring these new ideas to bear on production in the firms where they work. In this approach, workers invest in human capital accumulations to enhance their own productivity and earnings, made possible by the enhanced ability of firms to produce output. We note, however, that contemporary models of human capital accumulation tend to follow what we have described earlier as the Shell–Romer approach which recognizes that the increasing returns to scale that innovation makes possible lead to firms having market power, necessitating the use of models of imperfect competition.

We have argued earlier that economists have very little they can say about how new ideas are created, since this question properly belongs to the domain of cognitive psychology. The two approaches, then, focus on two distinct aspects of the way economic entities internalize and structure the application of new ideas to production. In this sense, the two approaches resemble the proverbial blind men and the elephant in highlighting different aspects of the same process. The Schumpeterian approach points up the importance of applications of new technological ideas in generating growth, while the Lucasian approach emphasizes the fact that new ideas must be communicated and embodied in the human beings who constitute the firm for them to have any positive effects on growth.

That the two approaches really are complementary is apparent from examining the sources of funding for research broadly defined and by the structural units

Endogenous Growth: Theory, Methods and Morphology
International Symposia in Economic Theory and Econometrics, Volume 35, 141–164

ISSN: 1571-0386/doi:10.1108/S1571-038620260000035019

of the economy in which the different kinds of research activities are done. The chart below (from the National Science Foundation, https://ncses.nsf.gov/pubs/ncses22209) shows the source of funds and performance sector for three broad categories of research: development, applied research, and basic research. From the NSF definitions,

> Development is the systematic use of the knowledge or understanding gained from research directed toward the production of useful materials, devices, systems, or methods, including the design and development of prototypes and processes.
>
> The objective of applied research is to gain the knowledge or understanding to meet a specific, recognized need. In industry, applied research includes investigations to discover new scientific knowledge that has specific commercial objectives with respect to products, processes, or services.
>
> The objective of basic research is to gain more comprehensive knowledge or understanding of the subject under study without specific applications in mind. In industry, basic research is defined as research that advances scientific knowledge but does not have specific immediate commercial objectives, although it may be performed in fields of present or potential commercial interest.

From the chart (Fig. 12), it is clear that development and applied research are funded almost entirely by industry, while basic research is funded by the federal government and universities. Development and applied research are carried out, for the most part, by industry, while basic research is carried out by universities. This dichotomy is entirely consistent with the two distinct approaches that economists have taken to modeling how the economy uses new ideas. What is missing, though, is any attempt to examine the economic structuring of how foundational knowledge generated by basic research finds its way into the firm. Much of the reason for this is likely due to the fact that universities don't function the way firms do, with their focus on profit maximization and relatively simple objectives like shareholder or stakeholder value maximization.

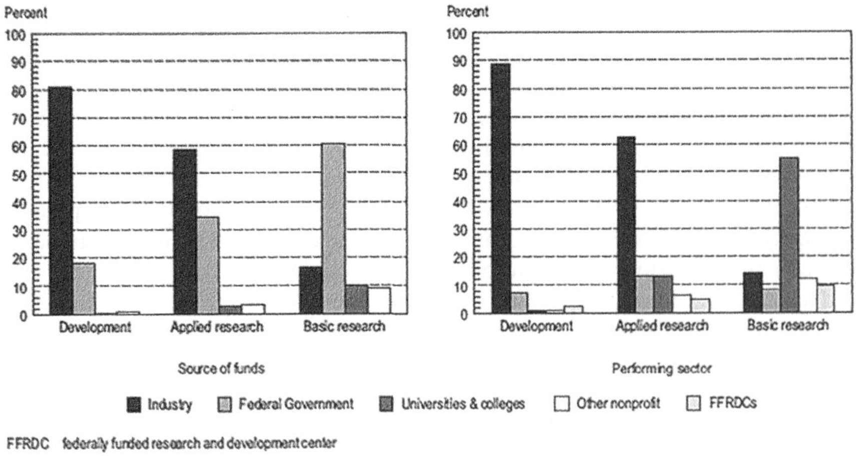

Fig. 12. U.S. Research Funding. *Source*: National Science Foundation, Division of Science Resources Statistics, *Naitonal Patterns of R & D Resources,* annual series. See appendix tables B-1 through B-8.

There have been a few papers published since the late 1990s that attempt to deal with the question of how research activities should be organized and rewarded. Among the most highly cited papers are Manso (2011), Aghion et al. (2008), and Stern (2004). All of these papers make the fundamental point that standard profit motives don't incentivize basic research. Rather, there is an inherent preference for this kind of work that motivates scholarship and scientific inquiry.

We examine each of these major papers in chronological order, turn to a new paper that links these issues of compensation and the organization of basic research with the received endogenous growth framework, and finally, present a new model of the agency relationships at work in university settings that combine both the creation of new knowledge and the embedding of this new knowledge in human capital through teaching.

INCENTIVES TO INNOVATE

Stern's early work on compensating innovation provided an empirical examination of the trade-off between what he called "the taste for science" and the fact that scientific breakthroughs generate greater productivity and, hence, potential gains to compensation for research. Stern's empirical model posits that firms engaged in R&D differentially adopt approaches that either do or do not support basic research by their employees. Workers in the science-based firms have preferences over both compensation and research directly, and Stern allows for heterogeneity in preferences in the sense that scientists of higher ability put more weight on the research component. Firms in the model benefit from the quality of the scientific talent they hire, but, if they take an approach supportive of basic research, they also incur a cost for activities like conference travel and independent, possibly non-germane work by their scientists. Hence, firms in the model face a key trade-off between benefitting from the outputs of more talented scientists but needing to support the preference-induced costs associated with hiring higher ability researchers.

For specificity, we reproduce Stern's reduced form econometric model here. The model posits a large number of firms, indexed by j, who can choose whether the orientation of their R&D efforts, which Stern splits into two categories: scientific or non-scientific. This distinction is implemented in the model via a dummy indicator variable, SCI = 1 if the firm's R&D has basic research components or SCI = 0 if it does not.

Firms then hire researchers from a population of workers indexed by I. For simplicity, Stern assumes they hire a single researcher with an observable (but random) ability γ_i. The firm's ability to hire qualified researchers is constrained by a firm-specific distribution of possible abilities denoted by $g_j(\gamma)$ which is bounded below by zero and has mean $\bar{\gamma}_j$. Each workers utility from a job offer is given by

$$U_i = \alpha_0 + \alpha_s \gamma_i \mathrm{SCI}_j + w_j,$$

where w_j is the wage paid by firm j. The rationale for the second term derives from (as Stern notes) the priority-based reward system prevalent in scientific research.

Firms in the model earn profits given by

$$\pi_{ij} = \gamma_i \left[\beta_0 + \beta_S \mathrm{SCI}_j \right] - w_{ij} - \delta \mathrm{SCI}_j.$$

This specification of the profit function reflects the assumption that the firm's scientific orientation enhances the productivity of the researchers it hires, even as it pays a fixed cost δ for providing this environment. Because the firm's scientific orientation enables it to attract more productive researchers, it generates a surplus. Stern assumes this surplus is split between the firm and researcher using a Nash bargaining solution with bargaining power given by a parameter $\vartheta \in (0,1)$ (see Stern and references therein for details on this). This bargaining process determines a wage function of the form

$$w_{ij}^{*} = \gamma_i \beta_0 + \gamma_i \left[\vartheta \beta_s - \alpha_s \right] \mathrm{SCI}_j.$$

The wage equation also determines the conditions under which a firm will invest in basic research:

$$\mathrm{SCI}_j = 1 \text{ if } f \bar{\gamma}_j > \frac{\delta}{(1-\vartheta)\beta_s - \alpha_s}.$$

This condition derives from the requirement that the firm's expected profit from hiring scientific researchers is positive, and it states that the cost–benefit ratio from providing an environment amenable to basic research is smaller than the expected quality of its hires. Stern interprets this as indicating "a structural positive relationship between the firm's expected ability to recruit high-quality scientists and its adoption of a science-oriented research strategy" (p. 13).

As Stern notes, while many earlier studies have found a significant positive relationship between scientific innovation and productivity, this work has been based on confounding both applied and basic research activities. In principle, one can control for the biases generated by this confounding in the data, using instrumental variables that are correlated with ability in cross-sectional regressions, or by working with panel data. Instrumental variables work well in these kinds of labor market analyses when workers are relatively homogeneous, or when other control variables for things like educational attainment and relative socioeconomic status are available. This approach is not particularly effective, though, when looking at entry-level markets for scientists, since newly minted Ph.D.s don't vary much in educational attainment.

The second approach is to work with panel data. This kind of data will control for the biases from estimates that confound the effects of applied versus basic research, though, as Stern notes, the usual method of working with this kind of data involves looking at people who switch jobs, under the assumption that switching indicates an initial mismatch due to unobserved ability. For these studies, though, the fact that job switching is endogenous and can occur for reasons that may not be related to ability, the estimates coming from these studies can also be problematic.

Stern uses a different approach based on the fact that markets for new Ph.D.s generally involve job applicants receiving multiple offers. In this case, the number and qualitative characteristics of the offers a candidate receives are a signal of the ability the market perceives in the individual job candidate. Stern uses a collection of data compiled by himself of graduate students in biological sciences to run his wage regressions based on a subsample of the data of individuals who had multiple *private* sector offers of employment who subsequently accepted one of these offers. While Stern's methodology is interesting in its own right, it is far enough afield of what we are doing in this book that we refer the interested reader to the article directly.

Stern's bottom-line finding, however, is significant: on average, private sector firms that employee biological science Ph.D.s and allow these individuals to pursue their own basic research interests extract a 25% reduction in the wages they pay relative to firms that do not permit this kind of research freedom. This indicates that the preference component in individual basic research efforts plays an important role in incentivizing this kind of work. To the extent that we can extrapolate these findings to non-profit university employment, it also suggests that field preferences play a major role in determining the substantial pay differentials that exist between the various disciplines.

The Aghion et al. paper builds on earlier work by Aghion and Tirole (1997) in taking a property law approach toward understanding the incentive differences at work between basic and applied research. In particular, their key assumption is that scientists involved in basic research value having control over the projects they pursue, with freedom to follow discoveries wherever they may lead. The paper cites Stern's work as indicating that scientists willingly accept lower compensation in order to avoid the practicality constraints of applied research. The control issue is highlighted in the differences in intellectual property (IP) protection afforded to the results of applied research versus the relative lack of such protection for basic research results. We note that part of the motivation for this work was the unfolding consequences of legislation in the United States[1] allowing for the patenting of certain basic research results. As Aghion et al. note, evidence from the biological sciences pointed to a skewing of incentives for basic research in this field away from fundamental problems toward projects with potentially valuable near-term payoffs, such as the human genome project.

The model Aghion et al. construct has, at its core, the interaction between uncertainties in the ultimate value of different lines of research and the costs of pursuing this research, which depend in large measure on the difference in academic wages versus private sector wages for comparable talent. The specific model assumes that ideas get developed sequentially based on previous ideas, undergoing k steps of research activity before culminating in a final, economically useful research product which has an assumed payoff V. Scientists in the model can choose to work in an academic environment, where they control the kind of research they engage in, or in the private sector, where an entrepreneur

[1]Specifically, the passage of the Bayh-Dole Act in 1980 which allowed academic institutions to patent the results of research done using government funds.

dictates which research strategies the scientist pursues based on the quickest route to a monetary payoff. In this framework, scientists working in academia will earn lower wages than those in the private sector because of their preference for the freedom to pursue their own research strategies.

In the simplest formulation of the Aghion et al. model, they assume that each scientist examining an idea at a stage earlier than the final stage k has the same probability p of advancing the idea to the final stage. In this case, the expected payoff for a scientist advancing an idea from stage $k-1$ to stage k in the private sector is

$$E\left(\pi_k^p\right) = pV - w_p,$$

where π_k^p is the entrepreneur's profit at stage k, and w_p is the private sector scientific wage. The expected payoff in the academic setting is

$$E\left(\pi_k^a\right) = \alpha pV - w_a,$$

where π_k^a is the academic institution's payoff from advancing the idea to stage k, w_a is the scientific wage in academia, and α is the probability that the scientist's research methods are appropriate for advancing the idea from stage $k-1$ to stage k. Aghion et al. assume that academic wages are equal to the scientist's reservation wage (from, e.g., driving a cab). Similarly, the value of the idea to academic organizations is assumed to be the same as it is to the entrepreneur (and hence the consideration of possible IP protection for the product of academic inquiries). Wages in the private sector are assumed to be given by $w_p = w_a + z$, where z is a premium the entrepreneur must pay for depriving the scientist of the freedom to choose his or her own research projects.

In this simplified setting, Aghion et al. show that the private sector will yield a higher payoff than academia if and only if

$$(1-\alpha)pV > \left(w_p - w_a\right) = z,$$

or

$$pV > z.$$

From this, the basic intuition of the tradeoff between academic freedom and entrepreneurial control is apparent. The private sector will be more attractive the greater the value of the final product, and the higher the probability of its outcome. This captures the standard intuition about the distinction between basic and applied research stated earlier in the NSF definitions.

By recursively following the logic above, letting $E\left(\pi_k^j\right) = \Pi_k^j$ for $j = a,p$, Aghion et al. observe that at each stage k,

$$\Pi_{k-1}^p = p\Pi_k^p - w_p,$$

$$\Pi_k^a = \alpha p \Pi_k^a - w_{a.}$$

As before, the private sector yields a higher payoff than academia if and only if $p\Pi_k^p > z$. Since $\Pi_k < V$ it follows that if the private sector is value maximizing at any stage $k - 1$, it will be value maximizing at stage k. Since Π_k^p declines the further back in time one goes, this implies that it becomes progressively harder for the private sector to outperform academia. Aghion et al.'s first proposition then states that it cannot be value maximizing to have academia operating at later stages of the research process. Their second proposition then states that any research program with a sufficiently large number of stages will not be viable if it is located exclusively in the private sector. This result follows from consideration of the *ex ante* value of having a project done completely in the private sector. Letting $\Omega(allprivate)$ denote this value, it is given by

$$\Omega(\text{allprivate}) = p^k V - \left(1 + p^{k-1} + \cdots + p\right) w_p.$$

Clearly, for V fixed, if k is large enough, this expression must become negative.

As Aghion et al. note, this proposition doesn't establish the necessity of an academic sector, since it may be that research lines that are not profitable for the private sector are also not profitable if started in academia. To show that there are parameter values for which this is not the case, Aghion et al. consider the case where the reservation wage of scientists $w_a = 0$. In this case, the *ex ante* value of doing a k-stage project in academia is

$$\Omega(\text{allacademia}) = (\alpha p)^k V.$$

This is always positive, so the project is worth undertaking. The following sections of the paper consider optimal transition points from academic development to private development and find that this transition point will be earlier the large V is, or the smaller α or z is, which is quite intuitive.

Aghion et al. expand on this analysis in two directions. First, they allow for the possibility that multiple scientists can work on the same problem in parallel, with the probability of success then modeled as independent draws. In this setting, the probability of success given n scientists is

$$\varphi(n) = \left[1 - (1-p)^n\right].$$

The expected profit in the private sector in this setting for a k-stage project completed in that sector is given by

$$E\left(\pi_k^p\right) = \left[1 - (1-p)^n\right] V - n w_p.$$

From this expression, one can calculate the optimal number of scientists to employ (ignoring integer restrictions) as

$$n_k^p = \frac{\ln\left(\dfrac{\beta V}{w_p}\right)}{\beta},$$

where $\beta = -\ln(1-p)$. A similar calculation for the optimal number of scientists employed in an academic setting when the last stage of a k-stage project is completed there gives

$$n_k^a = \frac{\ln\left(\frac{\alpha\beta V}{w_a}\right)}{\beta}.$$

Aghion et al. argue that assuming an optimal number of scientists are employed by academia can be justified on funding grounds, where a benevolent social planner determines the level of funding needed for academic support based on optimality considerations. Given this assumption, the calculations show that the optimal number of scientists employed in academia can be greater than or less than those employed in the private sector, depending on academic productivity levels α and academic compensation relative to the private sector. With these preliminaries, the paper then shows that in this setting, there will also be an optimal transition point at which a project should be moved out of academia into the private sector, as in the simpler representative scientist model.

Aghion et al. model the possibility of granting IP protection to academic research outputs by viewing this as early privatization of the research project, that is, moving the project into private sector development before the optimal transition point. In the simple representative scientist model, early privatization always generates a higher probability of success, though it can occur that the higher labor costs associated with this strategy make the overall project infeasible. The paper demonstrates this with a pair of examples. This result, however, comes about as a direct result of the single scientist assumption. In the more general independent draws model, the fact that the number of scientists employed is endogenous means that early privatization can stymie innovation because fewer scientists end up being employed.

Building on this set of results, Aghion et al. turn next to a model in which scientists can pursue multiple research strategies, with some positive probability that different strategies can generate high value "offspring" projects that are themselves further developed. While we don't pursue this analysis in detail, it yields the result that the private sector develops narrowly focused projects, with the narrowness of focus enforced by firms' supervisory activities. This narrowness of focus, in turn, means that privatization cuts off the possibility of new and important discoveries, in ways that academic development of these projects would not. This result captures the empirical observation that chance favors a prepared mind in matters of intellectual inquiry.

To summarize, the key finding of the Aghion et al. paper is that when projects are not follow-on work on existing, protected embodiments of older ideas, they are more likely to be developed in an academic environment where the scientific talent working on these projects retains full control. These results are developed in the context of different organizational structures that incentivize academic research in section 5 of the paper. This analysis looks at the costs and benefits to entrepreneurs (broadly defined to include academic administrators) of becoming informed about the practical value of research projects. When this cost is low and the value of the project is high, the entrepreneur will find it desirable to incentivize researchers to pursue a practical research strategy that brings the project to fruition faster. How much incentive is needed to divert scientific talent away from other research strategies depends on the degree of preference that scientists have for maintaining control of their own research. As the authors note, though, this analysis doesn't change the basic results of the paper delineating the boundaries between basic and applied research. We would add that these extensions, though interesting, don't provide the kind of detailed and plausible explanation for the differences between universities and firms that Manso's harnessing of optimal search and agent models does, so we turn to this next.

Manso (2011) uses a clever embedding of the well-known two-armed bandit model in a principal-agent framework to examine incentives for research risk-taking in a university-like setting. The motivation for this work is the fact that basic research outcomes are highly uncertain (even ambiguous), while incremental or applied research outcomes are typically more predictable. As Manso notes, the two-armed bandit problem has been widely used to study optimal decision-making under ambiguity when the decision-maker has to choose between allocating additional resources to a relatively known outcome (exploitation) or to a new, unknown outcome (exploration), using Bayesian updating to capture what is learned from exploration. In Manso's model, risky exploration corresponds to blue-sky basic research, while incremental research on known issues corresponds to exploitation. Manso sets up the agency relationship by assuming there are two periods and that the agent in the model faces two stochastic possibilities, success or failure. The agent must choose between shirking (i.e., doing nothing), exploitation where the probability of success is known, or exploration, where the probability of success is unknown. The principal allocates resources in the model in the form of compensation for the agent based on the expected return from the research activities.

Formally, Manso considers a two-period agency model in which the principal hires an agent to conduct basic research. The agent in the model can take one of three possible actions. The first, shirking, involves doing nothing and imposes no private costs on the agent. The second, undertaking incremental (or exploitative) research, imposes a private cost c_0. The third action, undertaking pioneering (or exploratory) research, imposes a private cost or $c_1 > c_0$. Corresponding to these actions is a likelihood of success, for which Manso assumes that the probability of success when shirking, or $p_0 < E[p_i]$ for $i = 1, 2$, where $E[p_i]$ is the unconditional expectation of the probability of success under strategy i. For the agent, Manso models the action choice as a two-armed bandit problem. The choice of action 1 corresponds to pulling the arm with a known probability distribution, which Manso characterizes as the incremental research approach. For this action,

$$p_1 = E[p_1] = E[p_1 \mid S,1] = E[p_1 \mid F,1],$$

where $E[p_1 \mid X, j]$ is the expected probability of p_1 given event $X = S,F$ when the action taken was j. Here, S and F denote success or failure respectively.

For the second action, the probability of success is unknown and must be learned by experimentation. Here, Manso assumes that

$$E[p_2 \mid F,2] < E[p_2] < E[p_2 \mid S,2].$$

Letting $\langle i_k^j \rangle$ denote the agent taking action i in period 1 and then taking action j in period 2 if the first period action was a success or taking action k in period 2 if the first period action was a failure. The agent's expected payoff is then given by

$$EU\left[\langle i_k^j \rangle\right] = \left\{E(p_i)S + \left[1 - E(p_i)\right]F\right\} + E(p_i)\left\{E\left(p_j \mid S,i\right)S + \left[1 - E\left(p_j \mid S,i\right)\right]F\right\}$$
$$+ \left[1 - E(p_i)\right]\left\{E(p_k \mid F,\mathrm{i})S + \left[1 - E(p_k \mid F,i)\right]\right\}.$$

Manso focuses on two strategies, $\langle 1_1^1 \rangle$ and $\langle 2_1^2 \rangle$, which correspond to the agent pursuing incremental research in both periods, or doing pioneering research in the first period, followed by continue pioneering research in period 2 if the first period outcome is successful, but reverting to incremental work in period 2 if the first period outcome is failure. It is straightforward to show that the payoff to exploratory research is larger than that of incremental research if and only if

$$E(p_2) \geq p_1 - \frac{p_1\left(E[p_2 \mid S,2] - p_1\right)}{1 + \left(E[p_2 \mid S,2] - p_1\right)}.$$

Manso then assumes that the agent's actions are unobservable to the principal so that the principal must base compensation on observed output. This assumption generates a standard moral hazard problem, which we will comment on further below.

Wages in the model are thus contingent on outcomes – success or failure – in each period of the relationship. The principal offers the agent a contract with wage options given by

$$\boldsymbol{w} = \left[w_{F,} w_S, w_{SF}, w_{SS}, w_{FS}, w_{FS}\right],$$

where the subscripts F, S refer to failure or success. Manso assumes that agents have limited liability (i.e., wages must be non-negative) and that both principal and agent are risk-neutral.

Given this basic framework, the total expected cost to the principal for agent plan $\langle i_k^j \rangle$ is

$$W\left[\boldsymbol{w}, \langle i_k^j \rangle\right] = \left\{E(p_i)w_S + \left[1 - E(p_i)\right]w_F\right\} + E(p_i)\left\{E\left(p_j \mid S,i\right)w_{SS} + \left[1 - E\left(p_j \mid S,i\right)\right]w_{SF}\right\}$$
$$+ \left[1 - E(p_i)\right]\left\{E(p_k \mid F,i)w_{FS} + \left[1 - E(p_k \mid F,i)\right]w_{FF}\right\},$$

while the expected cost to the agent is

$$C\left[\left\langle i_j^k\right\rangle\right]=c_i+E(p_i)c_j+\left[1-E(p_i)\right]c_k.$$

Manso then defines an optimal contract as one that minimizes the total expected cost to the principal $W\left[w,\left\langle i_k^j\right\rangle\right]$ subject to the incentive compatibility constraints

$$W\left[w,\left\langle i_k^j\right\rangle\right]-C\left[\left\langle i_j^k\right\rangle\right]\geq W\left[w,\left\langle \ell_m^n\right\rangle\right]-C\left[\left\langle \ell_m^n\right\rangle\right].$$

where $\left\langle \ell_m^n\right\rangle$ is any other plan the agent might undertake. In Manso's framework, this is a linear program in six variables with 27 constraints. Given a solution to the cost minimization problem, the principal will then implement an action plan $\left\langle i_k^j\right\rangle$ to

$$\max_{\left\langle i_k^j\right\rangle} R\left(\left\langle i_k^j\right\rangle\right)-W\left[w\left(\left\langle i_k^j\right\rangle\right),i_k^j\right]$$

where $R\left(\left\langle i_k^j\right\rangle\right)$ is the principal's total expected revenue when the agent uses action plan $\left\langle i_k^j\right\rangle$ and $W\left[w\left(\left\langle i_k^j\right\rangle\right),\left\langle i_k^j\right\rangle\right]$ is the cost-minimizing contract that implements this plan.

Manso simplifies the exposition by assuming that the agent has zero reservation utility so that a participation constraint is unnecessary, given the limited liability assumption.

Manso then shows that if there is no cost to the agent of pursuing either strategy, then there is no conflict of interest between principal and agent, and the model reduces to a standard two-armed bandit problem where the only trade-off is between the returns to exploitation versus exploration. If it is costly for the agent to pursue exploration relative to exploitation, then the agency friction binds, and the principal must structure a contract with the agent that motivates the agent to exert effort.

As we noted above, the information asymmetry in Manso's model generates a moral hazard problem. This assumption might be viewed as problematic, since it seems to imply that research-oriented organizations don't review the actions of their employees. This is obviously not true, since standard promotion and tenure (P&T) review processes within universities go to considerable lengths to evaluate what faculty are working on and attempting to make judgments about the quality of the work. The problem that universities face here, though, is in the quality determination, so it is worth spending some time examining this issue.

The "publish or perish" dictum in academia is well-known, and in most university's P&T processes, quality-weighted publication counts play a central role in determining the outcome of an individual's review. Of course, this just raises the question of how to weight different journals or other research outlets in terms of quality. Libraries and publishers have developed a number of different systems for ranking journals, most of them based on the number of citations that published papers accumulate over time. Some of these systems are simply bibliometric, designed to tell publishers or libraries which journals are most widely used or purchased, and others (most notably the Web of Science) use multiple metrics derived from citation analysis to provide top quality information about the relative *scientific* importance of various journals. For evaluation purposes, though, even the best of these rankings delivers uncertain results.

One can see this fact at play in a couple of different ways. In physics and computer science, the research cycle is quite fast, particularly compared to the inherent lags involved in peer review and publication of papers (even in electronic form on the web). As a result of this, many physics and CS departments rely on the citation analysis generated by the arXiv preprint servers, since these capture the fast impact that breakthroughs in these areas have in stimulating further research. While these citation results are more useful than the ultimate peer-reviewed citations that accrue after a paper is formally published, the process within the arXiv can be biased by things as simple as the updating process the servers use. Specifically, the index listings of papers in the system are updated every day at 4 PM. As this fact became known in the communities using these servers, competition developed to see who could get their new paper into the index most quickly, since being at the top of the index generated more views and hence, more possible citations.

A second example comes from the field of economics. Many top-rated economics departments consider publishing in the so called top five journals – *Quarterly Journal of Economics, American Economics Review, Review of Economic Studies, Econometrica*, and *Journal of Political Economy* – as the gold standard for determining top-quality work. However, in a recent paper, Heckman and Moktan (2020) (entitled "The Tyranny of the Top Five") showed that these journals only managed to capture half of the important, breakthrough publications in economics. The other important results they identified were published in respected field journals, of which there are many in economics.

A related issue in fields like economics where the research cycle is slow is the fact that it takes time for new papers to be cited, since the diffusion of new knowledge in this field is significantly slower than it is in areas like physics or computer science. Since P&T decisions generally need to be made well before the full impact of a publication becomes apparent, the uncertainty about quality in the process remains. This is one of the major reasons why the Nobel Prize in economics looks more like a life-time achievement award than do the prizes in the physical sciences.

Manso's key results show that the optimal contracts for encouraging exploitation or exploration are quite different. For exploitation, the usual agency results apply: contracts reward early positive outcomes and punish perceived shirking using tools ranging from reductions in compensation or threats of termination. For exploration, the optimal contract encourages (or at least tolerates) early failures and rewards long-term success. Manso shows this by first classifying exploration strategies as either radical or moderate. Radical strategies are those for which

$$\frac{1-E(p_2)}{1-p_1} \geq \frac{E(p_2)E(p_2 \mid S,2)}{p_1^2}.$$

This condition states that the likelihood ratio between exploration and exploitation with failure in the first period is greater than or equal to the likelihood ratio between exploration and exploitation with two consecutive successes. Manso calls this radical because it implies that the exploratory strategy has a high expected probability of failure in the first period relative to the exploitative strategy. Manso's Proposition 2 states that to implement an exploratory strategy, the optimal contract will have

$$w_{FS} = \alpha_1, \text{ and } w_S = w_{SF} = w_{FF} = 0.$$

If exploration is moderate, then

$$w_{SS} = \alpha_2 + \frac{p_1 - p_0}{E[p_2]E[p_2 \mid S,2] - p_0 p_1} \frac{p_1(1+E[p_2])c_1}{E[p_2]E[p_2 \mid S,2] - p_1^2}\left(\frac{c_2}{c_1} - \beta_2\right)^+.$$

Here,

$$\alpha_1 = \frac{c_1}{p_1 - p_0}$$

$$\alpha_2 = \max_{j \in \{0,1\}} \frac{(1+E[p_2])c_2 - p_0 c_j}{E[p_2]E[p_2 \mid S,2] - p_0 E[p_j]} + \frac{(E[p_2] - p_0)p_0\alpha_1}{E[p_2]E[p_2 \mid S,2] - p_0 E[p_j]}$$

$$\beta_2 = \frac{E[p_2](E[p_2 \mid S,2] - p_0 p_1) + E[p_2](p_1 E[p_2 \mid S,2] - p_0 p_1)}{(p_1^2 - p_1 p_0) + E[p_2](p_1^2 - p_1 p_0)}$$

and $(x)^+ = \max(x,0)$. On the other hand, if exploration is radical, then

$$w_F = \frac{p_1(1+E[p_2])c_1}{E[p_2]E[p_2 \mid S,2] - p_1 E[p_2]}\left(\frac{c_2}{c_1} - \beta_2\right)^+$$

and

$$w_{SS} = \alpha_2 + \frac{E[p_2] - p_0}{E[p_2]E[p_2 \mid S,2] - p_0 p_1} \frac{p_1(1+E[p_2])c_1}{E[p_2]E[p_2 \mid S,2] - p_1 E[p_2]}\left(\frac{c_2}{c_1} - \beta_2\right)^+.$$

Intuitively, the contract that implements exploration must first deter shirking or exploitation. Not rewarding failures in the first period deters shirking, while not rewarding success in the first period deters exploitation. Deferring compensation for a success in the first period is also optimal since second-period performance also provides information about which action plan the agent implemented in the first period. The remainder of Manso's paper examines which of the various incentive constraints bind in the various scenarios, and how relaxation of the commitment assumption (together with the possibility of termination) affect the optimal contract, and what happens if the principal has more information about the agent's actions and can give feedback to guide the agent's actions in the second period. We refer the interested reader to Manso's paper for this discussion and to the appendix of Manso's paper for detailed proofs of his propositions.

While Manso's model encompasses only two periods of interaction, the results here suggest that in an infinitely repeated relationship, the need to reward long-term investments combined with the well-known promise-keeping requirements of long-term contracts can be interpreted as tenure. In models of CEO compensation with termination, this friction takes the form of "golden parachutes" which fulfill the promise-keeping function of the contract. Universities do not pay golden parachutes, but the granting of tenure has the same effect of delivering on promised future compensation without any concurrent productivity demands. This should be compared with conventional "expectations of employment" that are part of many employment contracts. While these have a similar flavor to formal tenure, they don't carry the kinds of legally binding promises of employment that formal tenure contracts do.

ROLE OF ACADEMIA

As we've documented above, economists have paid a good bit of attention to questions about research incentives and the differences between basic and applied research in their impact on growth. But there does not appear to be much work examining the incentives at work within academic organizations, nor does there appear to be much in the way of analysis looking at how these incentive structures or organizational differences impact the standard endogenous growth story. Indeed, a Google Scholar search on "basic research incentives" and "endogenous growth" returns only one page of hits. Similarly, a search on "endogenous growth models" and "academic organization" only returns a single page of hits. The related search on "endogenous growth" and "academic organization" returns six pages of hits, but for both of these searches, the hits returned deal largely with regional issues or the sociology of academia rather than research impacts on endogenous growth.

Two papers that are relevant are Akcigit et al. (2011) and Marchiori and Minelli (2023). Akcigit et al. work in a continuous time endogenous growth framework based on Romer's monopolistic competition model where the spillover and division of labor effects generate increasing returns. The model includes a specific academic sector consisting of labs financed by taxation. Private firms in the model can also engage in basic (as opposed to applied) research, with the key difference in the effects of the two distinct sources of basic research being that firms can patent direct applications of their basic research outcomes. This limits the spillover effects of non-academic research. The incorporation of these effects in the Romerian endogenous growth model is fairly mechanical, though the paper builds in a lot of detail about things like buyouts, equilibrium firm entry and exit decisions, and labor market heterogeneity in order to accommodate the empirical analysis that makes up the bulk of the paper. We do note, however, that research wages in this paper are the same for firms or academia, and there is no specific consideration of preferences for research in the model as there is in Stern's work, or the Aghion et al. paper. One of the key things the empirical specification of the model accomplishes is an analysis of the effects of government funding on growth, through the channel of support for academic research. The calibrated simulations of the model show that, in the baseline model, academic research accounts for 26% of the observed growth in the economy, while accounting for 64% of the overall basic research undertaken (consistent with the data presented earlier). The model also implies that at an optimum, the fraction of GDP allocated to basic academic research should be on the order of 10%, which is roughly triple the current allocation in the U.S. economy, according to the National Science Foundation (see https://ncses.nsf.gov/pubs/nsf23339). Since the theoretical model the authors use is largely derivative of related Romerian models, we forego a detailed examination of the mathematics of the model and refer the reader to the paper for details.

The Marchiori–Minelli (MM) model seems to be one of the few that actually examine how different incentive mechanisms in academic organizations affect endogenous growth. We characterize MM as a model of European academic organization based on their assumption that the typical university is publicly funded and makes use of targeted publication outlets for evaluating faculty productivity. Within this framework, MM also assume that scientific quality comes in different, privately known degrees of ability. Researchers in the model get positive utility from reputation, which is based on their scientific achievements, while the effort they put into research generates a disutility cost which is lower for higher ability types. MM then assume that research can be either incremental – a safe research strategy which leads to incremental gains to reputation – or pioneering – a risk strategy which can lead to reputation gains that exceed what can be achieved through the incremental approach.

Under a restriction on the probability of success in pioneering research and on the additional reputational boost given by publishing this research in top tier outlets MM show that "star" researchers will always work on pioneering projects. They then show that in the absence of evaluation criteria, there are cut-off values for ability such that low ability researchers always pursue incremental research, while those with high ability values pursue pioneering work with different degrees of effort.

In the formal model, research ability is a continuous random variable having a finite mean and variance. Ability type in the model is denoted by θ. The utility function for researchers of type θ is an increasing function of a measure of scientific reputation, denoted by z, money, denoted by m, and a decreasing function of effort, denoted by e,

$$U(z,e;\theta) = v(z) - C(e;\theta) + m.$$

The function v is assumed to be strictly increasing and strictly concave. The cost function C is strictly increasing and strictly convex in e for θ fixed and strictly decreasing in θ for fixed e. The authors also assume that $\frac{\partial^2 C(e,\theta)}{\partial e \partial \theta} < 0$ so that the marginal cost of effort is decreasing in ability, and Inada conditions in the form of $\frac{\partial v}{\partial z} \to \infty$ as $z \to 0$, and $\frac{\partial C}{\partial \theta} \to \infty$ as $\theta \to 0$.

MM's formal characterization of incremental versus pioneering research assumes that e units of effort – which can be interpreted as publishing papers in journals of differing levels of prestige – translates one-for-one into prestige z, while the same investment in pioneering research translates into $\gamma e > e$ units with probability μ and into nothing with probability $1-\mu$. With this specification, the expected utility payoffs to a type-θ researcher undertaking pioneering research (ignoring monetary compensation for the moment) is

$$V_1^{\theta}(e) = \mu v(\gamma e) - C(e;\theta).$$

The payoff to a researcher choosing to undertake incremental research is

$$V_0(e) = vz(e) - C(e;1)$$

where the subscript $i = 0,1$ on the expected utility function indicates whether the research program is incremental ($i = 0$) or pioneering ($i = 1$), and the research type with $\theta = 1$ can undertake either incremental or pioneering research for the same cost per unit of effort.

With this specification and assumptions, MM then show that for each research program, absent any evaluation criteria (and related monetary compensation), there are unique maxima $\hat{e}_0$ and $\hat{e}_1(\theta)$ for the two expected utility functions above. Letting $\hat{V}_1(\theta)$ be the indirect utility (evaluated at the maximal effort) for the researcher of type θ undertaking pioneering research, MM show that both $\hat{e}_1(\theta)$ and $\hat{V}_1(\theta)$ are strictly increasing in θ. This result, in turn, lets them define two cut-off thresholds $\bar{\theta}$ and $\underline{\theta}$ such that

$$\hat{V}_1(\underline{\theta}) = \hat{V}_0$$

and

$$\hat{e}_1(\bar{\theta}) = \hat{e}_0.$$

Here, $\hat{V}_0$ is the indirect utility of undertaking incremental research at the optimal level of effort. Researchers with abilities below $\underline{\theta}$ have a high cost of undertaking pioneering research, while those with abilities above $\bar{\theta}$ are "stars" who choose to pursue pioneering research. MM then impose the assumption that the expected indirect utility for stars pursuing pioneering research exceeds the indirect utility from pursuing incremental work. This captures the fundamental differences in preferences for basic over applied research.

Given this result, MM turn next to looking at the effects of imposing an evaluation procedure. The specific one they examine posits a one-off monetary premium paid if a threshold in a pre-determined quality metric is achieved. This metric may or may not coincide with the implied metric based on scientific consensus that determines the reputational payoffs in the model. This modeling choice is designed to capture the practice in a number of European countries of drawing up lists of A-level, B-level, etc., journals in different disciplines, and mandating certain numbers of publications in these journals for promotion, tenure, salary, and grants decisions.

The first key finding in the paper is that if the evaluation criterion is simply one of publishing some requisite quantity of work in non-quality weighted journals, the incentive scheme has the effect of inducing middle ability types – those for whom $\underline{\theta} < \theta < \overline{\theta}$ – who were previously pursuing some pioneering research now choose to "play it safe" and pursue only incremental work. Under the quantitative scheme, high ability types continue to pursue pioneering work. When the evaluation scheme is chosen to mirror the scientific consensus on research quality, the procedure has the effect of inducing middle ability researchers to put more effort into pioneering work. In terms of outcomes, the pure quantity-based evaluation procedure reduces the number of expected pioneering outcomes, while a quality-based evaluation procedure aligned with the scientific consensus increases this number.

MM then embed this basic research compensation analysis in the standard Romerian endogenous growth framework and show that the evaluation-induced average research productivity positively affects growth rates (as one would expect). The policy analysis in the paper demonstrates that quality-based evaluation procedures uniformly dominate the quantitative procedure regardless of the tax rates imposed to support public basic research.

RESEARCH AND TEACHING

Most work on endogenous growth accepts as established fact that ideas and human capital are complements. Indeed, this notion is part and parcel of Romer's breakout work on endogenous growth (see Romer, 1990a, 1990b), where the introduction of a potentially infinite set of new intermediate input goods in production is the direct result of investments in new scientific knowledge. Implicit in this view is the fact that before new knowledge can impact production, it must be embedded in the workers who create and operate the new technologies that encompass the new ideas generated by basic and applied research. On the applied side, Arrow (1962) posits his well-known learning-by-doing hypothesis for how this synthesis comes about. Recent work on how ideas from basic research get baked into human capital has focused on modeling the diffusion of knowledge into technology – see, for example, Braunerhjelm et al. (2008), Michel and Nyssen (2002), Langlois (2001), Acs et al. (2003), Klein and Sener (2023) – or on the role of education in creating human capital – see all of the many papers that cite the famous Lucas (1988) paper on the role of human capital in economic development. But there seems to be very little work, at least in the context of economic models of growth, that deal explicitly with the tradeoffs that faculty face between research and teaching activities.

That these two activities are intertwined is an obvious empirical fact in educational institutions around the world. On its face, this embedding of the two key functions of knowledge creation and dissemination might seem counterintuitive, if not counterproductive and it raises the question of why should the people who are good at doing basic research also have the responsibility for teaching the new ideas that come from research to students? We note that it is not unusual for universities to employ what are commonly called research scientists (or scholars, more generally) who, in fact, don't have teaching responsibilities. It is also a common observation that young people can get first rate college educations at small, liberal arts colleges whose faculty don't do much in the way of research. And yet, the standard model of combined research and teaching is the one that dominates in most university settings. So, we need to address the question of why this is the case.

One of the key contributors to the academic literature on this question is Richard Florida, who has argued that innovation and training go hand in hand, and this fact is responsible for the development of so called innovation corridors like Silicon Valley or the Route 128 corridor outside of Boston. This work is well summarized in Lee et al. (2010) who argue persuasively that innovation thrives in an environment where creative, educated people can freely share ideas. In many respects, this is the definition of a university. Other work has examined the question more directly by looking at whether students do, in fact, value the educations they get at R1 universities.

Indeed, there have been a number of studies over the past 20 years on the relationship between research productivity and rankings of schools in the popular press. A paper by Siemens et al. (2005) looks at the correlation between business school research productivity and popular rankings. The paper finds a strong relationship between where schools are ranked and the research productivity of their faculty. From the paper's abstract:

> This paper examines the relationship between an objective measure of research productivity in prestigious business journals from 1986–1998 and recent undergraduate and master's business school ratings determined by U.S. News & World Report. These findings are validated over separate sets of U.S. News measures for undergraduate and MBA programs, extended to a smaller set of MBA rankings from Business Week, and address institutions' residuals that indicate whether ratings of the schools are under- or overestimated when research productivity is used as a predictor. The relationship between discipline research productivity and undergraduate and master's business school program rankings also are examined. Results indicate that research productivity is strongly related to undergraduate program ratings with more than 50% of the variance in ratings explained by a school's research productivity scores. Research productivity is more strongly related to undergraduate business school program ratings/rankings than to master's programs ratings/rankings.

For the U.S. News & World Report rankings, the proximate cause of this correlation is the fact that 25% of the weight that goes into their ranking comes from surveys of peer reputation for the schools included in the rankings. This, however, doesn't explain the full strength of the correlation in the U.S. News rankings, nor does it factor into the rankings of business schools by Business Week magazine, which depend only on surveys of students, alumni, and employers for their rankings.

While these correlations suggest there is value for education in the research activities of faculty, the fact that reputation can be subject to self-fulfilling prophecies, and research subject to fads leads us to want to look more deeply into the connection between research and teaching.

While universities date back to the Middle Ages in Europe, the modern form of the university, with its emphasis on both research and teaching, arose in Germany and the UK in early 1800s.[2] The coincidence of this with the opening phases of the industrial revolution was not an accident. New technologies and new modes for organizing business activities brought with them the need for a literate and numerate workforce. While expansions in primary and secondary education fulfilled this need for workers on the lower end of the labor spectrum, the need for workers who could incorporate innovations flowing from basic research into industry was also important. This need accelerated through the early 20th century, particularly in the years immediately following World War II. To quote from Enders:

> In many industrial societies after World War II, the coincidence of various phenomena had contributed to a political climate that allowed for a substantial increase in the expenses for higher education and research: namely, the belief that so-called "blue-sky research" serves important societal needs for scientific and technological innovation; the boom of the economics of education – i.e., the belief that substantial educational investment is needed in order to ensure economic growth … (p. 7).

One finds additional support for the contention that research and teaching are jointly produced complements by looking at the tuition charged by different classes of educational institutions. Epple et al. (2006) studied the relationship between U.S. college/university tuition charges and the quality of student education (measured by peer quality) and found that the colleges in their data sample stratified naturally into six distinct tuition categories with close, increasing correlations in peer quality across the categories. Indeed, they interpret their model as one of differentiated product monopolistic competition, stating that

> Colleges with high quality have significantly more market power because they do not face competition from higher quality colleges. Hence, they can set tuitions above effective marginal costs and generate additional revenues that are used to enhance quality (p. 887).

A NEW TRADEOFF MODEL: RESEARCH VERSUS EDUCATIONAL ACTIVITY

Based on these findings of the relationship between basic research and education, we develop a new model which treats research and human capital production as a joint product but also recognizes the tradeoff that faculty face in how much effort they devote to each of these activities. Since, as we've seen from Manso's work on incentivizing innovation and the problems with evaluation studied by Marchiori and Minelli, managing the production of both research and teaching is complex – the so-called problem of herding cats – we follow Manso's lead in working with a principal–agent framework for our model.

The basic ideas behind the model are the following:

a. Ideas are generated by basic research, which is costly.
b. Ideas affect production by enhancing the productivity of both labor and capital.
c. Ideas cannot affect anything if they are not communicated and embedded in human capital, which is also costly.

[2]See Enders (2006).

d. The costly activities by which research gets done and communicated are carried out by universities which fund themselves by taking a share of the value of educated workers in production.
e. To model these ideas, we let q be a measure of technological quality which can be generated by having basic researchers invest a level of effort $r \in [0,1]$ in research activities. This investment yields a new stochastic technological quality conditional on the existing quality level. The distribution of this output is given by a probability measure $R(\tilde{q} \mid r_t, q_{t-1})$ with $R_r > 0$ and $R_q > 0$. The assumption that the production of technological quality is stochastic is based on the riskiness of research.

Education translates research results into human capital measured in efficiency units H_t. We assume that the production function for producing human capital is deterministic and depends on the level of effort put into education, $e_t = 1 - r_t$ (reflecting the faculty trade-off between research and teaching). We also assume that the production function for human capital $H(e_t)$ is humped shaped. This reflects the fact that in the absence of effective research, there are no new, useful ideas to communicate, in which case faculty teaching activities produce some base level H_0 of human capital. At the same time, if faculty devote all their time to research, teaching activities are ineffective and result in a less than optimal production of human capital. For example, we could specify $H_t = [1 + \delta r_t (1 - r_t)] H_0$.

Since some fraction of educated workers must work in the education sector in the future, we can define the measure of professors as $P_t = 1 - H_t$. Quality adjusted educated labor inputs to production are then $q_t H_t$.

The university captures a percentage of the capitalized value of human capital investments $\frac{W_t q_t H_t}{i}$ at time t, where i is the real interest rate and W_t is the wage. Call this fraction α and assume the university distributes a proportion ω of this to faculty, with the remaining $(1-\omega)$ going to fixed production costs. With the contract share ω depending on the realized innovation q, the principal's objective function is

$$Prin(r_t; q_{t-1}) = \frac{W_t}{i_t} \int \alpha(1 - \omega[q_t]) q_t H(r_t) dR(q_t \mid r_t, q_{t-1}).$$

Faculty preferences take the form

$$V(r_t; q_{(t-1)}) = \frac{W_t}{i_t} \int u(\alpha\omega[q_t] q_t H_t[r_t]) dR(q_t | r_t, q_{t-1}) - \psi(r_t).$$

where the function u is strictly increasing, strictly concave and satisfies $u'(0) = \infty$, and the function ψ is also strictly decreasing and convex and satisfies $\psi(0) = \infty$ and $\psi(1) = 0$. The assumptions on u are standard, while the assumptions on ψ mean that faculty incur no disutility if all their effort goes into research (i.e., research intensity is $r_t = 1$ and $e_t = 0$), while they incur infinite disutility when all effort goes into teaching. Since W_t and i_t are fixed for the agency analysis, we will specify $z_t = \frac{W_t}{i_t}$ going forward.

Since the human capital production function doesn't depend on q_t, we can write the principal's objective function as

$$Prin(r_t;q_{t-1}) = \alpha z_t H(r_t)\int(1-\omega[q_t])q_t dR(q_t|r_t,q_{t-1})$$

The agent's participation constraint is then

$$V(r_t;q_{t-1}) = z_t \int u(\alpha\omega[q_t]H_t[r_t]q_t)dR(q_t|r_t,q_{t-1}) - \psi(r_t) \geq \overline{V}.$$

The first-best case: To keep the analysis simple, we will assume that the agent (as well as the principal) is risk-neutral. For the first-best case, since the principal observes the action the agent takes and knows whether the resulting realization of q was due to lack of effort or chance, the compensation scheme can be made independent of the random state q. In this scenario, the first-best optimization problem becomes

$$\max_{\omega,r}\ (1-\omega)\overline{q}(r)H(r),$$

subject to

$$\alpha z\omega\overline{q}(r)H(r) - \psi(r) \geq \overline{V},$$

where $\overline{q}(r)$ is the conditional mean of q given the action r by the agent. The first-order conditions for this problem (letting λ be the Lagrange multiplier corresponding to the constraint) are

$$\alpha z\overline{q}(r)H(r) + \lambda[\alpha z\overline{q}(r)H(r)] = 0,$$

and

$$\alpha z(1-\omega)[H'(r)\overline{q}(r) + H(r)\overline{q}'(r)] +$$
$$\lambda\alpha z\omega[H'(r)\overline{q}(r) + H(r)\overline{q}'(r)] - \lambda\psi'(r) = 0.$$

From the first FOC, we have $\lambda = 1$. From the second FOC, we get (setting $\lambda = 1$):

$$\alpha zH'(r)\overline{q}(r) + \alpha zH(r)\overline{q}'(r) - \psi'(r) = 0.$$

By assumption, $\psi' < 0$ and $\overline{q}'(r) > 0$, from which it follows that $H'(r) < 0$, that is, the first-best solution does not have the university maximizing its human capital output. Rather, it sacrifices some quality of instruction in order to encourage research that advances technical knowledge. Note also, that because of the risk-neutrality assumption, the shares going to administration and faculty are indeterminate. We will address this issue below when we discuss production.

The second-best case: Maintaining the assumption that the agent is risk-neutral, the second-best problem assumes that the principal cannot observe the agent's actions and hence cannot determine whether the resulting output of q is due to effort or luck. In this case, the compensation scheme will be not a constant share of revenues, but a share given as a function of the observed output q. We will assume that the function $\bar{q}(r)$ is concave so that we can use the first-order approach to characterize incentive compatibility. The second-best optimization problem then takes the form

$$\max_{\omega(r),r} \alpha z H(r) E\{(1-\omega(q))q|r\},$$

subject to

$$z\alpha H'(r) E\{\omega(q)q|r\} + \alpha z H(r)\frac{\partial}{\partial r} E\{\omega(q)q|r\} - \psi'(r) = 0.$$

Under the assumption that the conditional measure $R(\cdot|r,q_{-})$ has a density, denoted by $f(\cdot|r,q_{-})$, the first-order conditions for this problem take the form[3]

$$-H(r)qf + \lambda H(r)qf + \mu\left[H'(r)qf + H(r)qf_r(r)\right] = 0,$$

plus the adjoint equation obtained by taking the partial derivate with respect to r directly. These two equations together will determine the compensation function $\omega(q)$ and the second-best optimal research effort r. We can rewrite the condition above as

$$1 = \lambda + \mu\left[\frac{H'(r)}{H(r)} + \frac{f_r}{f}\right].$$

Note that since f is a conditional density, we know that $\int f(q|r) = 1$ for all r. Hence, differentiating with respect to r yields $\int f_r(q|r) = 0$. We can use this fact by integrating the FOC above with respect to $f(q|r)dq$ to get $1 = \lambda + \mu\frac{H'(r)}{H(r)}$. From the incentive compatibility constraint, we have

$$\alpha z H'(r)\int \omega(q) qf(q|r)dq + \alpha z H(r)\int \omega(q) qf_r(q|r)dq = \psi'(r) < 0$$

Since the second term is the expected payoff to the agent from additional research, holding teaching output constant, our assumptions on the functions H and density f imply that this is strictly positive. In this case, it tells us that $H'(r) < 0$ which in turn implies that the multiplier $\lambda > 1$ and the marginal payoff to additional human capital production will be more than what it is in the first-best case. The fact that the function H is strictly concave also tells us that the optimal second-best level of research will be greater than it is in the first-best case. This is also apparent from the fact that in both first-best and second-best cases, the Lagrange multiplier λ is the agent's marginal utility of compensation at the optimum. Since the agent's utility function is concave, having $\lambda > 1$ in the second-best optimum means that compensation relative to first-best is smaller. This is offset (to maintain incentive compatibility) by allowing faculty to increase

[3]This is a calculus of variations problem, since we are taking variations with respect to the function $\omega(q)$

their research effort. This is intuitive, since in the absence of observable research effort and faculty disutility associated with teaching, it now costs more to motivate teaching effort.

We can now embed this compensation structure in a standard endogenous growth framework along lines similar to that of Marchiori and Minelli (2023), by letting firms' production functions take the form

$$Y_t = F(K_t, q_t H_t),$$

with the production function F being constant returns to scale. Quality adjusted per capita output is then

$$y_t = \frac{Y_t}{q_t H_t} = F\left(\frac{K_t}{q_t H_t}, 1\right) = f(k_t).$$

In a balanced growth steady state with quality growing as

$$q_t = (1+\varrho)^t q_0$$

we will have Y_t and K_t also growing at the same rate.

Since Euler's theorem on homogeneous functions implies that all of the output produced in a competitive equilibrium will be distributed to capital and workers, the compensation to the university must be funded entirely from the earnings of workers (i.e., tuition). Following Stern (2004), we assume that the compensation for university workers will be 75% that of educated production workers. While this is an obvious simplification of the fact that faculty salaries vary considerably, it is justified both by Stern's results and by the fact that faculty in disciplines with direct industry applications earn more than those in other disciplines. Thus, for example, Business School salaries are typically higher than Arts and Sciences college salaries.

Since the efficiency wage for workers is Wq, the total wage bill for workers will be WqH. With professors earning $0.75\,Wq$ as well, the wage bill for professors and administrators will be $0.75\,WqP$. From our assumption above, this will be equal to αWqH, from which it immediately follows that $\alpha = \frac{0.75P}{H}$. We can also use the production function to determine the wage in terms of capital, human capital, and the technical innovation. Replacing this in the compensation equalization condition (given that the faculty share ω of university revenues is indeterminate), we have $\omega WqP = 0.75qW$ or $\omega = \frac{1}{0.75P}$.

We can also modify the model to allow for external spillover effects that increase total factor productivity by specifying

$$Y_t = A(\overline{q_t})F(K_t, q_t H_t)$$

In this setting, the external effect based on the mean quality variable can also be internalized, but firms will then have increasing returns to scale technology and so would need to operate in a strategic environment such as in the Shapley–Shubik market game. In this setting, if firms operate competitively (taking the externality as given), profits will be strictly positive. Since the same tuition calculation above will hold here, there is scope for enhancing the compensation of research/education via the imposition of government taxes (as in Shell's original work) to support research and education. Finally, since (as we've noted before) the extension of this to a full endogenous growth model is largely mechanical, we leave it to future research to carry this forward.

CHAPTER 7

UNIFYING THE APPROACHES? TOWARD A MORPHOLOGY OF ENDOGENOUS GROWTH

To understand the *evolution, development*, and *diffusion* of endogenous growth models from Lucas and Romer onward, we utilize a *morphological* approach (for a detailed explanation of this approach, see Spear & Young, 2023). We set out several planes along which EG models can be analyzed in a comparative morphological perspective. These are:

(i) Sectors and returns to scale structure of EG models.
(ii) Areas of focus and analytical efficacy of EG models.
(iii) Stylized facts of growth.
(iv) Generations of EG models and population growth decline.
(v) Generalization of EG models.

SECTORS AND RETURNS TO SCALE

One-sector models were those with a single aggregate production function, as in Romer (1986b) or the AK-based approach of Barro (1990), Rebelo (1991), and Jones and Manuelli (1990). The two-sector model involved goods production and knowledge accumulation (often in the form of human capital). *Both* emphasized factors such as human capital and technological progress as factors impacting long-run growth. As seen in the previous chapters, one-sector models assumed a single aggregate production function converting inputs (labor and capital) to output, with no distinction between different types of capital or production processes. The most widely cited example is Romer (1986b), where knowledge spillovers from individual firms' investments in R&D led to economy-wide improvements in productivity. The AK models of Barro, Rebelo, and others also impacted on the diffusion of the one-sector EG approach.

Endogenous Growth: Theory, Methods and Morphology
International Symposia in Economic Theory and Econometrics, Volume 35, 165–170

ISSN: 1571-0386/doi:10.1108/S1571-038620260000035023

Two-sector models had a "goods sector" and a "knowledge sector," with the two sectors interacting. Perhaps, the best example of this is Lucas (1988) which incorporated the accumulation of human capital *both* in the development of new technology and goods production. Another type of two-sector approach included *both* physical and human capital accumulation and their impact on growth in the long-run, as in Bond et al. (1996).

The morphology of sectors *and* returns to scale in first-generation EG models is as follows. As can be seen, some models were initially presented in *both* CRS and IRS form, albeit the version applied in these cases followed the accepted conventional specification, and were not generalized to cover CRS, IRS, or even DRS.

A morphology of sectors and returns to scale in first-generation EG models shows that, in some cases, models were initially presented in *both* CRS and IRS forms, albeit the version *applied* followed the accepted conventional specification, and were not *generalized* to cover CRS, IRS, or even DRS. For example, Romer (1986a, 1986b) presents a *one-sector model* and provides *both* CRS and IRS versions of his model. Romer (1990a, 1990b), on the other hand, gives a *two-sector* IRS specification. In contrast to this, Lucas (1988) specifies both *two-sector* CRS and IRS models. Rebelo (1991) also gives a *one-sector* and *two-sector* CRS model. For their part, both Grossman and Helpman (1989) and Aghion and Howitt (1992) specify *two-sector* IRS models.[1]

AREAS OF FOCUS AND ANALYTICAL EFFICACY OF ROMER'S *FIRST-GENERATION* EG APPROACH

Over the first two decades after Romer (1990a, 1990b), the focus of the EG approach *widened* to include several areas on which models focused. These included:

(i) Technological progress and its adoption (Parente-Prescott, 1994; Stokey, 1995)
(ii) Human Capital accumulation (Acemoglu, 1996; Stokey, 1991)
(iii) Fertility choice (Becker et al., 1990; Soares, 2005)
(iv) Government spending and taxation (Bond et al., 1996; Perotti, 1993)
(v) Money and inflation (Chang et al., 2007)
(vi) Financial intermediation (Aghion et al., 1999; Levine & Zervos, 1998)
(vii) Trade and development (Yi, 2003)
(viii) Income distribution (Aghion, 2002; Krusell et al., 1987)
(ix) Search, matching, unemployment (Acemoglu, 1997; Laing et al., 1995)

After its introduction, Romer's EG approach was *applied* to a wide range of economic issues. But with *Jones' critique* (1995), Romer's *initial* approach was seen to be limited in its applicability, and alternate approaches (*second-* and

[1]See Boldrin et al. (2004) for details.

third-generation models, such as SEG) were considered more relevant to the explanation of long run growth processes.

STYLIZED FACTS OF GROWTH (JONES & ROMER, 2010; KALDOR, 1961)

The *original* set of stylized facts as described by Kaldor (1961, pp. 177–222) were essentially empirically based statements regarding economic growth in the long run. They were considered to fundamentally characterize developed economies and were often utilized to evaluate the efficacy of growth models. Kaldor's original six stylized facts were:

(1) Output per worker, or labor productivity, grows over time at a sustained rate.
(2) Capital per worker grows over time also at a sustained rate.
(3) The real interest rate or return on capital is stable.
(4) The capital–output ratio is stable.
(5) The shares of capital and labor in national income are stable.
(6) There are differences in growth rates across countries, ranging between 2 and 5 percent.

Some 50 years later, Jones and Romer (2010) in their AER *Macro* paper "The New Kaldor Facts" set out additional stylized facts of growth as follows:

(1) Increases in the extent of the market have brought about an increase in the flow of goods, ideas, finance, and people.
(2) Accelerating growth.
(3) Variation in growth rates.
(4) Large income and TFP differences.
(5) Increases in human capital per worker.
(6) Long-run stability of relative wages.

However, these "new" facts remain to be assessed against *new* phenomenon such as *declining population growth* in developed countries, some models of which will be presented below. These are first- to fourth-generation EG models and models with decreasing population growth.

In the taxonomy developed by Bond-Smith (2019, p. 1370), if entry were particularly attractive ($\sigma \geq 1$), the model degenerates to the standard Romer (1990a, 1990b) model with a scale effect such that growth is simply a result of increasing variety and a preference for variety. Similarly, for $\kappa = 1$, the model is the standard Schumpeterian model with its linear requirement on returns to knowledge. In this way, the Schumpeterian model can be thought of as a special case where the linear "critique" is simply a modeling trick to avoid dealing with explosive growth from excessive increasing returns. Finally, the semi-endogenous case is also nested in the 4G model twice. First, if parameters are defined such that start-up costs for new varieties of average quality are too low, then the rate of return from investing in new varieties could still exceed the rate of return from investing in quality improvements in the steady state. In this corner solution, no quality improvement occurs in the steady state and new varieties are only the result of population growth as in the semi-endogenous model.

He goes on to say (Bond-Smith, 2019, p. 1370):

> Second, if quality improvements are increasingly difficult to discover such that $\kappa < 1$, then the logic follows that researching quality improving ideas would eventually cease such that any new varieties only match existing quality, and growth is simply a result of increasing variety due to population growth. The requirement of no improvements to existing varieties seems particularly strict, but the invention of entirely new varieties is perhaps more semantic. On the other hand, if quality improvements are increasingly easy to find ($\kappa \geq 1$), but entrants compete away the excessive profits associated with those improvements, then it follows that non-explosive endogenous growth is sustained indefinitely. The parameters that define each generation within Peretto (2018) are described. As a result, the linearity critique is no longer a valid weakness for models of fully endogenous growth.

Tables 5 and 6 present a morphological approach encompassing both recent SEG models and EG and SEG models with *declining* population growth (derived from Jones, 2022b). As can be seen, SEG models were able to cover a range of *new* areas of economic inquiry regarding the impacts of declining population growth, AI, and uncertainty, among other processes.

GENERALIZATION AND FOURTH-GENERATION MODELS

In Chapter 4, Cozzi's (2017, 2023) efforts to *hybridize* EG and SEG models were dealt with. Here, we briefly deal with the efforts of Peretto (2018) and Massari and Peretto (2025) to *generalize* the approach to endogenous growth by introducing the notions of "Robust" and "Super Robust" endogenous growth. The model proposed by Peretto (2018) *generalizes* all earlier generational models and has thus been termed a fourth-generation model as noted above. But more is involved here. As Bond-Smith (2019, p. 1371) notes:

> The technique used in 4G models is a repetition of the free entry and imperfect competition technique applied now to "excessive" increasing returns to the scale of innovation. In much the same way as entry constrains the impact of increasing returns on prices, the entry of new ideas constrains the impact of excessive increasing returns or population on the production of

Table 5. Recent Morphology of SEG Models.

Recent Morphology of SEG Models (J/K/S and Y/P/AH/DT)		
Area	Impact of	Author(s)
Population and labor market	Declining population	Jones (2022a, 2022b)
	Aging population	Engbom (2019)
Automation and AI	Robotics	Acemoglu and Restrepo (2020)
	AI	Aghion et al. (2019)
Trade	Uncertainty	Handley et al. (2022)
	Competition and innovation	Autor et al. (2018)

Table 6. EG and SEG Model Comparisons.

EG and *SEG* Models with *Declining* Population (Jones, 2022a, 2022b)

R/AH/GH *EG*

(1) $Y_t = A_t^{\sigma} N_t$

(2) $\frac{\dot{A}_t}{A_t} = \alpha N_t$

(3) $N_t = N_0 e^{-\eta t}, \eta > 0$

(4) $\frac{\dot{A}_t}{A_t} = \alpha N_0 e^{-\eta t}$

J/K/S *SEG*

(5) $Y_t = A_t^{\sigma} N_t$

(6) $\frac{\dot{A}_t}{A_t} = \alpha N_t^{\lambda} A_t^{-\beta}$

(7) $N_t = N_0 e^{-\eta t}, \eta > 0$

(8) $\frac{\dot{A}_t}{A_t} = \alpha N_0^{\lambda} e^{=\lambda \eta t} A_t^{-\beta}$

where

Y_t = output

A_t = stock of ideas

N_t = population

σ = degree of increasing returns

η = exogenous rate of population decline

β = difficulty in finding new ideas

ideas. In Schumpeterian models the technique was incomplete since it applied only to variety expanding ideas due to population growth and required a linear assumption to prevent excessive increasing returns on quality improving ideas. The newest generation of models goes one step further by allowing entry to constrain the impact of increasing returns on the production of variety expanding ideas due to population and the impact of excessive increasing returns in the production of quality improvements.

Recognizing that this new approach is uniquely different to earlier generations, this class of models is referred to here as the "4G" class of fully endogenous growth models without scale effects. The unique characteristic of the new class of models is that some logical market mechanism achieves the required linearity in the steady state and only in the steady state without relying on the placement of an assumption about the particular form of a differential equation.

In particular, Peretto (2018) identifies that quality improving innovations generate an opportunity for product proliferation by expanding the size of the market for all suppliers. Product proliferation and changes in demand are market responses to match the effect of any non-linearity from quality improvement, taming excessive returns to achieve linearity in the steady state and only in the steady state as well as negate the scale effect. That is, the market does not allow quality improvements to sustain excessive returns, with new varieties emerging in response to quality improving innovations and in response to changes in population.

As a result, these models imply that the linearity assumptions of Schumpeterian models are merely simplifying rather than a factual description of knowledge production. In this way, the linear assumptions in Schumpeterian models are merely a technicality that limits their application in a particular way, rather than a strong criticism. As a result, this class of models offers a resolution to the long running dispute about how to correctly remove scale effects from models of endogenous growth by reducing the linearity critique to a mere technicality.

Going beyond the 2018 Robust EG approach, Massari and Peretto (2025) propose a *Super-Robust* EG Theory, which they term *SREG* (p. 13). In this paper, they propose a model allowing for varying aggregate returns to scale while keeping constant returns to innovation at the level of the firm. The approach encompasses knowledge that the firms accumulate which improve quality, identifying this as what drives growth. The model goes against the linearity assumption conventional in theories of growth and shows that non-linear production can yield growth rates that are constant. Their approach extends previous models to include returns to knowledge that are decreasing, where growth rates can be positive, zero, or negative depending on returns to knowledge: increasing ($\kappa > 1$), constant ($\kappa = 1$), or decreasing ($\kappa < 1$) accordingly. Indeed, as the author's note (Massari & Peretto, 2025, p. 4):

> Robustness has always been a main point of contention concerning endogenous growth. Stiglitz (1990) and Romer (1994) argued that the unwillingness to work with knife-edge assumptions on the engine-of-growth equations has prevented the development of endogenous growth models for decades, explaining the long gap between Solow (1956, 1957) and Romer (1986a, 1986b, 1986c, 1990a, 1990b).
>
> Several attempts had introduced key features of endogenous growth theory long before Romer, such as profit-driven private R&D investment for the purpose of accumulating knowledge, a non-rival and partially non-excludable factor, and monopolistic competition that allows for pricing above marginal costs to compensate R&D investment (see, among many others, Arrow, 1962; Grossman & Helpman, 1989; Judd, 1985; Nordhaus, 1969), the key to endogenous growth.
>
> In his account of the origins of the theory, Romer (1994, p. 18) says that "Nordhaus and Arrow both worked at a time when there was real concern about the knife-edge character of the assumptions about ϕ", where ϕ is the parameter measuring aggregate returns to knowledge in the engine-of-growth equation of his 1990 model of knowledge accumulation.
>
> Likewise, he says about Judd (1985) and Grossman and Helpman (1991) that "like Nordhaus and Arrow, they stayed well away from the case where ϕ was equal to 1." This standstill ended when Romer (1986b) proposed his first model in which a sustained rate of economic growth originates from the endogenous accumulation of technological knowledge according to a linear equation. Unsatisfied that the model could not handle profit-driven knowledge accumulation by firms, Romer developed the 1990 model, which shares the same linear mathematical representation of knowledge accumulation. Given the preference for simple models that produce a constant growth rate of income per capita, in those early days the theory of endogenous growth developed around the knife-edge assumption of constant returns to knowledge in knowledge accumulation, with the understanding that robustness was desirable but an unnecessary mathematical complication. In his recent and exhaustive review of the field, Bond-Smith (2019) argues that the tradeoff between getting rid of the knife-edge assumption and delivering constant growth rates lasted until Peretto's development of a model of robust endogenous growth (2018),
>
> This paper builds on this tradition and makes four main contributions… it goes beyond Peretto (2018) by showing that it is possible to obtain the same results even with decreasing aggregate returns to knowledge, thus overturning the conventional wisdom in growth theory. In this sense, endogenous growth theory becomes super-robust.

To sum up, Endogenous or New Growth Theory has come a long way since the days of Romer and the AK theorists such as Barro and Rebelo, among others. In the *morphological* survey provided above, we have tried to illustrate just how far the *theory* and its *associated models* have progressed in terms of scope, method, and applications.

APPENDIX 1

Participants in the Uzawa Summer Seminars, Selected Years: Names, Institutions, Dissertations (See Table 7)

Table 7. Participants in the Uzawa Summer Seminars.

Date	Name	University	Dissertation (Date Submitted)
1964	Cass	Stanford	Studies in the theory of optimum economic growth (1965)
	Douglas	Stanford	Studies in monetary dynamics (1966)
	Goldman	Stanford	Economic growth and international trade: a study in the theory of economic development
	Oniki	Stanford	A theoretical study on the demand for education (1968)
	Ryder	Stanford	Optimal accumulation and trade in an open economy (1967)
	Shell	Stanford	Patterns of technical change and capital accumulation (1965)
	Teubal	Chicago	Inflation, unemployment, and economic growth (1967)
1965	Akerlof	MIT	Wages and capital (1966)
	Chaudhuri	MIT	Planning in a multi-regional economy: a case study of India (1966)
	Krishna	Chicago	Production relations in manufacturing plants: an exploratory study (1967)
	Levy	Yale	Racial imbalance act of Massachusetts (1969)
	Nordhaus	MIT	A theory of endogenous technical change (1967)
	Sheshinski	MIT	Essays on the theory of production and technical progress (1966)
	Stiglitz	MIT	Studies in the theory of economic growth and income distribution (1966)
1967	Burton	Northwestern	The development process in a dual economy (1971)
	Calvo	Yale	Efficiency and optimality in a heterogeneous capital model – putty-clay (1974)
	Ethier	Rochester	Models of international trade and investment (1970)
	Mirman	Rochester	Two essays on uncertainty and economics (1970)
	Narayanan	Yale	The two-sector model of growth (1973)
	Nissen	Berkeley	Consistent and inconsistent intertemporal behavior (1968)
	Onitsuka	Chicago	International capital movements and economics growth (1970)
	Razin	Chicago	Investment in human capital and economic growth: a theoretical study (1969)
	Rhee	Kansas	Foreign debt and economic growth (1972)
	Sidrauski	Chicago	Rational choice and patterns of growth in a monetary economy (1967)
	Smith	Northwestern	On risk and optimal rates of resource utilization in a theory of the firm

APPENDIX 2

Papers Presented at the May 1988 Buffalo Conference and Their Impact

Below a listing including Google Scholar Citations (GSC), which contests Warsh (2006)'s assertion regarding their impact (p. 290):

Barro, R. (1990). Government spending in a simple model of endogenous growth. *Journal of Political Economy, 98*(5), S103–S125. GSC: 13895.

Becker, G., Murphy, K., & Tamura, R. (1990). Human capital, fertility, and economic growth. *Journal of Political Economy, 98*(5), S12–S37. GSC: 4272.

Jorgenson, D., & Yun, K.-Y. (1990). Tax reform and U.S. economic growth. *Journal of Political Economy, 98*(5), S151–S193. GSC: 203.

King, R., & Rebelo, S. (1990). Public policy and economic growth: Developing neoclassical implications. *Journal of Political Economy, 98*(5), S126–S150. GSC: 1724.

Krugman, P. (1988). *Endogenous innovation, international trade and growth.* Paper presented at the SUNY-Buffalo Conference on The Problem of Development. Published as Ch. 11 in Krugman (1990), Rethinking International Trade, MIT Press. GSC: 4.

Romer, P. (1990). Endogenous technological change. *Journal of Political Economy, 98*(5), S71–S102. GC: 44008.

Rosenzweig, M. (1990). Population growth and human capital investments: Theory and evidence. *Journal of Political Economy, 98*(5), S38–S70. GSC: 350.

REFERENCES

Abramowitz, M. (1952). Economics of growth. In B. Haley (Ed.), *A survey of contemporary economics* (Vol. 2, pp. 132–181). Irwin.

Abramowitz, M. (1956). Resource and output trends in the United States since 1870. *American Economic Review, 46*(2), 5–23.

Acemoglu, D. (1996). A microfoundation for social increasing returns in human capital accumulation. *Quarterly Journal of Economics, 111*(3), 779–804.

Acemoglu, D. (1997). Matching, heterogeneity, and the evolution of income distribution. *Journal of Economic Growth, 2*(1), 61–92.

Acemoglu, D. (2008). *Introduction to modern economic growth*. Princeton University Press.

Acemoglu, D., & Restrepo, P. (2020). Robots and jobs: Evidence from US labor markets. *Journal of Political Economy, 128*(6), 2188–2244.

Acs, Z., Audretsch, D., Braunerhjelm, P., & Carlsson, B. (2003). *The missing link: The knowledge filter and endogenous growth*. Center for Business and Policy Studies.

Aghion, P. (2002). Schumpeterian growth theory and the dynamics of income inequality. *Econometrica, 70*(3), 855–882.

Aghion, P., Akcigit, U., & Howitt, P. (2015). The Schumpeterian growth paradigm. *Annual Review of Economics, 7*(1), 557–575.

Aghion, P., Antonin, C., & Bunel, S. (2019). Artificial intelligence, growth and employment: The role of policy. *Economie et Statistique / Economics and Statistics, 510-512*, 149–166.

Aghion, P., Dewatripont, M., & Rey, P. (1999). Competition, financial discipline and growth. *Review of Economic Studies, 66*(4), 825–852.

Aghion, P., Dewatripont, P., & Stein, J. C. (2008). Academic freedom, private-sector focus, and the process of innovation. *The RAND Journal of Economics, 39*(3), 617–635.

Aghion, P., & Durlauf, S. (2005). Preface to the handbook of economic growth. *Handbook of Economic Growth, 1*, xi–xv.

Aghion, P., & Howitt, P. (1992). A model of growth through creative destruction. *Econometrica, 60*(2), 323–351.

Aghion, P., & Howitt, P. (1998). *Endogenous growth theory*. MIT Press.

Aghion, P., & Howitt, P. (2006). Joseph Schumpeter lecture on appropriate growth policy: A unifying framework. *Journal of the European Economic Association, 4*(2–3), 269–314.

Aghion, P., & Tirole, J. (1997). Formal and real authority in organizations. *Journal of Political Economy, 105*(1), 1–29.

Akcigit, U., Hanley, D., & Serrano-Velarde, N. (2011). *Back to basics: Private and public investment in basic R&D and macroeconomic growth*. 2011 Meeting Papers 1196, Society for Economic Dynamics.

Aoki, M. (1967a). Increasing returns to scale and the market mechanism. Ph.D thesis, University of Minnesota.

Aoki, M. (1967b). Increasing returns to scale and market mechanisms. Technical Report 6, IMSSS, Stanford, November.

Aoki, M. (1968). Dynamic processes and social planning under increasing returns. Technical Report 15, IMSSS, Stanford, June.

Aoki, M. (2013). communication October 15, 2013.

Arrow, K. (1959, December 15). *Economic welfare and the allocation of resources for invention*. RAND Research Paper P-1856-RC.

Arrow, K. (1962). The economic importance of learning by doing. *Review of Economic Studies, 29*(3), 155–173.

Arrow, K. (1998). *Innovation and increasing returns to scale. Increasing returns and economic analysis* (pp. 403–408). Palgrave Macmillan.

Assad, A. (2011). Richard E. Bellman. In A. Assad & S. Gass (Eds.), *Profiles in operations research* (pp. 415–446). Springer.

Atkinson, A., & Stiglitz, J. (1969). A new view of technological change. *Economic Journal, 79*(315), 573–578.

Autor, D., Dorn, D., Pisano, G., Hanson, G., & Shu, P. (2018). *Foreign competition and domestic innovation: Evidence from US patents*. 2018 Meeting Papers (No. 239). Society for Economic Dynamics.

Balassa, B. (1967). *Trade liberalization among industrial countries*. McGraw-Hill.

Bardhan, P. (2015a). *Communication 21 December 2015*.

Bardhan, P. (2015b). *Communication 23 December 2015*.

Barro, R. (1990). Government spending in a simple model of endogenous growth. *Journal of Political Economy, 98*(5), S103–S126.

Barro, R., & Becker, G. (1989). Fertility choice in an endogenous growth model. *Econometrica, 57*(2), 481–501.

Barro, R., & Sala-i-Martin, X. (1992). Convergence. *Journal of Political Economy, 100*(2), 223–251.

Becker, G. (1964). *Human capital*. Columbia University Press.

Becker, G., Murphy, K., & Tamura, R. (1990). Human capital, fertility, and economic growth. *Journal of Political Economy, 98(5), Part 2*, S12–S37.

Bellman, R. (1951). *On a general class of problems involving sequential analysis*. Rand Research Memorandum RM-647.

Bellman, R. (1952). On the theory of dynamic programming. *Proceedings of the National Academy of Sciences, 38*(8), 716–719.

Bellman, R. (1954a). Some problems in the theory of dynamic programming. *Econometrica, 22*(1), 37–48.

Bellman, R. (1954b). *The theory of dynamic programming*. Rand Paper P-550.

Bellman, R. (1954c). The theory of dynamic programming. *Bulletin of the American Mathematical Society, 60*(6), 503–515.

Bellman, R. (1956a). *Dynamic programming and its application to variational problems in mathematical economics*. Rand Paper P-796.

Bellman, R. (1956b). [1958] Dynamic programming and its application to variational problems in mathematical economics. In L. Graves (Ed.), *Proceedings of the eighth symposium in applied mathematics* (pp. 115–138). American Mathematical Society, University of Chicago, McGraw-Hill.

Bellman, R. (1957). *Dynamic programming*. Princeton University Press.

Bellman, R. (1963). *Dynamic programming and mathematical economics*. Rand Research Memorandum R-3539-PR.

Bellman, R. (1984). *Eye of the hurricane: An autobiography*. World Scientific.

Bellman, R., & Lee, E. (1984, November). History and development of dynamic programming. *IEEE Control Systems, 4*(4), 24–28.

Benhabib, J., & Perli, R. (1994). Uniqueness and indeterminacy: On the dynamics of endogenous growth. *Journal of Economic Theory, 63*(1), 113–142.

Ben-Porath, Y. (1967). The production of human capital and the life cycle of earnings. *Journal of Political Economy, 75*(4), 352–365.

Blackwell, D. (1961). On the functional equation of dynamic programming. *Journal of Mathematical Analysis and Applications, 2*(2), 273–276.

Blackwell, D. (1962). Discrete dynamic programming. *Annals of Mathematical Statistics, 33*(2), 719–726.

Blackwell, D. (1964a). Memoryless strategies in finite state dynamic programming. *Annals of Mathematical Statistics, 35*(2), 863–865.

Blackwell, D. (1964b). Probability bounds via dynamic programming. *Proceedings of Symposia in Applied Mathematics, 16*(1), 277–280.

Blackwell, D. (1965). Discounted dynamic programming. *Annals of Mathematical Statistics, 36*(1), 226–235.

Bloom, N., Jones, C. I., Van Reenen, J., & Webb, M. (2020). Are ideas getting harder to find? *American Economic Review, 110*(4), 1104–1144.

Boldrin, M., Chen, B.-L., & Wang, P. (Eds.). (2004). *Human capital, trade, and public policy in rapidly growing economies: From theory to empirics*. Edward Elgar Publishing.

Bond, E., Wang, P., & Yip, C. (1996). A general two-sector model of endogenous growth with human and physical capital: Balanced growth and transitional dynamics. *Journal of Economic Theory, 68*(1), 149–173.

Bond-Smith, S. (2019). The decades-long dispute over scale effects in the theory of economic growth. *Journal of Economic Surveys, 33*(5), 1359–1388.

Bourguignon, F. (1974). A particular class of continuous time stochastic growth models. *Journal of Economic Theory, 9*(2), 141–158.

Braunerhjelm, P. (2008). Entrepreneurship, knowledge and economic growth. *Foundations and Trends in Entrepreneurship, 4*(5), 451–533.

Britto, R. (1966). *Efficient allocation of resources in a growing economy*. PhD thesis. Brown University. Abstract published in: Doctoral dissertations in econometrics and mathematical economics, *American Economist* (1968) 12, 81.

Brock, W. (1971). Sensitivity of optimal growth paths with respect to a change in target stocks. In G. Brockman & W. Weber (Eds.), *Contributions to the Von Neumann growth model* (pp. 73–89). Springer.

Brock, W., & Gale, D. (1969). Optimal growth under factor augmenting progress. *Journal of Economic Theory, 1*(3), 229–243.

Brock, W., & MacGill, M. (1979). Dynamics under uncertainty. *Econometrica, 47*(4), 843–868.

Brock, W., & Mirman, L. (1970a). *The stochastic modified golden rule in a one sector model of economic growth with uncertain technology*. Cornell and Rochester mimeograph.

Brock, W., & Mirman, L. (1970b). *The stochastic modified golden rule in a one sector model of economic growth with uncertain technology*. Presented at the Econometric Society meeting, Detroit, December.

Brock, W., & Mirman, L. (1971). *Optimal economic growth and uncertainty: The Ramsey-Weizacker case*. Working Paper 7, MSSB Workshop on the Theory of Markets and Uncertainty, Department of Economics, University of California at Berkeley.

Brock, W., & Mirman, L. (1972a). Optimal economic growth and uncertainty: The discounted case. *Journal of Economic Theory, 4*(3), 479–513.

Brock, W., & Mirman, L. (1972b). A one sector model of economic growth with uncertain technology: An example of steady state analysis in a stochastic control problem. In A. Balakrishnan (Ed.), *Techniques of optimization* (pp. 407–419). Academic Press.

Brock, W., & Mirman, L. (1973). Optimal economic growth and uncertainty: The no-discounting case. *International Economic Review, 14*(3), 560–573.

Bruno, M., & Easterly, W. (1998). Inflation crises and long-run growth. *Journal of Monetary Economics, 41*(1), 3–26.

Calvo, G. (1974). *Efficiency and optimality in a heterogeneous capital model-putty clay*. PhD thesis, Yale University.

Calvo, G. (1976). Optimal growth in a putty-clay model. *Econometrica, 44*(5), 867–878.

Cannon, E. (2000). Economies of scale and constant returns to capital: A neglected early contribution to the theory of economic growth. *American Economic Review, 90*(1), 292–295.

Cass, D. (1965). Optimum growth in an aggregative model of capital accumulation. *Review of Economic Studies, 32*(3), 233–240.

Cass, D. (1966). Optimum growth in an aggregative model of capital accumulation: A turnpike theorem. *Econometrica, 34*(4), 833–850.

Chamberlin, E. (1933). *The theory of monopolistic competition*. Oxford University Press.

Chang, J., Chang, W., Lai, C., & Wang, P. (2007). Equilibrium dynamics in an endogenous growth model of money and banking. *Journal of Money, Credit and Banking, 39*(7), 1683–1710.

Cozzi, G. (2017). Endogenous growth, semi-endogenous growth… or both? A simple hybrid model. *Economics Letters, 154*(C), 28–30.

Cozzi, G. (2023). Semi-endogenous or fully endogenous growth? A unified theory. *Journal of Economic Theory, 213*(C), 105732.

Cutler, D. (1973). *Comprehensive identification of past MSSB projects and participants*. Memorandum, Center for Advanced Studies in the Behavioral Sciences, Stanford University.

Dinopoulos, E., & Thompson, P. (1999). Scale effects in Schumpeterian models of economic growth. *Journal of Evolutionary Economics, 9*(2), 157–185.

Dixit, A. (1990). Growth theory after thirty years. In P. Diamond (Ed.), *Growth, productivity, unemployment* (pp. 3–22). MIT Press.

Dixit, A., & Stiglitz, J. (1974). *Monopolistic competition and optimum product diversity*. Technical Report 153, Institute for Mathematical Studies in the Social Sciences, Stanford University, November.

Dixit, A., & Stiglitz, J. (1975). Monopolistic competition and optimum product diversity. Research Paper 64, Department of Economics. University of Warwick, February.

Dixit, A., & Stiglitz, J. (1977). Monopolistic competition and optimum product diversity. *American Economic Review*, *67*(3), 297–308.

Dobell, A. (1970). Optimization in models of economic growth. In T. Hull (Ed.), *Studies in optimization 1 (proceedings of the Toronto symposium 11-14 June 1968)* (pp. 1–27), Society for Industrial and Applied Mathematics.

Domar, E. (1946). Capital expansion, rate of growth, and employment. *Econometrica*, *14*(2), 137–147.

Doob, J. (1953). *Stochastic processes*. Wiley.

Drandakis, E., & Phelps, E. (1965). *A model of induced invention, growth and distribution*. Cowles Foundation Discussion Paper 186, July.

Dvoretsky, A., Kiefer, J., & Wolfowitz, J. (1957). The inventory problem I and II. *Econometrica*, *20*(2), 187–222 and 450–466.

Enders, J. (2006). The academic profession. *International Handbook of Higher Education* (pp. 5–21). Springer Netherlands.

Engbom, N. (2019). *Firm and worker dynamics in an aging labor market. No. 756*. Federal Reserve Bank of Minneapolis.

Epple, D., Romano, R., & Sieg, H. (2006). Admission, tuition, and financial aid policies in the market for higher education. *Econometrica*, *74*(4), 885–928.

Ethier, W. J. (1982). National and international returns to scale in the modern theory of international trade. *American Economic Review*, *72*(3), 389–405.

Fellner, W. (1961). Two propositions in the theory of induced innovations. *Economic Journal*, *71*(282), 305–308.

Fischer, S. (1988a). Recent developments in macroeconomics. *Economic Journal*, *98*(1), 294–339.

Fischer, S. (1988b). Symposium on the slowdown in productivity growth. *Journal of Economic Perspectives*, *2*(4), 3–7.

Fischer, S., & Merton, R. (1984). Macroeconomics and finance: The role of the stock market. *Carnegie Rochester Conference Series on Public Policy*, *21*(1), 57–108.

Frankel, M. (1955). Obsolescence and technological change in a maturing economy. *American Economic Review*, *45*(3), 296–319.

Frankel, M. (1961). Producer goods, consumer goods and acceleration of growth. *Economic Journal*, *71*(281), 1–19.

Frankel, M. (1962). The production function in allocation and growth: A synthesis. *American Economic Review*, *52*(5), 996–1022.

Frankel, M. (1965). Home versus foreign investment: A case against capital export. *Kyklos*, *18*(3), 411–433.

Frisch, R. (1933). Propagation problems and impulse problems in dynamic economics. *Business Cycle Theory, Part I* (Vol. *4*, pp. 305–336). Routledge.

Gelb, A. (1989). *Financial policies, growth, and efficiency* (Vol. *202*). World Bank Publications.

Gelfand, I., & Fomin, S. (1963). *Calculus of variations*. Prentice-Hall.

Gordon, R. (1961). Differential changes in the prices of consumers' and capital goods. *American Economic Review*, *51*(5), 937–957.

Greenwood, J., & Jovanovic, B. (1990). Financial development, growth, and the distribution of income. *Journal of Political Economy, 98(5), Part 1*, 1076–1107.

Grossman, G., & Helpman, E. (1991). Trade, knowledge spillovers, and growth. *European Economic Review*, *35*(2–3), 517–526.

Haavelmo, T. (1956). *A study in the theory of economic evolution*. North-Holland.

Hahn, F. (1995). On growth theory. *Economics in a Changing World: Volume 5 Economic Growth and Capital and Labour Markets* (pp. 85–100). Palgrave Macmillan.

Handley, K., Carballo, J., & Limao, N. (2022). Economic and policy uncertainty: Aggregate export dynamics and the value of agreements. *Journal of International Economics*, *139*(C), 103661.

Harrod, R. (1939). An essay in dynamic theory. *The Economic Journal*, *49*(193), 14–33.

Harrod, R. (1948). The fall in consumption. *Bulletin of the Oxford University Institute of Economics & Statistics*, *10*(5), 162–167.

Heckman, J., & Moktan, S. (2020). Publishing and promotion in economics: The tyranny of the top five. *Journal of Economic Literature, 58*(2), 419–470.

Hirshleifer, J. (1966). Discussion of Nelson-Phelps. *American Economic Review, 56*(1/2), 81–82.

Howard, R. (1960). *Dynamic programming and Markov processes*. Wiley.

Howitt, P. (1999). Steady endogenous growth with population and R. & D. inputs growing. *Journal of Political Economy, 107*(4), 715–730.

Inada, K. (1968). *Endogenous technological progress and steady growth*. Technical Report 9, IMSSS, Stanford University, January.

Inada, K. (1969). Endogenous technological progress and steady growth. *Review of Economic Studies, 36*(1), 99–107.

Ito, K. (1942). On stochastic processes. *Japanese Journal of Mathematics, 18*, 261–301.

Ito, K. (1951). On stochastic differential equations. *Memoirs of the American Mathematical Society, 4*, 1–51.

Ito, K. (1960). *Lectures on stochastic processes*. Tata Institute of Research.

Ito, K., & McKean, H. (1964). *Diffusion processes and their sample paths*. Springer.

Jeanjean, P. (1971). *Optimal growth with stochastic technology in a closed economy*. Berkeley Center for Research in Management Science Working Paper.

Jeanjean, P. (1972). *Optimal growth with stochastic technology in a multi-sector economy* [Ph.D. thesis]. University of California Berkeley.

Jeanjean, P. (1974a). Croissance optimale et incertitude: Un modèle a plusiers secteurs. *Cahiers du Séminaire d'Économétrie, 15*, 47–99.

Jeanjean, P. (1974b). Optimal development programs under uncertainty: The undiscounted case. *Journal of Economic Theory, 7*(1), 66–92.

Jones, C. (1994). Economic growth and the relative price of capital. *Journal of Monetary Economics, 34*(3), 359–382.

Jones, C. (1995). R & D-based models of economic growth. *Journal of Political Economy, 103*(4), 759–784.

Jones, C. (1999). Growth: With or without scale effects? *American Economic Review, 89*(2), 139–144.

Jones, C. (2022a). The end of economic growth? Unintended consequences of a declining population. *American Economic Review, 112*(11), 3489–3527.

Jones, C. (2022b). *The past and future of economic growth: A semi-endogenous perspective*. NBER Working Paper 29126. http://www.nber.org/papers/w29126

Jones, L., & Manuelli, R. (1990). A convex model of equilibrium growth: Theory and policy implications. *Journal of Political Economy, 98*(5), 1008–1038.

Jones, C., & Romer, P. (2010). The new Kaldor facts: Ideas, institutions, population, and human capital. *American Economic Journal: Macroeconomics, 2*(1), 224–245.

Jorgenson, D., & Yun, K.-Y. (1990). Tax reform and U.S. economic growth. *Journal of Political Economy, 98*(5), S151–S193.

Judd, K. (1985). Redistributive taxation in a simple perfect foresight model. *Journal of Public Economics, 28*(1), 59–83.

Kaldor, N. (1957). A model of economic growth. *The Economic Journal, 67*(268), 591–624.

Kaldor, N. (1961). Capital accumulation and economic growth. In D. C. Hague (Ed.), *The theory of economic growth* (pp. 177–222). St. Martin's Press.

Kaldor, N., & Mirrlees, J. (1962). A new model of economic growth. *Review of Economic Studies, 29*(3), 174–192.

Karlin, S. (1955). The structure of dynamic programing models. *Naval Research Logistics Quarterly, 2*(4), 285–294.

Kennedy, C. (1964). Induced bias in innovation and the theory of distribution. *Economic Journal, 74*(295), 541–547.

King, R., & Rebelo, S. (1990). Public policy and economic growth: Developing neoclassical implications. *Journal of Political Economy, 98(5), Part 2*, S126–S150.

Klein, M., & Sener, F. (2023). Product innovation, diffusion and endogenous growth. *Review of Economic Dynamics, 48*, 178–201.

Klenow, P., & Rodriguez-Clare, A. (1997). *Quantifying variety gains from trade liberalization*. University of Chicago mimeo.

Knight, F. (1944). Diminishing returns from investment. *Journal of Political Economy, 52*(1), 26–47.

Koopmans, T. (1965). *On the concept of optimal economic growth*. Paper presented at the Vatican Study Week, October 7–13, 1964, On the Econometric Approach to Development Planning, 225–300. Pontifical Academy of Science.

Kremer, M. (1993). Population growth and technological change: One million B.C. to 1990. *Quarterly Journal of Economics*, *108*(3), 681–716.

Krugman, P. (1988). Endogenous innovation, international trade and growth. Paper presented at the SUNY-Buffalo conference on the problem of development. Published as Ch. 11 in P. Krugman (1990). Rethinking International Trade, MIT Press.

Krusell, P., Ohanian, L., Ríos-Rull, V., & Violante, G. (1987). Capital-skill complementarity and inequality: A macroeconomic analysis. *Econometrica*, *68*(5), 1029–1053.

Lai, E., Riezman, R., & Wang, P. (2009). Outsourcing of innovation. *Economic Theory*, *38*(3), 485–515.

Laing, D., Palivos, T., & Wang, P. (1995). Learning, matching, and growth. *Review of Economic Studies*, *62*(1), 115–129.

Langlois, R. N. (2001). Knowledge, consumption, and endogenous growth. *Journal of Evolutionary Economics*, *11*(1), 77–93.

Lee, S., Florida, R., & Gates, G. (2010). Innovation, human capital, and creativity. *International Review of Public Administration*, *14*(3), 13–24.

Leland, H. (1974). Optimum growth in a stochastic environment. *Review of Economic Studies*, *41*(1), 75–86.

Levhari, D. (1966a). Further implications of learning by doing. *Review of Economic Studies*, *33*(1), 31–38.

Levhari, D. (1966b). Extensions of Arrow's "Learning by Doing". *Review of Economic Studies*, *33*(1), 117–131.

Levhari, D., & Srinivasan, T. (1969). Optimal savings under uncertainty. *Review of Economic Studies*, *36*(2), 153–163.

Levine, R., & Zervos, S. (1998). Stock markets, banks, and economic growth. *American Economic Review*, *88*(3), 537–58.

Li, C. (2000). Endogenous vs. semi-endogenous growth in a two-R&D-sector model. *The Economic Journal*, *110*(462), 109–122.

Ljungqvist, L., & Sargent, T. (2018). *Recursive macroeconomic theory*. The MIT Press.

Lucas, R. (1985). *On the mechanics of economic development*. Manuscript. Prepared for the Marshall Lectures, Cambridge University, May. University of Chicago.

Lucas, R. (1987). *Models of business cycles*. Blackwell.

Lucas, R. (1988). On the mechanics of economic development. *Journal of Monetary Economics*, *22*(1), 3–42.

Lucas, R. (2001, April). *Professional memoir*. Lecture given at Trinity University.

Lucas, R., & Moll, B. (2014). Knowledge growth and the allocation of time. *Journal of Political Economy*, *122*(1), 1–51.

Malinvaud, E. (1965). *Croissances optimales dans un modele macroeconomique*. Paper presented at the Vatican Study Week, October 7–13, 1964, On the Econometric Approach to Development Planning, 301–384. Pontifical Academy of Science.

Malthus, T. (1926). *First essay on population, 1798*. Macmillan.

Manso, G. (2011). Motivating innovation. *The Journal of Finance*, *66*(5), 1823–1860.

Marchiori, C., & Minelli, E. (2023). Talent, basic research and growth. *Journal of Economic Theory*, *213*(C), 105721.

Massari, F., & Peretto, P. (2025). Super-robust endogenous growth: Theory and estimation. *SSRN Electronic Journal*, *10*(2139), ssrn.5260756.

McCallum, B. (1996). Neoclassical vs. endogenous growth analysis: An overview. NBER Working Paper 5844.

McKenzie, L. (1968). Accumulation programs of maximum utility and the Von Neumann facet. In J. Wolf (Ed.), *Value, capital and growth* (pp. 353–383). Edinburgh University Press.

McKenzie, L. (1999). *The first conferences on the theory of economic growth*. Rochester Center for Economic Research, RCER Working Paper 459, University of Rochester, January (1998, December 16).

Merton, R. (1969). Lifetime portfolio selection under uncertainty: The continuous-time case. *Review of Economics and Statistics*, *51*(3), 247–257.

Merton, R. (1970). *Analytical optimal control theory as applied to stochastic and non-stochastic economies* (Ph.D. thesis). MIT.

Merton, R. (1971). Optimum consumption and portfolio rules in a continuous time model. *Journal of Economic Theory, 3*(4), 373–413.

Merton, R. (1973). *An asymptotic theory of growth under uncertainty*. Sloan School Working Paper 673-73, MIT.

Merton, R. (1975). An asymptotic theory of growth under uncertainty. *Review of Economic Studies, 42*(3), 375–393.

Michel, P., & Nyssen, J. (2000). On knowledge diffusion, patents lifetime and innovation based endogenous growth. In D. Encaoua, B. Hall, F. Laisney, & J. Mairesse (Eds.), *The economics and econometrics of innovation* (pp. 55–81). Springer.

Mirman, L. (1970a). *Two essays on uncertainty and economics* (Ph.D. thesis). University of Rochester.

Mirman, L. (1970b). *The steady state behavior of a class of one-sector growth models with uncertain technology*. Mimeographed, Department of Economics, University of Rochester.

Mirman, L. (1971). Uncertainty and optimal consumption decisions. *Econometrica, 39*(1), 179–185.

Mirman, L. (1972). On the existence of steady state measures for one sector growth models with uncertain technology. *International Economic Review, 13*(2), 271–286.

Mirman, L. (1973). The steady state behavior of a class of one-sector growth models with uncertain technology. *Journal of Economic Theory, 6*(3), 219–242.

Mirman, L. (2014). communication, June 15.

Mirman, L., & Zilcha, I. (1975). On optimal growth under uncertainty. *Journal of Economic Theory, 11*(3), 329–339.

Mirman, L., & Zilcha, I. (1976). Unbounded shadow prices for optimal stochastic growth models. *International Economic Review, 17*(1), 121–132.

Mirman, L., & Zilcha, I. (1977). Characterizing optimal policies in a one sector model of economic growth under uncertainty. *Journal of Economic Theory, 14*(2), 389–401.

Mirrlees, J. (1964a). *Optimum planning for a dynamic economy* (Ph.D. thesis). University of Cambridge.

Mirrlees, J. (1964b). *Optimum economic policies under uncertainty.* Paper presented at Rochester-SSRC conference, on Mathematical models of economic growth.

Mirrlees, J. (1964c). *Structure of optimum policies in a macroeconomic model with technical change.* Paper presented at the Econometric Society meeting, Zurich.

Mirrlees, J. (1965a). *Optimum accumulation under uncertainty*. Paper presented at the First World Econometric Society meeting, Tokyo.

Mirrlees, J. (1965b). *Optimum accumulation under uncertainty*. Unpublished manuscript.

Mirrlees, J. (1967). Optimum growth when technology is changing. *Review of Economic Studies, 34*(1), 95–124.

Mirrlees, J. (1974). Optimal accumulation under uncertainty: The case of stationary returns to investment. In J. Dreze (Ed.), *Allocation under uncertainty* (pp. 36–50). Macmillan.

Mirrlees, J. (2014). communication, September 4.

Mirrlees, J., & Stern, N. (1973). *Models of economic growth: Proceedings of a conference held by the International Economic Association, Jerusalem, 1970*. Macmillan.

Muth, J. (1961). Rational expectations and the theory of price movements. *Econometrica, 29*(3), 315–335.

Nelson, R. (1962). Introduction. In R. Nelson (Ed.), *The rate and direction of inventive activity: Economic and social factors* (pp. 3–16). Princeton University Press for NBER.

Nelson, R. R., & Phelps, E. S. (1965a, August). *Investment in humans, technological diffusion and economic growth*. Cowles Foundation Discussion Papers 189.

Nelson, R., and Phelps, E. (1965b, December). *Investment in humans, technological diffusion and economic growth*. Rand Corporation Paper 3295.

Nelson, R., & Phelps, E. (1966). Investment in humans, technological diffusion, and economic growth. *American Economic Review, 56*(2), 69–75.

Newhouse, A. (1958). Review of Bellman's dynamic programming. *American Mathematical Monthly, 65*, 788–789.

Nordhaus, W. (1969). An economic theory of technological change. *American Economic Review, 59*(2), 18–28.

Olson, L., & Roy, S. (2006). Theory of stochastic optimal economic growth. In R. Dana, C. Le Van, T. Mitra, & K. Nishimura (Eds.), *Handbook on optimal growth* (pp. 297–335). Springer.

Parente, S., & Prescott, E. (1994). Barriers to technology adoption and development. *Journal of Political Economy*, *102*(2), 298–321.

Park, K. (1987). *A theory of on-the-job learning* [PhD dissertation], manuscript. The University of Chicago.

Peretto, P. (1998). Technological change and population growth. *Journal of Economic Growth*, *3*(4), 283–311.

Peretto, P. F. (2018). Robust endogenous growth. *European Economic Review*, *108*(C), 49–77.

Peretto, P., & Smulders, A. (1998). *Specialization, knowledge dilution, and scale effects in an IO-based growth model*. Working Papers 98-07, Duke University, Department of Economics.

Perotti, R. (1993). Political equilibrium, income distribution, and growth. *Review of Economic Studies*, *60*(4), 755–776.

Pesch, H. J. (2012). *Carathéodory on the road to the maximum principle*. Optimization Stories, Documenta Mathematica, 317329.

Pesch, H., & Plail, M. (2009). The maximum principle of optimal control. *Control and Cybernetics*, *38*(4), 973–995.

Pesch, H., & Plail, M. (2012). *The cold war on the maximum principle of optimal control* (pp. 331–343). Documenta Mathematica, ISMP.

Phelps, E. (1960a). *Optimal inventory policy for serviceable and reparable stocks*. Rand Paper P-1996, June.

Phelps, E. (1960b). *Capital risk and household consumption path: A sequential utility analysis*. Cowles Foundation Discussion Paper 109, December.

Phelps, E. (1961). *The accumulation of risky capital: A discrete-time sequential utility analysis*. Cowles Foundation Discussion Paper 10, February.

Phelps, E. (1962a). The accumulation of risky capital: A sequential utility analysis. *Econometrica*, *30*(4), 729–743.

Phelps, E. (1962b). *Optimal decision rules for the procurement, repair or disposal of spare parts*. Rand Memorandum RM-2920-PR.

Phelps, E. (1964, October). *Models of technical progress and the golden rule of research*. Cowles Foundation Discussion Paper 176.

Phelps, E. (1966). Models of technical progress and the golden rule of research. *Review of Economic Studies*, *33*(2), 133–145.

Prescott, E., & Boyd, J. (1986, April). *Dynamic coalitions, growth and the firm*. Federal Reserve Bank of Minneapolis Working Paper 100, Minneapolis, MN.

Puterman, M. (1994). *Markov decision processes: Discrete stochastic dynamic programming*. Wiley.

Radner, R. (1963, January). *Notes on the theory of economic planning*. Technical Report 9, Center for Research in Management Science, University of California at Berkeley.

Radner, R. (1964, February). *Dynamic programming of economic growth*. Technical Report 17, Center for Research in Management Science, University of California at Berkeley.

Radner, R. (1966). Optimal growth in a linear-logarithmic economy. *International Economic Review*, *7*(1), 1–33.

Radner, R. (1967). Dynamic programming of economic growth. In E. Malinvaud & M. Bacharach (Eds.), *Activity analysis in the theory of growth and planning, proceedings of a conference held by the international economic association* (pp. 111–141). St. Martin's Press.

Radner, R. (1971). Balanced stochastic growth at the maximum rate. In G. Bruckmann & W. Weber (Eds.), *Contributions to the Von Neumann growth model* (pp. 39–62). Springer.

Radner, R. (1972). Optimal steady state behavior of an economy with stochastic production and resources. In R. Day (Ed.), *Mathematical topics in economic theory and computation*. SIAM Publications.

Radner, R. (1973). Optimal stationary consumption with stochastic production and resources. *Journal of Economic Theory*, *6*(1), 68–90.

Ramsey, F. (1928). A mathematical theory of saving. *Economic Journal*, *38*(152), 543–559.

Razin, A. (1969). *Investment in human capital and economic growth: A theoretical study*. PhD thesis, University of Chicago.

Razin, A. (1972a). Optimum investment in human capital. *Review of Economic Studies*, *39*(4), 455–460.

Razin, A. (1972b). Investment in human capital and economic growth. *Metroeconomica*, *24*(2), 101–116.

Razin, A. (2008). Review of Helpman's book: The mystery of economic growth. *Israel Economic Review, 5*(2), 129–139.

Rebelo, S. (1991). Long-run policy analysis and long-run growth. *Journal of Political Economy, 99*(3), 500–521.

Report of the Ann Arbor Meeting. *Econometrica, 24*(2) 198–210.

Report of the North American Regional Conference, Detroit, *Econometrica, 39*(4), 293–315, 344–350.

Ricardo, D. (1895). *The first six chapters of the principles of political economy and taxation of David Ricardo, 1817*. Macmillan.

Rivera-Batiz, L., & Romer, P. (1991). Economic integration and endogenous growth. *Quarterly Journal of Economics, 106*(2), 531–555.

Rodrik, D. (2008). The real exchange rate and economic growth. *Brookings Papers on Economic Activity, 2008*(2), 365–412.

Romer, P. (1983). *Dynamic competitive equilibria with externalities, increasing returns, and unbounded growth* (Order No. T-28814). ProQuest Dissertations & Theses Global (303206758). https://www.proquest.com/dissertations-theses/dynamic-competitive-equilibria-with-externalities/docview/303206758/se-2

Romer, P. (1984). *Externality and increasing returns in dynamic competitive analysis*. University of Rochester Working Paper, September.

Romer, P. (1985). *Increasing returns and long run growth*. Rochester Center for Economic Research Working Paper No. 27.

Romer, P. (1986a). Increasing returns and long-run growth. *Journal of Political Economy, 94*(5), 1002–1037.

Romer, P. (1986b). *Increasing returns, specialization, and external economies: Growth as described by Allyn Young*. Rochester Center for Economic Research Working Paper No. 64.

Romer, P. (1986c). *Growth based on increasing returns due to specialization*. Rochester Center for Economic Research Working Paper No. 70.

Romer, P. (1987a). Crazy explanations for the productivity slowdown. In S. Fischer (Eds.), *NBER macroeconomics annual* (pp. 163–202). MIT Press.

Romer, P. (1987b). Growth based on increasing returns due to specialization. *American Economic Review, 77*(2), 56–62.

Romer, P. (1988a). *Capital accumulation in the theory of long run growth*. Rochester Center for Economic Research Working Paper No. 123.

Romer, P. (1988b, May). Summary of Paul Romer's endogenous technological change. In I. Erlich, G. Hariharan, & R. Lutter (Eds.), *The problem of development: Exploring economic development through free enterprise* (pp. 46–56). Proceedings of conference Part I, SUNY.

Romer, P. (1988c, May). Endogenous technological change. In I. Erlich, G. Hariharan, & R. Lutter (Eds.), *The problem of development: Exploring economic development through free enterprise* (pp. 271–315). Proceedings of conference Part II. SUNY.

Romer, P. (1989a). *What determines the rate of growth and technological change?* (Vol. *279*). World Bank Publications.

Romer, P. (1989b). *Endogenous technological change*. NBER Working paper 3210.

Romer, P. (1989c). *Increasing returns and new developments in the theory of growth*. NBER Working paper 3098.

Romer, P. (1989d). *Human capital and growth: Theory and evidence*. NBER Working paper 3173.

Romer, P. (1989e). Capital accumulation in the theory of long run growth. In R. Barro (Ed.), *Modern business cycle theory* (pp. 51–127). Harvard University Press.

Romer, P. (1990a). Endogenous technological change. *Journal of Political Economy, 98(5), Part 2*, S71–S102.

Romer, P. (1990b). Capital, labor, and productivity. *Brookings Papers on Economic Activity. Microeconomics*, 337–367.

Romer, P. (1991). Increasing returns and new developments in the theory of growth. In W. A. Barnett (Ed.), *Equilibrium theory and applications: Proceedings of the sixth international symposium in economic theory and econometrics* (Vol. *6*, pp. 83–100). Cambridge University Press.

Romer, P. (1993). Idea gaps and object gaps in economic development. *Journal of Monetary Economics, 32*(3), 543–573.

Romer, P. (1994). The origins of endogenous growth. *Journal of Economic Perspectives, 8*(1), 3–22.

Romer, P. (2014). Human capital and growth: Theory and evidence. *Annals of Economics and Finance, 15*(1), 765–816.
Romer, P. (2015). Mathiness in the theory of economic growth. *American Economic Review, 105*(5), 89–93.
Rosenzweig, M. (1990). Population growth and human capital investments: Theory and evidence. *Journal of Political Economy, 98*(5), S38–S70.
Ryder, H. (1965, January). *Optimal patterns of foreign trade and investment in a two sector model of capital accumulation, II*. Technical Report 8, University of Chicago.
Ryder, H. (1967a). *Optimal accumulation and trade in an open economy*. PhD thesis, Stanford University.
Ryder, H. (1967b). Optimal accumulation and trade in an open economy of moderate size. In K. Shell (Ed.), *Essays on the theory of optimal economic growth* (pp. 87–116). MIT Press.
Samuelson, P. (1965). A theory of induced innovation along Kennedy-Weisäcker lines. *Review of Economics and Statistics, 47*(4), 343–356.
Samuelson, P. (1967). The monopolistic competition revolution. In R. Kuenne (Ed.), *Monopolistic competition theory: Studies in impact*. Wiley.
Samuelson, P. (1976). The periodic turnpike theorem. *Nonlinear Analysis, Theory, Method and Applications, 1*(1), 3–13.
Sandmo, A. (1970). The effect of uncertainty on saving decisions. *Review of Economic Studies, 37*(3), 353–360.
Sato, K. (1966). Discussion of Shell's paper. *American Economic Review, 56*(1/2), 78–80.
Schultz, T. (1963). *The economic value of education*. Columbia University Press.
Schumpeter, J. (1942). *Capitalism, socialism and democracy*. Harper & Brothers.
Schumpeter, J. (1996). The fundamental phenomenon of economic development: The theory of economic development (1934). *Manz Wirtschaft, 3*, 182–214.
Shapley, L., & Shubik, M. (1977). Trade using one commodity as a means of payment. *Journal of Political Economy, 85*(5), 937–968.
Shell, K. (1965a). *Patterns of technical change and capital accumulation*. PhD thesis, Stanford University.
Shell, K. (1965b, December 29). *Inventive activity and capital accumulation*. Paper presented at ASSA-AEA session "Capital theory: technical progress and capital structure".
Shell, K. (1966). Toward a theory of inventive activity and capital accumulation. *American Economic Review, 56*(1–2), 62–68.
Shell, K. (1967a). Optimal programs of capital accumulation for an economy in which there is exogenous technical change. In K. Shell (Ed.), *Essays on the theory of optimal economic growth* (pp. 1–30). MIT Press.
Shell, K. (1967b). A model of inventive activity and capital accumulation. In K. Shell (Ed.), *Essays on the theory of optimal economic growth* (pp. 67–85). MIT Press.
Shell, K. (1969 [1967]). Technological knowledge and economic growth. In Planning for advanced skills and technologies. UN [presented in May 1967].
Shell, K. (1973). Inventive activity, industrial organisation and economic growth. In J. Mirrlees & N. Stern (Eds.), *Models of economic growth* (pp. 77–100). Macmillan.
Shell, K. (2013). Communication, October 26.
Sheshinski, E. (1967). Optimal accumulation with learning by doing. In K. Shell (Ed.), *Essays on the theory of optimal economic growth* (pp. 31–52). MIT Press.
Sidrauski, M. (1967). Rational choice and patterns of growth in a monetary economy. *American Economic Review, 57*(2), 534–544.
Siemens, J., Burton, S., Jensen, T., & Mendoza, N. (2005). An examination of the relationship between research productivity in prestigious business journals and popular press business school rankings. *Journal of Business Research, 58*(4), 467–476.
Smith, A. (1776). *An inquiry into the nature and causes of the wealth of nations: Volume One*. A. Strahan and T. Cadell.
Snowden, B., & Vane, H. (1999). *Conversations with leading economists*. Edward Elgar.
Soares, R. (2005). Mortality reductions, educational attainment, and fertility choice. *American Economic Review, 95*(3), 580–601.
Solow, R. (1956). A contribution to the theory of economic growth. *Quarterly Journal of Economics, 70*(1), 65–94.

Solow, R. (1957). Technical change and the aggregate production function. *Review of Economics and Statistics, 39*(3), 312–320.

Solow, R. (1961). A note on Uzawa's two-sector model of economic growth. *Review of Economic Studies, 29*(1), 48–50.

Solow, R. (2000). *Growth theory: An exposition* (2nd ed.). Oxford University Press.

Solow, R. M. (1994). Perspectives on growth theory. *Journal of Economic Perspectives, 8*(1), 45–54.

Spear, S., & Wright, R. (2001). An interview with Karl Shell. *Macroeconomic Dynamics, 5*(5), 701–741.

Spear, S., & Young, W. (2014). Optimum savings and optimal growth: The Cass–Malinvaud–Koopmans nexus. *Macroeconomic Dynamics, 18*(1), 215–243.

Spear, S., & Young, W. (2015). Two-sector growth, optimal growth, and the turnpike: Amalgamation and metamorphosis. *Macroeconomic Dynamics, 19*(2), 394–424.

Spear, S., & Young, W. (2018). Macroeconomic dynamics survey: Endogenous growth theory and models: The "first wave," 1952–1973. *Macroeconomic Dynamics, 22*(6), 1695–1720.

Spear, S., & Young, W. (2023). *Overlapping generations: Methods, models and morphology*. Emerald Publishing Limited.

Stern, N. (1991a). Public policy and the economics of development. *European Economic Review, 35*(2–3), 241–271.

Stern, N. (1991b). The determinants of growth. *The Economic Journal, 101*(404), 122–133.

Stern, S. (2004). Do scientists pay to be scientists? *Management Science, 50*(6), 835–853.

Stiglitz, J. (1969). *A note on behavior towards risk with many commodities*. Cowles Foundation Discussion Paper 262.

Stiglitz, J. (1990). Some retrospective views on growth theory. In P. Diamond (Ed.), *Growth, productivity and unemployment* (pp. 50–68). MIT Press.

Stokey, N. (1991). Human capital, product quality, and growth. *Quarterly Journal of Economics, 106*(2), 587–616.

Stokey, N. (1995). R&D and economic growth. *Review of Economic Studies, 62*(3), 469–489.

Stokey, N. (2025). Lucas on economic development. *Journal of Political Economy, 133*(11), 3449–3493.

Stokey, N., & Lucas, R. (1989). *Recursive methods in economic dynamics*. Harvard University Press.

Swan, T. (1956). Economic growth and capital accumulation. *Economic Record, 32*(2), 334–361.

Tukey, J. (1942). Some notes on the separation of convex sets. *Portugaliae Mathematica, 3*(2), 95–102.

Uzawa, H. (1961a). On a two-sector model of economic growth. *The Review of Economic Studies, 29*(1), 40–47.

Uzawa, H. (1961b). Neutral inventions and the stability of growth equilibrium. *The Review of Economic Studies, 28*(2), 117–124.

Uzawa, H. (1963). *Optimal growth in a two-sector model of capital accumulation*. Technical report 121, Institute for Mathematical Studies in Social Sciences, Stanford University.

Uzawa, H. (1964). Optimal growth in a two-sector model of capital accumulation. *The Review of Economic Studies, 31*(1), 1–24.

Uzawa, H. (1965). Optimum technical change in an aggregative model of economic growth. *International Economic Review, 6*(1), 18–31.

Uzawa, H. (1969). Symposium on the theory of economic growth. *Journal of Political Economy Part 2, 77*(4), 573–574.

von Neumann, J. (1945). A model of general economic equilibrium. *The Review of Economic Studies, 13*(1), 1–9.

Von Weizsäcker, C. (1966). Tentative notes on a two-sector model with induced technical progress. *Review of Economic Studies, 33*(3), 245–251.

Wald, A. (1950). *Statistical decision functions*. Wiley.

Wang, P. (2010). *Endogenous growth theory*. Department of Economics, Washington University in St. Louis.

Warsh, D. (2006). *Knowledge and the wealth of nations: A story of economic discovery*. Norton.

Weitzman, M. (1998). Recombinant growth. *The Quarterly Journal of Economics, 113*(2), 331–360.

Wiener, N. (1923). Note on a paper of M. Banach. *Fundamenta Mathematicae, 4*(1), 136–143.

Wilson, R. (1977). The effect of technological environment and product rivalry on R&D effort and licensing of inventions. *Review of Economics and Statistics, 59*(2), 171–178.

Xie, D. (1991). Increasing returns and increasing rates of growth. *Journal of Political Economy*, *99*(2), 429–435.

Xie, D. (1994). Divergence in economic performance: Transitional dynamics with multiple equilibria. *Journal of Economic Theory*, *63*(1), 97–111.

Xie, X., & Wang, H. (1994). On effects of foreign direct investment on economic growth. *International Business Research*, *2*(4), 100–108.

Yi, K. (2003). Can vertical specialization explain the growth of world trade? *Journal of Political Economy*, *111*(1), 52–102.

Young, A. (1991). Learning by Doing and the Dynamic Effects of International Trade. *Quarterly Journal of Economics*, *106*(2), 369–406.

Young, A. (1993). Invention and bounded learning by doing. *Journal of Political Economy*, *101*(3), 443–472.

Young, A. (1998). Growth without scale effects. *Journal of Political Economy*, *106*(1), 41–63.

Young, W. (2014). *Real business cycle models in economics*. Routledge.

Printed and bound by CPI Group (UK) Ltd, Croydon, CR0 4YY

15/09/2026

14962484-0001